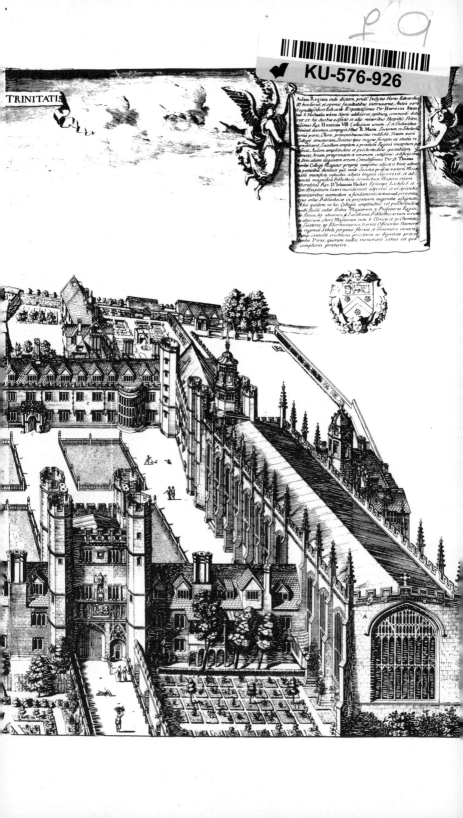

DR BENTLEY

by the same author

THE POLITICAL THOUGHT OF S. T. COLERIDGE
FROM WATERLOO TO PETERLOO
CAMBRIDGE LIFE
LIFE IN REGENCY ENGLAND
EUROPE IN THE EIGHTEENTH CENTURY

Fiction

THE SMARTEST GRAVE

Richard Bentley, 1662–1742

Portrait by John Thornhill, 1710, when Bentley was 48.
By Bentley's own request, this portrait hangs in the Master's
Lodge, Trinity College.

(*By permission of the Master and Fellows*)

DR BENTLEY

A Study in Academic Scarlet

by R. J. WHITE

His sins were scarlet, but his books were read.
From an epitaph proposed for himself by Hilaire Belloc

MICHIGAN STATE UNIVERSITY PRESS · 1968

Library of Congress Card Catalog Number 67-30680

First published in the United States of America 1968
Copyright © 1965 by R. J. White
Printed and bound in Great Britain

Contents

Illustrations

ENDPAPERS

A view of Trinity College drawn and engraved by David Loggan, first published as Plate xxix in his *Cantabrigia Illustrata* (Cambridge, 1690). It gives a picture of the College as it was at the time of Sir Isaac Newton.

ACKNOWLEDGMENTS

Special acknowledgment and thanks are due to the Master and Fellows of Trinity College, Cambridge, for permission to reproduce the portraits (plates 1 and 6) of Richard Bentley and Joanna Bentley which hang in the Master's Lodge; and also for the Roubiliac bust and for Bentley's letter of proposal of marriage, both in the Wren Library.

Acknowledgments are also due to Dr R. H. Glauert for the original of plate 5, the Master's Lodge; to H. R. Creswick Esq. and W. G. Rawlings Esq., and the University Library, Cambridge, for plates 9, 10, and the endpapers; to Dr John Keast-Butler for plate 12; to R. S. Don Esq. for plate 13; and to Edward Leigh Esq. for the photographs of the subjects of plates 2, 3, 4, 8, 11.

To
CLIVE & LUBA PARRY
under whose hospitable roof much
of it was written

In ye afternoon when it was to be voted, ye Houses were very full, and there was ye greatest appearance of Scarlet that perhaps had ever been seen in ye memory of Man.

> From an eye-witness account of the scene at the passing of the Grace depriving Dr Bentley of his degrees, October 17, 1718.

Preface

James Henry Monk, dean of Peterborough, published his *Life of Richard Bentley* in 1830, and with the exception of Jebb's little volume in 1882 there has not been another book-length study of the man in English since.[1] The present volume is not intended to be a formal biography. Monk's work, some 300,000 words in length, learned, exhaustive, and equally weighty in judgment,[2] remains – and will continue to remain – the standard 'life', the great repository. Monk missed very little, and it is unlikely that much remains to be discovered. There is still, however, something to be said by the historian of education and ideas. Bentley was something other than (one hesitates to say more than) a genius of classical learning. He was the pioneer of the natural sciences at Cambridge; the man who first brought Newtonian science (as the great man himself hoped it might be brought) 'to work with considering men for the belief of a Deity'; the precursor of twentieth-century Miltonic criticism; the stormy petrel of academic politics for nearly half a century in an age when the academic world needed, above all else, a lively troubling of the waters. It might even be suggested without undue irreverence that he was wasting his time in 'conjectural criticism', which, as Dr Monk thought, should have been 'rather the sport and amusement, than the serious and staple occupation of a genius like Bentley's'.

Monk was disposed to think that 'he did not correctly understand the nature of his own qualifications'. The great man himself, on at least one occasion, expressed some misgivings. His daughter, Joanna Bentley, had been 'lamenting to her father that so little of his talent had been given to original work'. After a period of thoughtful, and embarrassed, silence, he rejoined: 'Child, I am sensible I have not always turned my talents to the

[1] Jacob Mähly published his *Richard Bentley, eine Biographie*, at Leipzig in 1868.
[2] The one-volume quarto edition weighs 6 lb. Dr Nares' *Burleigh*, in reviewing which Lord Macaulay first had recourse to this mode of computation, weighed 60 lb.

proper use for which I should presume they were given me; yet I have done something for the honour of my God and the edification of my fellow creatures; but the wit and genius of those old heathen beguiled me, and as I despaired of raising myself up to their standard upon fair ground, I thought the only chance I had of looking over their heads was to get upon their shoulders.'[1] Monk's strictures, however, unlike the regrets of the beloved 'Juggy', have a flavour of moral reprobation befitting a dean dedicating his labours to a bishop of London in 1830. He regretted that Bentley's powers 'were not always exerted in the field where they were most capable of benefiting the world'. Beguiled by 'those old heathens', he was too fond of displaying his ingenuity and quickness, 'often at the expense of sound judgment and correct taste; and his learning was too much employed in defending his fanciful alterations of the text of a Latin poet when it ought to have been devoted to maintain and illustrate truth. . . .' In other words, he would have done better to go on delivering himself of Boyle Lectures 'for proving the Christian religion against notorious infidels', or excogitating his *Thoughts on Free-thinking* against Anthony Collins and his like, rather than producing fanciful editions of Horace and Homer and Milton's *Paradise Lost*. One suspects that the dean of Peterborough thought such avocations would not only have gained for him an immortal name in Christian apologetics, but would have kept him out of mischief with the fellows of Trinity and the vice-chancellor. He might even have been more regular in his attendance at chapel, instead of gazing out of the window of the Master's Lodge while the bell was ringing, thinking himself 'better employed writing paraphrases on the profane authors', though Monk does not exactly say so.[2] As it was, he gained a reputation not as a pillar of the Church but as a flying-buttress.

In the course of my studies for this book I have met with nothing but kindness, indeed generosity, from Trinity College, and especially in working over much of the material which

---

[1] The story comes from the *Memoirs* of Richard Cumberland, son of Joanna, the favourite daughter whom Richard Bentley called 'Jug', or 'Juggy', a well-favoured and lively-minded woman who much resembled her father.

[2] The scandalous alibi comes from a manuscript record of Bentley's prosecution before Bishop Greene in 1733 among the Bentley papers at Trinity College Library.

Monk used among the papers in the Wren Library. It has been endlessly inspiriting to encounter the manuscript memorials of the men engaged in battles long ago, from the bold and beautiful hand of Bentley himself to the crabbed and tireless lucubrations of Dr Colbatch. Roger North said of the Wren Library at Trinity that the beautiful room 'touches the very soul of any who first sees it'. Reading there under the eye of Roubiliac's fine bust of Richard Bentley is veritably to learn what Henry James might have called the lesson of the Master. To the Librarian, Dr C. R. Dodwell, perhaps I may be allowed to send the message which Bentley sent to Henry Dodwell in the postscript of a letter to Dr Bernard in 1691. *Doctissimum et integerrimum Dodwellum meo nomine salute: cujus judicium de his libris libenter scire velim.* To Dr Dodwell I owe permission to produce a photographic facsimile of Richard Bentley's letter proposing marriage to Joanna Bernard, perhaps the most interesting treasure I brought away from the Wren Library. I am indebted to Mr A. Halcrow, the sub-librarian, for drawing my attention to this document, and for many another act of kindness and patience. Mr Halcrow also gave me of his skill as a photographer.

In the matter of illustrations, by the courtesy of Lord Adrian I was enabled to secure photographic reproductions of the fine portraits of Dr Bentley and his wife which hang in the Master's Lodge; while to Dr R. H. Glauert, Junior Bursar of Trinity, I owe much assistance in the task of assembling photographic illustrations of the College, including two (of the bowling green and the chapel) generously supplied by old members of Trinity, Dr John Keast-Butler and Mr R. S. Don. Dr Robert Robson was kind enough to advise me about College pictures in general. Two pictures of special interest, those of Bishop John Moore and Conyers Middleton, I owe to the kindness of Mr H. R. Creswick, Librarian to the University. The portrait of Sir Thomas Gooch, which hangs in the University Combination Room, I owe to the good offices of Mr J. W. Woodcock of Downing College.

In the matter of proof-reading I am under a special obligation to the Master of my own college, Professor Keith Guthrie, who enabled me to remove a number of blemishes. For those that may remain I need hardly say that I alone am responsible. My wife, too, helped me considerably in the proof-reading, and in the making of the index, for which – and much else – I am infinitely grateful.

Finally, I wish to record my gratitude to Professor D. F. McKenzie of the Victoria University of Wellington, for generously allowing me to consult the typescript of his unpublished work on the history of the University Press, whereby I was able to acquire invaluable detail on the celebrated labours of Bentley as 'Second Founder of the Press' in 1696.

April, 1965   R.J.W.

DR BENTLEY

1

Introduction:
The Missing Statue

The age is past in which men rendered a cheerful justice to the labours of the classical scholar.

DE QUINCEY (1830).

When the old Master of Trinity died, they buried him under a small plain stone in the north-east corner of the chapel. In the brief inscription the fellows made no reference to his ever having been their master. Only in the shorthand of the initial letters, STPR, they let it be recorded that he had been *Sanctæ Theologiæ Professor Regius*, or Regius Professor of Divinity. Perhaps they were embarrassed. It is understandable.

For one thing, he was not a 'regularly bred Trinity College man'. He had been bred at St John's, next door, and 'Johnian pigs' were a byword to the Trinitarians. Nor had he been chosen as master by the fellows of Trinity. He had been set over them by the Crown, in accordance with the statutes of that royal foundation. Finally, he had not been Master of Trinity College for the last eight years of his life, having been deprived of that dignity in 1734. Since the sentence of deprivation passed upon him in that year, he had been no more than a squatter in the Master's Lodge, a squatter whom no one dared to eject. In the summer of 1742 they carried him out of it from the dark bedroom in the dark bedroom.

It is probable that few people who visit Trinity College chapel in Cambridge, that sombre yet elegant monument to the rational pieties of Walpoleian England, know that he lies there, or, if they were to come upon his grave, would know who he was. Entering by the tall bright ante-chapel, the visitor runs the gauntlet of the rather more than life-size marble statues of

Bacon and Barrow, Tennyson, Whewell and Macaulay, where they stare at each other from their marble thrones under the presidency of Trinity's greatest son, Sir Isaac Newton. Do these massive men sometimes, on moonlight nights, debate the absence of their great compeer from their ranks? Sir Isaac, towering above them all on his plinth, his neat head, his 'silent face', and his lithe body fresh-chiselled as if Roubiliac laid down his chisel but yesterday, gazes far beyond them, past screen and stall and organ-loft, to the place where Bentley's bones lie isolate. Newton knew the man, knew him before the stormy days of his reign as master, when Richard Bentley had preached to London audiences in the defence of religion against infidels, recruiting the findings of Newtonian science to the cause of Christian advocacy. Perhaps Newton's gaze across Trinity chapel, as he watches serenely the light refracted from the prism in his hand, expresses also some slight regret over the gap in the college pantheon.

It needed an historian to state the case for Bentley's commemoration among the mighty dead. More than a century after Bentley's funeral, Lord Macaulay wrote a private letter to William Whewell, the reigning master, pleading for a statue of Richard Bentley to be added to those of Bacon and Newton, the only great Trinity figures whose statues stood in the college ante-chapel at that time. Regardful of historical perspective, Macaulay declared that only Bentley was fit to share the honours of these two giants. Not that he would rank Bentley's *Phalaris* with Newton's *Principia*, or Bacon's *Novum Organum*. 'In the registers of all the colleges of Cambridge and Oxford we shall find nobody, Milton excepted, who is worthy to be *terzo fra cotanto senno*', but unfortunately Milton's parents 'were so stupid and perverse as to send him to Christ's'. Macaulay makes no mention of the fact that Bentley was bred among the pigs of St John's. He eschews the argument that Bentley should be commemorated in Trinity's holy of holies 'in his character of Master of a College'. He bases his claim squarely upon Bentley's unrivalled supremacy in the field of classical scholarship, 'the greatest man in his own department that has appeared in Europe since the revival of letters'. True, that department might not be the highest, but it is nevertheless the peculiar glory of

18

Trinity College. It was Richard Bentley who made it so, laying upon the scholarship of Trinity men 'a peculiar character which may be called Bentleian'. Newton and Bentley may fairly be classed together in one particular, at least; 'they were the two intellectual founders of our college'. In the sciences in which Bacon and Newton were the great masters, the college may have been equalled, even surpassed. 'But, in the studies from which Bentley derives his fame, we are, I believe, unrivalled.' And surely, Macaulay pleads, 'if there be in the world a place where honour ought to be paid to pre-eminence in classical learning, that place is our ante-chapel'.

Macaulay appears to have been alone in his advocacy. The fellows of Trinity preferred to put up a statue to the pious, learned, and munificent Isaac Barrow. Adam Sedgwick probably expressed the sentiments of all but the most virulent anti-Bentley diehards, when he said that, in estimating Bentley's grade 'on a merely intellectual scale', it might be well to forget that 'he was our master during a very long period of broils and litigation, produced, in part at least, by his own acts of tyranny and dishonesty', though when comparing him with Isaac Barrow as a suitable subject for honourable commemoration in the college chapel, 'they ought not, I think, to be forgotten altogether'. Nor were they. Nor are they still.

It may be that the Trinity men who resisted persuasion by the great historian will be proved to have been wise in their generation after all. A hundred years after the death of Macaulay, perspectives have greatly changed. No doubt it remains true that Richard Bentley did lay a peculiarly Bentleian impress upon classical studies, not only at Trinity College but in the world at large. Yet the pre-eminence of those studies, which Richard Bentley did so much to refine and enlarge, has vastly diminished. Even the marbled heroes of Trinity College chapel might more readily expect by now to be asked to make room in their ranks for another man of science or a mathematician. Bacon and Newton are household names. They changed the world in which we live. Tennyson and Macaulay celebrated these changes, after their fashion. Compared with these, Bentley's name strikes not at all, or but ambiguously, on the general ear. Three

19

centuries after his birth, and more than two centuries after his death, his name is held in high honour only within the small circle of scholars who devote their lives to the study of ancient literature.

There is a sense, of course, in which the life of a great scholar must ever be at odds with immortality. His work, which lends meaning to his life, is largely concerned with the establishment of precise and accurate knowledge of the minutiae of his subject, and this must ever remain a closed book to the minds of common men. And it is in the minds, the imagination and the memory of common men that immortality is nourished. Dr Johnson rejoiced to concur with the common reader; and even if the common reader of his day meant something a good deal more homogeneous and refined than the merely literate reading-public of our own, it nevertheless remains true – as he himself put it – that it is upon the common sense of the common reader, after all the subtilty, the refinements and the dogmatism of learning, that all claim to the honours of immortality must finally rest. Lighting upon a tattered copy of Thomson's *Seasons* in the window-seat of a country inn, Coleridge cried: '*That* is true fame!' It is unlikely that anyone ever came upon Bentley's *Phalaris* in a tavern, although there is a story that Maitland was assisted to his life's work by lighting upon a copy of Bishop Stubbs' *Constitutional History* one day in a London club. After all, the *Phalaris* is one of the few works that its author wrote in English, and in a fine, downright, racy English at that. Its subject was one that might be expected to engage the interest of most decently educated people: the bogus claims of the world's earliest literature to be the best. *Phalaris* was indeed a hefty blow on behalf of the 'Moderns' in the Battle of the Books, a contest which raged up and down the literary landscape during most of Bentley's life-time. Swift's coarse and savage satire, *The Battle of the Books*, is a set-text for schoolboys, but the *Dissertation upon the Epistles of Phalaris*, that great locker of powder and shot for the destruction of pretentious ignorance, and one of the world's greatest monuments of critical art, remains a closed book even among the learned.

The truth is that if the work of a great scholar is to strike upon the common ear and to achieve immortality in the common memory, at least three requirements must be fulfilled. It must relate to some subject of common and undying concern to men's business and hearts; it must be transmuted into the living forms of art by the power of creative imagination; and there must exist a public for its reception and recognition. The work of Richard Bentley fails in all three particulars. By far the greater part of what he wrote remains, and is likely to remain, veiled in what Gibbon calls 'the decent obscurity of a learned language'. What he wrote in English – *Phalaris, The Confutation of Atheism,* and a few sermons – remains a massive contribution to the critical and controversial literature of subjects in which mankind has largely ceased to interest itself. His English style, and his critical brilliance, once earned him a claim to a volume in the English Men of Letters Series. But the educated public, which acclaimed *Phalaris* and the Boyle Lectures on behalf of Christianity, has dwindled to a tiny minority in a world which has long since turned to other men and other matters. Praise of Bentley in such a world must be taken on trust. Even so the tributes of the learned to the greatness of their learned predecessors are never beyond suspicion in a world which is accustomed to hear cobblers advocating the superior qualities of leather. A. E. Housman, who belonged to the Bentley tradition not only in scholarship but in academic temper, describes him quite simply as 'the greatest scholar that England or perhaps Europe ever bred'. The general mind has not yet turned from Housman's *A Shropshire Lad* to Professor Housman's *Junii juvenalis saturæ*, nor has it turned from Lewis Carroll's *Alice in Wonderland* to revel in the Rev Charles Lutwidge Dodgson's *Elementary Treatise on Determinants.* The nearest thing that Richard Bentley ever provided in the way of bait for the great leviathan was his 'improved' version of Milton's *Paradise Lost.*

For the name and fame of Richard Bentley to be known and appraised by his fellow countrymen now, his story must be told within a wider, and at the same time more personal, context than the world of pure scholarship and academic controversy. It must be told as the story not only of a prince among scholars but as a man among men. For Bentley was a great man simply in the sense that he shared fully the commonest features of our common humanity, the broadest human instincts, passions and

21

failings. Pope, Mallet, Warburton, all of whom hated him, conspired to compose a portrait of a cantankerous pedant, a wicked old recluse beleaguered by his outraged enemies in the Master's Lodge at Trinity College, an ancient hermit-crab among the rocks of some remote academic shore, a scaly reptile hoarding its venom in order to squirt it in the direction of the metropolitan world of polite society – the world of wit and fashion to which his ill-conditioned nature rendered him alien.

> While Bentley, long to wrangling schools confined,
> And but by books acquainted with mankind. . . .

Like the portrait composed by Hazlitt and John Stuart Mill of the elderly Jeremy Bentham, this was a travesty of an old man by younger men whose memories of their subject were inevitably short. By the 1730s, when the onslaughts of *The Dunciad* were composed, Bentley was in his seventies, and near his death. Pope was his junior by a quarter of a century. When Bentley became Master of Trinity, Warburton was a child of two. What these caricaturists either did not know, or chose to forget, was that their *bête-noire* had played his full part in the world of men and affairs before they were born or while they were young men. The friend of John Evelyn, the intellectual associate of Wren and Locke, of Stillingfleet and Newton, was well enough acquainted with the larger affairs of mankind for many years before his destiny confined him (if it ever did) to 'wrangling schools' or limited his acquaintance with his fellow men (if it ever did) to the instruction to be gained from books. All through his youth and his early middle age, he lived in the central stream of the life of his age.

And what an age! The earliest age of the Royal Society (of which he became a fellow when he was thirty-three), of Newtonian science, of the triumph of the 'Moderns' (to which he made the greatest single contribution by his *Phalaris* when he was thirty-three), of the Glorious Revolution – which made the fortune of his country as the greatest power in Europe, which, in those days, meant the world. It was the watershed of modern history. On its slopes were poised the contending forces of almost all the great antagonisms that have occupied the world ever since. In England, the contest between arbitrary power and personal liberty was more than half over; that between science and religion had hardly begun. Fundamental conflicts frequently disguised themselves here beneath the guise of local, and often trivial, factions: High Church v. Dissent, Whigs v. Tories, Ancients v. Moderns. The English were the most contentious, and, at the same time, the least malignant people in the world. They fought each other at court and in the courts, in Senate and pulpit, in the ephemera of the press and in fat folio volumes. The only place where they declined to fight each other any more was on the battlefield. They had had two civil wars within the century, and they were resolved at almost any cost to have no more. And, it seems, the more remote and unthinkable the notion of drawing the sword became, the more ferocious grew the warfare of the pen. Divines pounded each other to mincemeat over a point of theology; scholars beat each other into the dust over the reading of some ancient text which probably never had any clear meaning even to its ancient author; politicians hounded their enemies into exile or on to the scaffold. *Væ victis*. . . . In 1662, the year of Richard Bentley's birth, the government imposed a statutory censorship of the press. The Licensing Act, however, was allowed to lapse in 1695, just in time for the contest of Boyle v. Bentley. *Phalaris* came out two years later, the master-stroke in the Battle of the Books. It is scarcely surprising that a Yorkshire man and a scholar, coming to manhood in these years, should have assumed a life-long posture of contention.

Bentley's first biographer, the Rev Dr James Henry Monk, writing from his deanery at Peterborough on the eve of the Victorian age, records a widespread opinion that Richard Bentley's talents were better adapted for military command than for the peaceful pursuits of a Regius Professor of Divinity. Certainly, 'Major-General Bentley' is a credible conception. 'Slashing Bentley', as Alexander Pope called him, came of good yeoman stock. Both his grandfathers had served the king in the great Civil War. Captain James Bentley, his father's father, died a prisoner in the hands of the Parliament, and suffered greatly in his estate for the Royalist cause. Major Richard Willie, his mother's father, after whom his illustrious grandson was named, is said to have held his commission in the Royal army likewise.

Yeoman stock, militant forebears, the general turbulence of the age, all these may be allowed to account for something. One thing only is certain: Richard Bentley possessed the temperament of man the fighting animal. The language of war came readily to his lips at all times. When he received his first serious set-back at the hands of the Seniority of his college, he was heard to declare: 'From henceforth, farewell peace to Trinity College. . . .' And he meant it. He declared war on the fellows forthwith, and pursued it with little intermission for more than forty years. Threatened with legal action for his abuse of statutes, he would lay his hand on his thigh and make reference to his 'rusty sword'. Not for him the envenomed darts of an Alexander Pope. Rather, as Swift wickedly satirized him in *The Battle of the Books*, his weapons of offence more closely resembled a flail and a chamber-pot. He laid about him with the gusto of a good Yorkshire man at single-stick. And as he flailed, so he railed in racy, earthy English yeoman manner. 'Dog' and 'Rat' were his mildest epithets for the learned men who crossed him. It has been truly said that he treated his opponents as if they had been corrupt readings in an old manuscript. If Bacon wrote philosophy like a Lord Chancellor, Bentley conducted personal controversy like a militant philologist.

He was relentless – until he had won (which he nearly always did). Like the celebrated Yorkshire professional on the game of cricket, he might have said: 'We don't play this game for foon. . . .' After battle, however, he was generally willing to forgive and forget. He bore no malice, and found it difficult to make out why his prostrate adversaries bore any. He sneered at Pope's *Iliad* that it was a very pretty poem, but that he must not call it Homer, and then wondered why he was pilloried in *The Dunciad*. 'I spoke against his Homer,' he concluded, 'and the portentous cub never forgives. . . .' Nor, despite much provocation, did he ever actually lay hands on his adversaries. He is known to have employed constables to exclude an enemy from attendance at a college meeting. He ordered his servants to refuse admission to the vice-chancellor's constables when they came to arrest him at his lodge. When one of them managed to get in, he was locked in the dining-room to cool his heels for four hours. And whether it was the Master of Trinity, or one of his servants, who fired the bullet that was later discovered embedded in the wall of the vice-chancellor's study at Caius, will never be known. Certainly the angle at which it rested was consonant with its having come from the adjoining house which bears the name of the Holy and Undivided Trinity. Bentley was prepared to fight about anything – or nothing. Everything, it seemed, could be fought over, and most things were. His contest with the Oxford scholars in *Phalaris* was concerned with issues of genuine intellectual importance. His long struggle with the fellows of Trinity represented a complex concern with both personal power and academic progress. His deathless vendetta with Dr Colbatch degenerated into a relentless pursuit through the courts for a fee of 3s 6d.

He kept it up to the end of a very long life, and he died in possession of the field. His masterful and aggressive nature thrived with the years. 'His spirit, daring even to rashness, self-confident even to negligence, and proud even to insolent ferocity,' Macaulay wrote, was in the end to produce a 'besotted reliance on his own powers and his own luck.' And yet, in Bentley, *hubris* never evoked *nemesis*. Twice tried for his 'irregularities', deprived for some five years of all his degrees, ultimately sentenced to be deprived of his mastership, he continued to live at the Master's Lodge until his death at the age of eighty, because no one dared to turn him out. He started smoking at seventy, and late in life he developed a nice taste in claret, which, he was fond of saying, 'would be port if it could'. There he sat in his old bed-gown, his wide-brimmed hat over his eyes, spoiling his grandchildren, and indulging in his broad north-country speech with its 'thou's' and 'thee's', the most learned man in all England, and the most masterful. His domestic life with his womenfolk – his beautiful younger daughter Joanna (or 'Jug', as he called her), and his amiable wife, had always been in strict contrast with his public life, idyllic in its harmony and mutual devotion. And year in, year out, through forty years of academic warfare at Cambridge, he had remained in amicable correspondence with the most eminent classical scholars in Europe, among whom his reputation never suffered one iota of diminution in its lustre. The severest exigencies of total war were powerless to check more than momentarily his output of scholarly works. Indeed, it seemed that he timed the publication of his brilliant contributions to scholarship as a succession of *coups de foudre* in the higher strategy of his endless campaign against his enemies.

It cannot fairly be said that Bentley mellowed with the years. 'We may strip him of his titles,' Conyers Middleton wrote, 'but we never can of his insolence; he has ceased to be a Doctor, and may cease to be a Professor, but he can never cease to be Bentley. There he will triumph over the University to the last; all its learning being unable to polish, its manners to soften, or its discipline to tame the superior obstinacy of his genius.'

'Drink your wine, sir,' he commanded a visitor, the eminent botanist, Philip Miller, who persisted in trying to pick the brains of the old Aristarch over the port. 'Drink your wine, sir.'

And finally, when persistence persisted:

'Walker – our hat!'

Walker was not the butler, as might be supposed, but the vice-master.

2

The Man from the North

Very little is known of the first twenty years of Richard Bentley's life. There was no particular reason why anyone should have made notes on the unremarkable youth of a Yorkshire lad of obscure family in the years between the Blessed Restoration which brought in King Charles II and the Glorious Revolution which turned out King James II. Even in the West Riding of Yorkshire there were more interesting and important things to take note of. Perhaps that is why the image of Richard Bentley remains, in so far as it remains at all, as that of an eighteenth-century figure, a man of the Augustan Peace and the age of Walpole. These were the years of his fame, and of his notoriety, when the world took note of him. But the years that made him, the lost years of his childhood and youth, belonged to the turbulent times of the Restoration and the Revolution, of the Dutch wars, the Exclusion Bill, the Seven Bishops, the Green Ribbon Club and Judge Jeffreys. The bells had scarcely ceased to ring for the return of the king when he was born, and he died in the year that Sir Robert Walpole fell. It is easy to forget that, although he lived more than forty years of his life in the eighteenth century, he was a toddler when Bunyan published *The Pilgrim's Progress*, he was a newly-fledged Master of Arts when Newton brought out the *Principia*, he entered into deacon's orders in the years of Locke's *Essay Concerning Human Understanding*. All the great formative intellectual influences of his lifetime were at work before, in his late thirties, he went to be Master of Trinity.

The basic facts of his youth are few and simple. Born in his maternal grandfather's house at Oulton, near Wakefield, in 1662, he was sent to a village school and then to the Wakefield Grammar School. At the age of fourteen he went as a subsizar, to St John's College, Cambridge. He graduated Bachelor of

Arts at eighteen, and at twenty he went to be master of the
school at Spalding. Thence he was rescued by Edward Stillingfleet, dean of St Paul's, a fellow Johnian, to serve as domestic
tutor to his son. This was in 1682. With Stillingfleet as his
patron and employer, the young scholar set forth into the world
of learning and affairs, and never looked back. It is a pity that
the record is so bare, more especially since biographers have
learnt to look for the formative moulds of a man's character in
heredity and early environment. One thing is certain; Richard
Bentley was no infant prodigy. That he learnt his Latin
accidence at his mother's knee led Monk to record it as remarkable 'that the most celebrated scholar of modern time received
the first rudiments of his classical education from a female'. But
those educational inequalities between the sexes which Monk
took for granted in the early nineteenth century were by no
means typical of an earlier time. 'The mother is the best
teacher', declared Thomas Tryon in his *New Method of Educating
Children*, in 1695, and certainly most children received their
earliest instruction in the home. There was nothing very remarkable about this for children who lived in the remote villages
and lonely farmhouses of old England. No doubt Sarah Willie,
daughter of a prosperous stone-mason, was 'a woman of
exceedingly good understanding', and it is likely enough that
her son Richard, like many other distinguished men, owed much
of his intellectual character to a remarkable mother.

'The bias of his taste and genius' was greatly strengthened by
his attendance at Wakefield Grammar School where, we learn,
he acquired 'singular reputation for his proficiency as well as for
his regularity'. Coming from his favourite grandchild, Richard
Cumberland, many years later, rather than from a headmaster's
report, this testimony tells us as much, and as little, as most
lapidary inscriptions. Wakefield was an excellent school. It gave
two Regius professors of Divinity to the two ancient universities in one generation. Bentley's opposite number at Oxford was
John Potter, later Archbishop of Canterbury. Potter was the
father of that member of the Hell Fire Club who wrote the
Essay on Woman, which got John Wilkes into trouble a century
later. It is a pity that next to nothing is known about John
Baskerville, who presided over the studies of these distinguished

scholars, except that he was of Emmanuel College in Cambridge. Bentley retained affectionate and vivid memories of Wakefield Grammar School to the end of his days. He is said to have concerned himself generously with the interests of boys coming up to Cambridge from his old school. Little Richard Cumberland, standing by the old man's chair in the study of the Master's Lodge, listened to 'a complete and entertaining narrative of his schoolboy days, with the characters of his different masters very humorously displayed. . . .' In particular, the old scholar remembered being punished for not bawling out his lesson in chorus with his classmates. 'The dunces could not discover,' he protested, 'that I was pondering it in my mind, and fixing it more firmly in my memory than if I had been bawling it out amongst the rest. . . .' One sees him there, mute among the crowd of bawling boys, sons of English craftsmen and yeoman farmers, reluctant heirs to a mighty heritage, chanting the elements of the tongue of Virgil and Horace, Cicero and Caesar. For Latin was still the language of all scholarship whatever. Proficiency in Latin was the essential passport to the world of learning.

There was no question of a boy's going, as we would say, on to 'the classical side'. There was no other 'side'. To grind into young heads the grammar of the ancient languages, was what 'grammar' schools were for. That Richard Bentley came away from Wakefield Grammar School highly proficient in this drill is all that one can safely say of his schooldays. He was not simply a lad with a special gift for linguistics, or the possessor of the secret of a clever trick like an expertise in mental arithmetic or the mechanics of music. His mother and his school, between them, had put into his hands the elementary tools of scholarship. What he might do with them would depend upon the bias given to his strong natural powers by his future environment, and upon his capacity for hard work. He is the classic example of Dr Johnson's definition of genius: 'a mind of large general powers, accidentally directed to some particular direction'. Wherein lay the accidentality that directed his strong general powers towards unsurpassed achievements in the sphere of classical learning is beyond the scope of analysis. In that day and age, the field of classical scholarship offered unique opportunities for a genius like that of Richard Bentley, with its blend of acute critical power, detailed analytical energy, and boldly intuitive apprehension. In a later age he might have become a great man of science.

It would be pleasant to think that the youthful Bentley attended to some other things besides Latin and Greek, that he roamed the Yorkshire moors and dales, haunted by the cry of the curlew and uplifted by the song of the larks above the peat and the heather. We know nothing of this, and it is likely that he knew even less. For one thing, 'Nature' had yet to become Wordsworthian. It was still rather 'awful', more especially among the crags and fells of northern England. North of the Trent, large areas still remained shaggy with heath and forest, wasteland scarcely touched as yet by the hand of man. People did admire rural scenery even in the seventeenth century, preferably at a safe distance from the mountains and the sea, but on the whole they admired nature after it had been put in order. Rural landscape was appreciated chiefly by visitors from the towns rather than by those who had to live in it. The ploughman wearily plodding his homeward way was truly weary, with little time or inclination to revel in rural charms. As for scrambling about among romantic ruins, the heart and the imagination athirst for the glamorous associations of an older world, this had to await the magical impulse of Walter Scott. The wild, the picturesque, or the simply old, were not much appreciated by those who lived among them in the seventeenth century, nor even by the itinerant visitor. Celia Fiennes, riding through England in the latter years of the century (she was born in the same year as Richard Bentley), fills her journals with details of 'modern' improvements of which she highly approved, but spared little sentiment for the monuments of the older world that was already being improved out of existence. The English in that age of rapidly increasing wealth and amenity would have understood the man from Detroit who asked the headmaster of Eton, 'Why not pull the old place down and build a new one?' One of the first things that Richard Bentley did when he became Master of Trinity College, was to tear out the tapestries and the leaded lights of the Master's Lodge and replace them with the latest thing in wainscot and plaster and sash-windows. To imagine Bentley the schoolboy, or the undergraduate, revelling in the rurality and the ruins of the West Riding, would be to ignore the spirit of the England of his youth.

It would also be to ignore the laborious and desk-bound character of boyhood in days before 'youth' as an estate of the realm had been invented. Schooling was a full-time occupation. The schoolboy's hours of 'minding his book' were, like those of the labourer and the artisan, all the hours of daylight. Holidays, even university vacations, were short and rare, especially for poor boys whose homes were at a distance. The boy was not only the father of the man, he was generally regarded as the man in miniature. Children were expected to grow up, and did grow up, much earlier than in later times. Their lives were laborious, exacting and harsh, whippings were prompt and regular, organized games non-existent. It was a regimen suited to the production of a hardy and competitive race of men.

The house in which Richard Bentley was born on January 27, 1662, is depicted in Monk's *Life*. It is a two-storied place with an attic-window in a high gable above the rest. By the time when Monk's sketch was made, the six front windows had been squared with plain stone mullions and transoms, and fitted with largish panes. The elevation is faced with ashlar or very neat plaster, the roof looks like slate, and the chimneys are the neat clay-potted stacks which took over from the squat and ornamental brick towers in the eighteenth century. What the place looked like when young Bentley knew it, is not easy to conjecture. Since its owner was a master-mason, and quite capable of setting modern improvements afoot ahead of the generality who lived in houses of this type, it may have looked very much as it is here depicted. It may have lacked the high gable-end and faced the world as a three-up and two-down house of a country craftsman or yeoman farmer. Certainly Bentley came from a substantial yeoman background: 'that respectable class which has supplied every profession with many of its brightest ornaments', as Monk observes. The Bentleys were a numerous yeoman family who had possessed small parcels of land at Heptonstall, near Halifax, for many generations. The name crops up no less than forty-two times in the baptismal registers of the chapelry of Heptonstall between 1599 and 1660. Captain James Bentley, the father of Thomas who married the stone-mason's daughter, had been sufficiently well-endowed to be recorded as having suffered the destruction of his house and the confiscation of his estate at the hands of the Parliament. It seems fairly safe to say that, on his father's side, Richard Bentley came of a family that had come down in the world by reason of its loyalty to the royal martyr.[1] Perhaps that is why Thomas Bentley, his father, married the stone-mason's daughter as his second wife in the year 1661, by which time the Act of Indemnity and Oblivion had made it apparent (as was bitterly observed) that there was to be oblivion for the king's friends and indemnity for his enemies. Perhaps that is why we hear so little of Thomas Bentley, the dim figure who left his son to be brought up by his father-in-law at Oulton. His martyrdom does not, however, appear to have been complete, for we know that he left his house and a small estate at Woodlesford to his eldest son by his first marriage when he died in 1675. We owe almost everything we know about the Bentley ancestry and its substance to Richard Cumberland, and Cumberland has been proved inaccurate in several particulars. After all, he was concerned to repudiate the slander that the distinguished scholar was a person of low extraction, and a man is not on his oath in lapidary inscriptions, especially as regards biographical detail. It is not uncommon for English families to make out that they have come down in the world by misfortunes incurred for noble causes.

To attempt to account for Richard Bentley's aggressive character by reference to an unfortunate childhood or unhappy family associations would be a hazardous game. To impute his failings to a lack of love in his infancy would be to libel his mother, Sarah Willie, the good Latinist, and her father, the kindly stone-mason, for whom Richard was the apple of his eye. It is true that his father was an elderly man when the child was born, and died when the boy was thirteen. Richard was the eldest child of his father's second marriage, and his mother was

[1] The Bentleys seem never to have been 'gentry' but they may possibly have been backwoodsmen of a region where, as Professor J. H. Hexter has put it, it was notoriously 'easy to go to pot on a stagnant rent-roll' in the early seventeenth century, and where there seems to have been some connection between the backwardness of the North and the military support enjoyed by the king. (See J. H. Hexter's *Reappraisals in History*, 1961, pp. 129–31.)

a young woman of nineteen. There were still four other children of this second brood to follow before the death of Thomas Bentley in 1675. At his father's death, the Woodlesford property went to the eldest son of Thomas Bentley's first marriage, and Richard's future became the concern of his mother and her father, Richard Willie, the mason. It is to these two that he was to owe every influence and endeavour that turned him from the obscure and laborious life of a Yorkshire farmer or a local craftsman, the most likely course of life for the eldest son of a second marriage in that time and place. Whether his father, during the thirteen years after the boy's birth, showed him much love or exercised much control over him, we are in no position to judge. Did the growing boy rebel against the discipline exerted by an elderly man confronted with a fresh horde of youngsters late in life? Did he resent his father's attachment to the offspring of his first marriage? Did he sense neglect or disregard from that quarter? We can know nothing of all this. Certainly his young mother and her father gave him all their loving care both before and after his father's death. He was born in grandfather Willie's house. He was given grandfather Willie's Christian name. It was grandfather Willie who got him to Wakefield Grammar School, and then to St John's College, Cambridge. Grandfather Willie left him two-thirds of his property at Oulton with the reversion of the whole. The other third went to Sarah, the mother of his favourite grandson.

The fact that Richard Willie, late 'Major' Willie in the king's service, was a stone-mason by trade, may help to account for the suppressed note of rejoicing in the *Biographia Britannica* when, in 1748, it recorded that the late Dr Bentley of Trinity was a person of very low extraction. The master's grandson, Richard Cumberland, took considerable umbrage at this, and was to be chided by James Henry Monk in 1830 for deeming it 'more honourable to his ancestor to have been born of gentle blood than to have raised himself from obscurity by the force of genius and merit'. Monk also conjectures, rather contradictorily, that Richard Willie appears to have been a person of more consideration than his trade of mason might imply, since he had been a cavalier with a major's commission in the royal army. For a lad whose maternal grandfather was a stone-mason to become

C

Regius Professor of Divinity and Master of Trinity would appear to have required some ingenious explanation. Yet even at the time when Monk was composing his celebrated biography, the son of a north-country carpenter, William Whewell, was Master of Trinity, and the recently deceased President of Queen's, Isaac Milner, was the son of a weaver from Leeds. Many a fellow of a college in the eighteenth century made his way to eminence from a humble home. The ancient grammar schools, sizarships, Holy Orders, provided a career open to talent that is often under-rated in a later age of state-pensioners. Nor need the trade of stone-mason at any time be held in low esteem. For centuries it had ranked among the higher crafts, and in country places – as at Higher Bockhampton in Dorset – it might very well denote a general builder, a man of some substance, employing his own labourers. When Richard Willie died, he left a pleasant house, outbuildings, and seven acres of land to his daughter and her son.

Young Bentley made his way from Wakefield to Cambridge when he was fourteen. His father had died in the previous year, and it may be that his grandfather took action at once for the boy's further education out of a desire to see him established in the world during his own lifetime. The boy's proficiency must have warranted the move. The average age for admission to a Cambridge college was at that time seventeen. Richard Bentley's admission to St John's College at fourteen was exceptional: perhaps that is why his age was given as fifteen on the college books. That there was no hard and fast rule may be gathered from the fact that his contemporary, William Wotton, was admitted at St Catharine's at the age of ten. Wotton, of course, was a child prodigy who could read Latin, Greek and Hebrew at six. Bentley had no such precocity. He went up as a subsizar. He was not to receive recognition in terms of college awards until the end of his second year. In those days, such awards were made after, and not before, admission. The fact is that Richard Bentley was in for the frugal, and often squalid, life of the typical 'poor scholar' for whom the medieval universities were intended. Any delusions of grandeur which he may have harboured (and it is unlikely that he harboured many) must be postponed to a distant futurity. When, some quarter of a century later, they came to fruition, he was to indulge them with a vengeance. As master of a college he was to prove something of a champion of undergraduate amenities, a championship which may have owed something to his own undergraduate experience of hardship.

What was it like to go up to Cambridge from a Yorkshire grammar school in the year 1676? In the days of steam-locomotion or the internal combustion engine, pre-admission interviews and Open Scholarship examinations, books about university life and hints for freshmen, translation from the West Riding to the Fens is scarcely a plunge into the unknown. In 1676 it was, even at the purely physical level, very much of an adventure. No doubt the young Richard Bentley rode pillion from Wakefield down to Doncaster, and thence by stage-wagon along the Great North Road through Bawtry, Grantham, Stamford and Huntingdon. The stage-wagon was a kind of hooded barge, drawn by six, eight, or even ten horses, on very wide wooden wheels bound with strips of iron designed to serve as rollers for levelling out the road surface. Since the stage-wagon had no springs, and the roads in summer were rutted into a series of ridges of the consistency of iron, passengers generally preferred to plod along beside the high wooden wheels for a considerable portion of the journey in order not to be shaken to pieces. The journey from Doncaster to Cambridge, in a succession of these slowly lumbering wagons, would take the best part of a week, or more, the poorer passengers dossing down among the sacks of merchandise, or in hay-lofts above the horses. Stage-coaches had been turned off the roads since the beginning of the century, for they were supposed to cut up the non-existent road-surfaces. The mail-coach was not yet invented. All that was to be said for the stage-wagon was that it was comparatively safe and cheap. The well-to-do traveller rode horseback, hiring and baiting horses at every stage. The stage-wagon, with its large team of high-collared horses, its high-piled merchandise, its whip-cracking carters and outriders, was more like a caravan. It was unlikely to attract footpads and highwaymen, and, if you were prepared to walk over the worst stages, you got there in the end. Sensible people stayed at home. It is readily to be understood that vacation travel by poor students at the university was at a premium.

'Going up' in 1676, there was no question of alighting jocund at 'the *Hoop*, famous inn', which stood where King and Harper's now stands. Rather, you were likely to be dumped down on Peas Hill or in the Market Place, along with the coals and corn and sacks of general merchandise. Physically bruised and battered, you crept away with your small portmantle to discover the semi-fortified house of bright Tudor brick beside the river which bore the name of St John the Evangelist, or whatever.

Migration strange for a stripling of the hills,
A northern villager. . . .

3

Cambridge

The main lines of Cambridge's central topography were already established. The river had been confined within its modern channel, the island behind Trinity was gone, and the beginnings of the 'Backs' were in sight, with groves and gardens and lime-walks lately planted. Except for the four nineteenth-century foundations,[1] the colleges were all present and correct, many of them very lately embellished with modern additions like the third court and the library of St John's, and the handsome work of Christopher Wren at Pembroke and Emmanuel. There was a great deal of huddle and muddle surviving from old times, the maze of shops and dwelling-houses crowding into the Market Place behind St Mary's the Great and lining either side of Bridge Street. What the place principally lacked was light and air and spaciousness. High walls shut away Peterhouse and the grim rotundity of the Church of the Holy Sepulchre. The main thoroughfares were unpaved lanes petering out like farm-tracks into the country. Cows and sheep grazed the greens and the 'pieces' by Christ's and Jesus, and the Leys beyond Pembroke Hall. Part of the charm of Cambridge in the later seventeenth century must have consisted in the presence of handsome build-ings in the rural setting of a fenland town.

Beyond the turreted gate-house tower of St John's, the third of its cobbled courts, backing on to the river, had just been com-pleted at a cost of a little more than £5,000. The Bridge of Sighs and the New Court (sometimes known as 'the Wedding Cake') were yet a century and a half away. All across the river was pasture and wilderness and the fellows' garden. Away to the south, along the river bank, the roofs and towers of neighbouring Trinity were still open to the western meadows. It was in the

---

[1] Downing, Selwyn, Girton and Newnham. New Hall and Churchill also founded in the present century.

year of Richard Bentley's arrival at St John's that Wren began the construction of the noble library which was to close the riverside aspect of Trinity like some golden Venetian palace. St John's had recently put up its Jacobean-Gothic library in gabled brick. Indeed, at the time when young Bentley first set eyes on the place, the whole of the southern and western aspects of the college must have looked very pink and new indeed. The house of St John the Evangelist had been building throughout the century with handsome rapidity. The date on the high gable of Bishop Williams' fine new library above the river is 1671. Even the statue of the foundress, the Lady Margaret Beaufort, mother of King Henry VII, set in the niche above the entry to the screens, was only two years old in 1676.

Likely enough, however, subsizar Richard Bentley was lodged somewhat aside from these splendours. Such third-class citizens of the republic of learning were lodged in odd holes and corners. Wordsworth's 'nook obscure' was to be over the kitchens. In Bentley's day, most of the poor scholars lived, two, three or four to a room, in the 'Labyrinth', a *congeries* of somewhat squalid lodgings on the north side of the first court, where Sir George Gilbert Scott's chapel now rears its Victorian-Gothic tower. These ancient rookeries, which extended as far as Bridge Street, were typical abiding places of the poor scholars of the medieval university. Life there must have resembled the overcrowded garret life of the student-quarter in medieval Paris or eighteenth-century Edinburgh: merry, rowdy, rough and stinking. Reading by a farthing dip in a horn-lantern, blowing on one's nails, stamping one's feet all winter long; stifling under the tiles in the summer days; and always haunted by the stench of the river. Loneliness, the solitude of the freshman in digs, was unknown. Like another man from the north, a century later, young Bentley could have reported:

> Some friends I had, acquaintances who then
> Seemed friends, poor Simple schoolboys, now hung round
> With honour and importance: in a world
> Of welcome faces up and down I roved;
> Questions, directions, warnings and advice
> Flowed in upon me, from all sides. . . .

And beyond the gates, as at all time, the 'motley spectacle' to delight the freshman's opening eyes:

> Gowns grave, or gaudy, doctors, students, streets,
> Courts, cloisters, flocks of churches, gateways, towers. . . .

An undergraduate of St John's in the later seventeenth century had good reason to be proud of his college, even if it was his lot to live the life of a sizar or subsizar. It was the most populous college in the university. Out of a total university population of some 2,500 (including servants), nearly 400 were Johnians. The average annual intake over the years 1661–80 was 65, and in point of numbers the college was not to be overtaken by the giant Trinity until late in the eighteenth century. One's company, as a sizar or subsizar, was likewise extremely numerous, for about half the undergraduates of St John's at that time belonged to this category. The college catered extensively for scholars of slender means, and it had a strong and lively connection with the northern parts of England. On admission, a student of St John's might – like Abraham de la Pryme, who arrived in 1690 – expect to be examined not only by his tutor, but by the Senior Dean, the Junior Dean, and finally by the master. According to de la Pryme, they 'all made me construe a verse or two in Greek Testament, except the Master who asked me both in that and in Plautus and Horace, too'. Thereafter, his studies – and indeed his life in general – passed under the supervision of a tutor.

What Cambridge made of a young man in those days already depended principally upon his college, and what his college made of him depended upon his tutor. The undergraduate would attend some professorial lectures in the outer world of the university, but the main part of his instruction and intellectual exercise took place within the walls of his college, where the tutor had tended to supply closer and more rigorous supervision of the young man's studies than the university professors or readers. The colleges had their own lecturers and were tending to assume the whole burden of instruction, leaving the university little to do but to grant degrees. The college tutor bore little resemblance to the 'admin. man' that he has tended to become in the twentieth century, the gentleman who writes testimonials and fills up forms for the Ministry of Education. He was more like 'M' tutor' at Eton or a house-master at a public school. He combined the role of the modern college tutor with that of the director of studies and the Cambridge supervisor. Like the college tutor at all times, he stood *in loco parentis* to his pupils, but he also lived with them as a parent lives with his children or a master with his apprentices, and often in the same 'chamber'. His eye was upon his pupils by day and by night, seeing that they said their prayers, read their Scripture, and minded their manners and morals. His authority over the young men, or boys (for the undergraduate sometimes came up at fourteen or even younger) had for long been corporal as well as spiritual and intellectual. 'I would rather he were fairly buried than lost for lack of correction', Margaret Paston said of her son Clement in requesting his master to 'truly belash' him, for 'so did his last master . . . the best he ever had at Cambridge'. True, that was in the fifteenth century, but the college tutors of Bentley's youth inherited the old schoolmasterly prerogatives and duties, even if they were less regularly exercised.

The college tutor read with his pupils daily in his room rather than 'supervised' them by hearing and discussing a weekly essay. They produced 'College Exercises' rather than essays. They construed texts; they attended to their tutor's readings from prescribed works, for a 'lecture' still meant literally a 'reading'. In the later eighteenth century, an Oxford man who was first trained in the 'professorial' university of Glasgow, was to deride the notion that a lecturer who reads and interprets some book, probably written in a foreign or dead language, to his pupils – or, since it would give him less trouble, makes them interpret it to him – is giving a lecture. This was the kind of thing that caused his students to desert his lectures, 'or perhaps attend upon them with plain enough marks of neglect, contempt and derision', so that he had to employ college discipline in order to compel regular attendance and decent and respectful behaviour during his performance, whereas 'after twelve or thirteen years of age, provided the master does his duty, force or restraint can scarce ever be necessary to carry on any part of education'.[1] It was in the intimacy of college tutorials rather than in the formal university lecturing to large audiences that

[1] Adam Smith, *The Wealth of Nations*, Book V, Ch. I, Part III, Art. 2.

this kind of education was achieved. Those dons who were not regularly engaged in this close and intimate college work, but spent their lives shut up in their rooms with their books, with little other diversion but dinner in hall, and port in the Combination Room, comprised the under-employed class of fellows who became notorious for 'port-and-prejudice' in the eighteenth century. Occasionally one would hang himself in his rooms, like the professor of Hebrew, Dr Sike, 'sometime this evening, before candlelight, in his sash'. That was on a May evening, at Trinity, in 1712. On a day in August 1716, Mr Rud wrote in his diary: 'This day Mr Sam Aubrey, Fellow of Jesus Coll., was found hanged in his study after he had been missed 5 or 6 days. He was near 60 years of age, but had always been look'd upon as a sort of a craz'd man.'

The Master of St John's in Bentley's time was Francis Turner. He, and his predecessor, Peter Gunning, and his successors, Humphrey Gower and Robert Jenkins, between 1661 and 1727, contrived to turn St John's into a stronghold of Tory politics and High Church Anglicanism. Francis Turner was a son of one of Archbishop Laud's chaplains, and he was to become Bishop of Ely and one of the Seven who petitioned King James II against the Declaration of Indulgence in 1688. He was fairly typical of the Tory-Anglican ethos of St John's in the later seventeenth century. When it came to swearing oaths of allegiance and supremacy to Dutch William, many of the clergy refused. St John's numbered twenty-eight of its fellows as nonjurors in the reign of William III – a larger sacrifice to High Tory principles in church and state than was made by the whole of the University of Oxford and the rest of the Cambridge colleges combined. The sacrifice was not particularly painful for the individuals concerned, for, although the writ of *mandamus* was issued from the Court of King's Bench for the exclusion of twenty fellows of St John's in 1693, its execution was delayed on technical points until 1717, by which time quite a number of them were dead. Even those who still lived might be successful in retaining their college-rooms. One, at least, simply went on writing his books under the somewhat boastful title *socius ejectus*.

The young Richard Bentley, whose forebears had served the

royal martyr, sword in hand, might be expected to have con-
curred heartily in the prevailing sentiments of his seniors. Not a
word or a line has survived from his college days for our information on the point. He was never a fellow of his college, and in the
Tory-testing years that followed the Revolution of 1688–9, he
was in the service of that moderate Tory churchman, Edward
Stillingfleet, dean of St Paul's, who, so far from suffering as a
non-juror, entered into the see of Worcester, at the recommenda-
tion of Gilbert Burnet, in 1689. Bentley postponed ordination
until the Revolution was safely over and he was twenty-eight
years old. In any case, he was never of the stuff of which martyrs
are made. It seems likely that, along with a host of sensible men,
he underwent a steady conversion to Whiggery as the Cavalier
cause fell into ruin with the Romish follies of the later Stuarts.
From his college days at Cambridge we have only a single
college-exercise. It took the form of an English Ode on the
frustration of 'The Papists' Conspiracy by Gunpowder'. It is
rather a tribute to the patriotism of an average Englishman than
an avowal of political or religious principles.

> Such devilish deeds to *Angli* done!
> Such black designs on Albion!

The Roman pontiff is charged with having 'hurl'd religion
upside down'. It was not to be supposed that *English* kings
should have been borne in a Roman triumph, nor that their subjects were so degraded by sin as to require

> . . . the Roman purgatory fire
> To make the Senate-house a pile
> And Senate a burnt off'ring for the isle.

He was never a poet, and Dr Monk rightly declined to regret
that none of his Latin verses of this period have been preserved.

Bentley's period at Cambridge (1676–80) was cast in one of
the most exciting epochs of the university's intellectual history.
For centuries the universities of the west had lived on Aristotle,
Holy Scripture and the logic-chopping of the schoolmen. The
Trivium confined the studies of the Cambridge scholar on his
way to the status of Bachelor within the bounds of Grammar,
Logic and Rhetoric. The content of learning was 'given'. What

was imparted was the rationale of expounding and defending it. The purpose of education was not to extend man's knowledge of the natural world, its structure, its working, its history. The purpose of university education was to train men to understand, and to hand on, a propositional view of life, here and hereafter, as Aristotle, scripture and the schoolmen had revealed it. Examinations were really tests of the student's fitness to grasp and state and defend necessary theses, and especially to meet and defeat objections. Candidates entering upon these verbal contests, known as 'Acts' and 'Opponencies', which were conducted like public tournaments in the presence of referees, known as 'Moderators', might best be likened to advocates rehearsing the technique of deploying the resources of logic and rhetoric. Long after the medieval world-outlook had broken down and the medieval Trivium had been burst asunder by the arrival of subjects which could by no stretch of the imagination be included under the heads of Grammar, Logic and Rhetoric, examinations continued to be – at least in part – conducted by verbal disputation. The last 'Act' was kept, in the ancient style, at Cambridge in 1839. What had happened to break up the old order was the transformation of the university from a closed shop training clerks, or clergy, into an intellectual replica of modern society with its learned laity and its diversity of interests. Men were no longer concerned to 'understand' everything in terms of a set of *a priori* concepts drawn from Aristotle, the scriptures, or the schoolmen. Many of the things that now interested them were not to be profitably treated in those terms, but required to be understood in their own terms. It would be time enough to consider them *sub specie aeternitatis* when sufficient was known about them by the patient processes of empirical inquiry. A provisional synthesis might be run up here and there, but it was to be honestly regarded as purely provisional, hypothetical. Western man's education over the last five centuries has taught him to live with the provisional. He has learnt to live in a mining-camp instead of the city of God.

Cambridge, in Bentley's young days there, was experiencing one of the earlier phases of this momentous transition. The old order still survived in many aspects of life, but it was undergoing challenge and change at every turn. When John Milton went up in 1625 he found to his disgust that the old Trivium of Grammar, Logic and Rhetoric still dominated the intellectual scene. Four years of undergraduate life devoted to the pursuit of this curriculum, punctuated by Acts and Opponencies on such theses as 'Day is more excellent than Night' or 'The Music of the Spheres', were more than sufficient to turn him into a champion of 'fresh woods and pastures new'. Dry, dull, dead and deadening he found it all, and being John Milton he did not hesitate to say so. The everlasting disputations on 'Commonplaces' which did duty for college teaching and university examination struck him as a more fitting occupation for fiends in hell, a subject on which he was an authority.

But Cambridge has never been as far behind the times as clever undergraduates, unwise in their generation, like to make out, and even less so than nineteenth-century historians, looking back through the righteous reformist haze of Victorian England, liked to believe. For one thing, university statutes laying down curriculum, prescribing lectures and set-books, tell less than half the story of what goes on in the way of education at Cambridge at any time. Cambridge consists not only of the university but of the colleges, and it is in the colleges that the young receive their education. This was already true by the seventeenth century, by which time colleges and college tutors were broadening and deepening the studies of their pupils far beyond the range of the medieval university. Richard Holdsworth, a fellow of Bentley's college of St John's, is perhaps the most notable example. 'The studies which Holdsworth[1] prescribed for his pupils,' Dr Curtis[1] writes, 'are much fuller, more thorough, and more comprehensive than those offered in the public schools or the universities.' And then there remains that great field of 'extra-statutory education' which has in most ages supplemented the formal studies of young men in the older universities. Because a subject was not formally taught does not mean that it could not be learnt. A man could always 'divert', as John Wallis, that stern critic of Cambridge in the early seventeenth century, so often

[1] Mark H. Curtis, *Oxford and Cambridge in Transition, 1558–1642* (Oxford, 1959), Ch. IV. In Chapter IX of this valuable work, Dr Curtis gives a picture of seventeenth-century university education far beyond the somewhat narrow confines of statutory provisions.

put it. At Cambridge, he tells us, he had 'imbibed the principles of what they now call the new philosophy. For I made no scruple of diverting from the common road of studies then in fashion to any part of useful learning. . . . On the same account, I diverted also to astronomy and geography, as parts of natural philosophy, and to other parts of mathematics, though at that time they were scarce looked upon with us as academical studies.'[1] The world beyond the walls of the university was in a ferment of revolutionary change and humming with the quest for 'natural knowledge'. It was, indeed, the wind of change blowing from beyond the academic walls that was making the university a lively and enlivening place when Bentley came up in 1676.

The impact in England of the civil wars, the Interregnum, and the Restoration, upon the ancient universities has often been deplored, more especially in respect of the way in which the contending factions in church and state screened the personnel of the colleges in accordance with their own interests, excluding some men for unsound opinions, imposing others for their reliability. In 1644 the Parliament appointed the earl of Manchester to the charge of a commission to inquire into the soundness of Cambridge in respect of the Covenant. The imposition of fellows by royal mandate, after 1660, was part and parcel of the remodelling of corporations in the interests of Tory politics. 'Exclusion' was a regular policy on all sides, employed on behalf of the Covenant, the Anglican monopoly, and the Revolution monarchy of William III. There was always something that had to be 'subscribed' by office-holders in church and state, on pain of forfeiture. Vicars of Bray were common enough, but very far from universal. All this was bad for university studies. It might put out good men and bring in bad ones. But, on balance, it was more invigorating than it was detrimental to the quality of academic life. Many of the 'new' men who came in were forward-looking, and this appears to have been especially true of the changes brought about in the period of the parliamentary supremacy and the 'oversight' of Cambridge by the earl of Manchester. And, as has so often been the case, Cambridge met the tonic impact of changes from without by a lively impulse

[1] Quoted Curtis, ibid, p. 247.

from within. In Bentley's undergraduate days, mathematics under the stimulus of the work of Isaac Barrow was already beginning its phenomenal advance to the pre-eminence it was to attain among Cambridge studies. Newton already occupied Barrow's chair as Lucasian Professor of Mathematics. By 1694, a Newtonian 'question' could stand as a subject for disputation in the schools. The authority of Aristotle had been badly shaken by the scandalous onslaught of Ramus,[1] but tutors still advised their pupils against attacking him too openly in examinations.

There were as yet no laboratories, but the Baconian emphasis on observation and experiment was already being felt in every field of study. The Cambridge Platonists, with their dislike of dogmatism – whether Roman or Genevan – and their attachment to free and rational inquiry, preferred the 'new philosophy' of Descartes to that of Bacon, since Bacon seemed to divorce theology and philosophy while Descartes provided a consistent and theistic interpretation of the universe. Indeed, the cosmological physics of Descartes became the fashion with 'the Brisk part of the University' in the 1660s and 1670s, more especially after the publication of Rohault's exposition in his *Traité de Physique* in 1672. Isaac Newton's *Principia* was not published until 1687, although the great man had been imparting the new light fragmentarily from the Lucasian chair since 1669, light that was gradually to throw the Cartesian vorticist physics into the shade which awaits all purely rational and deductive systems, however beautiful. But the fact that Newtonian physics were soon to discredit the Cartesian vorticist physics need cast no discredit upon Cambridge scholarship for its attachment to Descartes in the years preceding the Newtonian victory. Rather it was a sign and a symptom of emancipation from the tyranny of Aristotle and of the new spirit of intellectual adventure. There is no reason to suppose that the young Bentley

---

[1] Peter Ramus, author of *Aristotelicæ animadversiones*, among numerous anti-authoritarian works, was the sixteenth-century humanist who at his inception as Master of Arts at Paris had defended the thesis that everything Aristotle had said was false. His ideas were popular at both Oxford and Cambridge, where (as Mullinger said) 'to be well up in Ramus was regarded . . . as equivalent to being a good logician'. So much for the notion that the ancient universities in the sixteenth century were blindly loyal to Aristotle, whatever might be required by their statutes.

adopted the physics of Descartes, but it is more than probable that he attended Newton's lectures. When, in 1692, he came to deliver the Boyle Lectures in defence of Christianity, it was to Newton that he turned for his arguments from physics and cosmology. As Master of Trinity College he was to promote the cause of 'natural knowledge' along the line of observation and experiment, in the Baconian and Newtonian style, by setting up both an observatory and a chemical laboratory. What precisely Richard Bentley did with his time as an undergraduate, apart from routine studies, must remain a matter of speculation, but his attachment to the cause of the natural sciences throughout his later career, not to mention his application of the Newtonian rigour in close and precise examination of data in advance of any indulgence in generalization, announces clearly his intellectual parentage in the lively and forward-looking Cambridge of the later seventeenth century. There is a profound sense in which *Phalaris* may be said to represent the Newtonian revolution in classical studies, if not in literary criticism in general.

During these years, Bentley grew into the tall, lean, gangling youth, florid of countenance and high-mettled of temperament, who was to become the terrible master. He already showed the outward and visible signs of the embattled Aristarchus. His was a numerous year. The numbers graduating BA in 1680 stood as a record for more than a century, and there were many among them who were to make their mark in later life. Bentley does not appear to have made any life-long friends among them. No doubt he saw much of William Wotton, the youthful prodigy of St Catherine's Hall, whose name was to be immortally linked with his own in the Battle of the Books. He also seems to have made at least one enemy in Richard Johnson, a contemporary Johnian, and later to be the Master of Nottingham School, who was to lie in wait for him as scholar and critic with a book called *Aristarchus Anti-Bentleianus*.[1] Such is Johnson's personal spleen in this odd performance that it seems almost certain that the quarrel must have begun when they were undergraduates. Whatever may have been the case in the matter of personal feuds and friendships, Bentley the undergraduate must have benefited from what Dr Monk calls 'the collision of talent

[1] See below, p. 157.

inevitable in so large a society. . . .' At Wakefield he had been a big fish in a little pond. At Cambridge he was subjected to the healthy stimulus of finding himself a little fish in a big pond. He prospered to the point of election to a Dowman scholarship at the end of his second year, an award which seems to have come his way because there was no candidate available from Pockling-ton School, for whose scholars it was intended. He also received at about the same time one of the Yorkshire scholarships founded by Sir Marmaduke Constable. In his final examination he was placed sixth in the honours list.

Examination results in those days are of little service in assessing a scholar's intellectual standing. The reliability of class-lists was vitiated by the intrusion of tutorial advice and by favouritism. The vice-chancellor, and the two proctors, enjoyed the privilege of nominating one candidate each to the list of honours, and the names of these honorary 'Senior Optimes' were allowed to appear second and third to the name of the first man in the list. This might be taken to mean that Bentley was really the third man on the list of honours for his year rather than the sixth. For what it may be worth, then, it might be said that he graduated Third Wrangler, an achievement of high distinction, but scarcely meaningful in modern terms since comparisons between conditions then and now are, to say the least, distinctly odious. Of one thing, however, there can be no doubt at all. His academic record had put him in the running for election to a fellowship of his college. But here the luck of his Yorkshire origins deserted him. It had served him well in his candidacy for both the Dowman and the Constable awards. Now it proved an obstacle to his advancement. The statutes of St John's College at that time, and for long after, rationed fellowships by counties. In framing the first statutes of the college John Fisher, who came from Beverley, had sought to make sure that half the scholars and fellows of St John's should be northerners. There were already two Yorkshiremen holding fellowships at the college when Bentley became eligible. He hung on for two years, and then, in 1682, he went off to be Master of Spalding Grammar School.

St John's College has ever borne a high reputation for looking after its own. The mastership of Spalding School was in its gift, and Bentley was scarcely in a position to look a gift-horse in the mouth. Probably neither he nor the college regarded the appointment as more than a pied-à-terre. At any rate, in little more than a year, during which he must have suffered a lean time – for there was no proper schoolhouse at Spalding to accommodate the master, and he had been impelled to sell his interest in grandfather Willie's bequest of the Oulton property in order to lay in a stock of books – his college recommended him to Dr Edward Stillingfleet, the dean of St Paul's, and a former fellow of St John's, who was looking for a domestic tutor for his younger son. Bentley promptly packed up his books and his slender wardrobe, and set out for the dean's house in Park Street, Westminster. A brisk young bachelor of twenty, he had come to the first turning-point of his career.

4

The Life of Learning

When, nearly twenty years later, Richard Bentley was appointed
Master of Trinity, Bishop Stillingfleet is reputed to have said:
'We must send Bentley to rule the turbulent fellows of Trinity
College. If anybody can do it, he is the person; for I am sure that
he has ruled my family ever since he entered it.' The story may
not be true *au pied de la lettre*, but it contains a substantial truth
all the same. The bishop's domestic tutor was a very masterful
young man. When his patron became Bishop of Worcester he
made Bentley his chaplain. 'My Lord,' a certain nobleman is
said to have observed to the bishop, after sitting next to Bentley
at dinner, 'that chaplain of yours is a very extraordinary man.'
Stillingfleet agreed, adding, 'Had he but the gift of humility, he
would be the most extraordinary man in Europe.' No doubt the
bishop was entertained by the young man's brisk certitudes, for
he was in a position to check them and to command a sufficient
respect for his own authority. After all, he had been a domestic
tutor himself in his youth. To the end of his days he did everything in his power to promote Richard Bentley's interests. His
liking and admiration for his young protégé were warmly
reciprocated. He was the best friend Bentley ever had; and when
Bentley came to write the bishop's epitaph, he did it in the
noblest Latin periods, enumerating all the heads for an article in
a biographical dictionary, and concluding with ECCLESIÆ
ANGLICANÆ DEFENSOR SEMPER INVICTUS.

His personal tribute, however, had been recorded during the
bishop's lifetime, in the Preface to his *Dissertation upon the
Epistles of Phalaris*:

> I shall always esteem it both my honour and my happiness to
> have spent fourteen years of my life in his family and
> acquaintance, whom even envy itself will allow to be the glory

of our church and nation; who, by his vast and comprehensive genius, is as great in all parts of learning as the greatest next to himself are in any.

This great and good man was of Yorkshire descent, though he was born in Dorset. At the age of thirty he became rector of St Andrew's, Holborn, and in 1678 dean of St Paul's. He was a peacemaker, an inspired middleman – in the best sense a 'trimmer'. One of his earliest works was his *Irenicum* (1654), a somewhat optimistic attempt to effect a reconciliation between Presbyterians and Prelatists, the two leading factions in the religious life of England during the troubled times of the early Stuarts and the Interregnum. Stillingfleet's efforts were never likely to succeed. There was no room for Presbytery in England, once its powerful anti-Roman impulse had spent itself, usefully if somewhat hysterically, in the age of Laud. When the king came back in 1660, he brought with him the bishops and the Prayer Book and the rural civil service of Anglican parsons – brothers, sons and cousins of the squires. At a higher level it was soon evident that the work of Cranmer and Hooker and the Caroline divines had come to harvest in a Catholic reformed church of England which held the hearts of the people and conformed perfectly to the hierarchical structure of rural society. Little wonder that Stillingfleet's most notable work was not *Irenicum* but *Origines Sacrae* (1662), a piously learned attempt to place the Anglican church upon its true historical basis in the earliest religious life of the English people.

When Bentley entered his household Edward Stillingfleet was the foremost scholarly divine of his age; the champion not only of Christianity against deists and materialists (a cause which Bentley was to serve in turn), but of the Anglican church against a reviving romanism under the patronage of the later Stuart kings. He was indeed the great middleman of the Anglican supremacy in the critical years of the English revolution. He was one of the seven bishops who stood up to James II in 1688, and he was promoted to the see of Worcester when William III was safely installed in 1689. He then turned to the task of confuting what he took to be the anti-Trinitarianism of John Locke. Unfortunately (and understandably) he had not

51

understood Locke's position, and came off worst in the encounter. Stillingfleet looked what he was: a scholar and a gentleman. He was tall and well-proportioned, of an open and fresh-complexioned countenance, impressive-looking in the original sense of 'awful'. In conversation he is said to have been cheerful and discreet, obliging and very instructive. He bore the nick-name 'The Beauty of Holiness'. In his later years he suffered much from the gout; indeed it killed him at the age of sixty-four.

To live in the household of this ornament of church, state and society on terms, if not of familiarity, at least of mutual regard, was a privilege of which an ardent young scholar like Richard Bentley could be expected to take full and fruitful advantage. He was now placed in ideal circumstances for the flowering of his genius. His patron received him on a footing of friendly solici-tude. His duties were agreeable and not excessively arduous. At his patron's table he encountered the first literary society in London. Most important of all, he had the run of a library which excelled almost anything in private hands at that time. It was during these years at Park Street, at the bishop's palace at Worcester, and at the University of Oxford (whither he accom-panied his pupil in 1689), that he laid the foundations of that massive learning which, in the perspective of nearly 300 years, was to lead A. E. Housman to describe him as Europe's greatest scholar. It is easy to overlook the magnitude of Bentley's achievement between his twentieth and his thirtieth years, the years when he was taking in rather than giving out. Between his engagement by Stillingfleet in 1682 and his appointment as Boyle lecturer in 1692, he was only once in print, and that was when at the age of twenty-nine he contributed a learned Latin 'letter' as an appendix to another man's book. Even as late as 1699, within a few months of his installation as Master of Trinity, he could truly protest, 'I have never published anything yet, but at the desire of others!' He was no youthful prodigy panting for proofs. He was a patient apprentice equipping him-self painfully for the life of learning.

Painfully because while he was tutor to James Stillingfleet he was himself, quite informally, pupil to *Ecclesiæ anglicanæ defensor*. The library at Park Street was the wondrous workshop of *Origines sacrae*, replete with the materials for historico-theological studies. Bentley was never to become a great theologian. His services to Christianity were popular rather than professional, although he was to carry off the Regius chair of Divinity at Cambridge (by sharp practice); and even at the height of his success in the quarrel over *Phalaris* his enemies were to sneer at him as an upstart theologian, the amanuensis to a bishop daring 'to start up Professor of Divinity'. Bentley, while avowing that he would never account it any disgrace to have served the bishop of Worcester in any capacity of a scholar, denied that he had ever been his lordship's amanuensis. Nor had he, although he probably assisted Stillingfleet in his theological researches. The point is that he availed himself of his opportunities to make himself proficient in Hebrew and the earliest authorities for the study of the Scriptures. It was in this that the young man at large in the marvellous library at Park Street spent laborious days.

The average young scholar in his middle twenties might have contented himself with the nodding acquaintance with Hebrew and modern rabbinical learning that he had brought away from Cambridge. Bentley was intent on going to the roots of the subject. For Greek and Latin studies the scholar had at any rate a few lexicons and dictionaries, although the apparatus of class-ical scholarship was to remain rudimentary until the early decades of the eighteenth century. For fundamental Old Testa-ment studies such aids were not only rudimentary, they were almost non-existent, and the scholar had still to make his own tools. The sort of activity this involved is revealed to us by the account Bentley was to give of his labours in these early days, an account which forms part of the prelude to his *Proposals* for printing a new edition of the Greek New Testament in 1720. Before he was twenty-four, he tells us, he had made himself 'a sort of Hexapla; a thick volume in quarto, in the first column of which he inserted every word of the Hebrew Bible alphabetically; and in five other columns all the various interpretations of those words in the Chaldee, Syriac, Vulgate Latin, Septuagint, and Aquila, Symmachus and Theodotion, that occur in the whole Bible'. Apart from Arabic, Persic and Ethiopic, he 'read over the whole Polyglot'. In a second quarto volume he entered all the various lections and emendations of the Hebrew text drawn out of the ancient versions.

James Stillingfleet went up to Wadham College in 1689, accompanied – as was not unusual at that time, and for long after – by his private tutor.[1] Whether the bishop left it to the tutor to decide between Oxford and Cambridge as his son's university is uncertain. What is certain is that Richard Bentley's name was entered on the books of Wadham, and that he was incorporated MA Oxon at the same time. In the following year he entered into Holy Orders, all uncertainties about the future security of the clergy of the Church of England having been lately dispelled by the flight of James II and the establishment of 'Our Great Restorer', King William III. The Rev Richard Bentley, Master of Arts of both universities, chaplain to the bishop of Worcester, twenty-eight years of age, tall, mettlesome and bright-eyed, despite the fact that he was a master of Greek, Latin, Hebrew, Chaldee and Syriac, found himself at a single stride on the steps of the Bodleian Library, that Eldorado of books. As Thomas de Quincey, another Oxford man and a classical scholar, was to put it many years later: 'No man ever entered those sacred galleries so well qualified to make a general use of their riches. . . . Golden schemes floated in Bentley's mind; for he was a golden scholar, and these were the golden hours of his early manhood.' No longer was he the solitary young man ruling quartos in a private library at Westminster. He had come to the mighty crossroads of classical learning.

Learned men were all about him, men who thought nothing of devoting their whole lives to huge tasks of erudition, tasks which we of a later age are tempted to liken to setting the mountains in labour for the bringing forth of a mouse, or sifting colossal dust-heaps for a small and solitary nugget of pure gold. The mouse might die under the pressure of another tome on a library shelf, and the nugget roll into some crevice behind the shelving, but the mountains had been shifted, the dust-heaps sifted, and the aristocrats of learning had taken their exercise, displayed their expertise. It might seem that they had won the

[1] Young William Pitt was accompanied by his tutor, the Rev Edward Wilson, when he went up to Pembroke College, Cambridge, in 1772.

prestige, dear to the hearts of all aristocrats, of having expended their energies in an activity insusceptible to the reproach of being useful to anyone. 'I have never done anything "useful", ' wrote the late Professor G. H. Hardy proudly in his 'Apology' for a mis-spent life as a pure mathematician. 'No discovery of mine has made or is likely to make, directly or indirectly, for good or ill, the least difference to the amenity of the world.' A later age may be inclined to agree with him. Yet this is only half, or rather less than half, the story of classical scholarship in the days when Bentley went to Oxford. The beaver-like and frequently contentious men who laboured beneath the dreaming spires and antique towers of the lovely town, burrowing, sifting, scribbling, collating and emending their precious texts, were employed upon the pioneer tasks of modern scholarship, the making of a world of humane learning that could only come into existence with the fashioning of tools and the presentation of decent texts. The ghastly pedantry which was to settle like a blight upon classical scholarship, especially at the hands of the Germans, was still a long way away. Bentley's youth was cast in the spring-time of modern classical scholarship, when the land was still to be cleaned and cultivated.

The world of the learned in Latin and Greek was still a paradigm of the world of educated men and women in general. They who devoted themselves to classical scholarship were not engaged in an esoteric activity remote from the intellectual life of society at large. Few persons of any cultivation had yet come to regard devotion to 'the Classics' as the rather odd activity of a rather odd minority. What are now known as the Classics were almost the only works of humane literature that were universally read. Men, and women, were nurtured on them, grew up with them, and lived their lives in a semi-classical context. One was apt to be regarded as ill-educated, almost illiterate, if one could not, on the appropriate occasion, quote – or at least recognise a quotation from – Horace or Seneca, Virgil or Ovid or Cicero. The classical dye that imbued the educated person's mind showed through in oratory, *belles-lettres*, letter-writing and polite conversation. To provide a new edition of a Greek or Latin poet was not simply a feat to be noticed in specifically learned journals, but a service to be rewarded by the interests and the

regard of the reading-public at large. For there was still one
reading-public; indeed it might almost be said that, above the
line of literacy, there was one world. The notion of two cultures
was still mercifully hidden in the womb of time. Living as we
do in the twilight of the classics of Greece and Rome, it is
difficult indeed to form a just impression of what these ancient
literatures once meant to ordinary educated men and women,
and of the respect paid by ordinary persons to the quotidian
activities of the classical scholar.

In these activities Bentley was to take his part with distinction.
He was to be known as Richardus Bentleius, for all the workers
in the preparing field were addicted to latinized names. Some
were ponderous, preposterous, even absurd: Wolfius, Croquius
and Torrentius, Rutgerius, Millius and Vossius, and – one is
tempted to add – Uncle Thomasius Cobleius *et al.* Some derived
their pedantic ring simply from the fact that 'ius' is a not
uncommon suffix in the German lands. Others, like Millius and
Vossius, were the adoptive Latinity of decent Englishmen like
Dr John Mill, principal of St Edmund's Hall, and Dr Isaac
Voss, canon of Windsor. If your name happened to be Henry
Dodwell, the eminent chronologist and author of *De Cyclis
Veterum*, with whom Richardus Bentleius disputed upon the age
of Pythagoras, you could conjugate it (as Richardus Bentleius
did not fail to do) into Dodwellus, Dodwellum, Dodwelli and
Dodwello. Thinking, talking and writing always in the ancient
tongues, scholars performed such feats of nomenclature in the
cause of the immortal republic to which they belonged, despising
the vernacular which impeded learned discourse and destroyed
universal amenity. When, as late as 1841, Dr Christopher
Wordsworth completed and published his brother John's edition
of the correspondence of Richard Bentley, he prefaced his work
with an impassioned plea for the continuance of this prudery in
the matter of vernacular tongues among the learned. 'When men
of learning have ceased to possess a common language,'
Dr Wordsworth declared, 'they will soon forget that they have
a common country; they will no longer regard each other as
intellectual compatriots; they will be Englishmen, Frenchmen,
Dutchmen, but not Scholars.' It was a waste of time for a scholar
to learn *living* languages, and most 'detrimental to the society

of which he is a member. . . . He sets an example which, if followed, must lead to the dissolution of the Literary Republic of which he is a citizen'. In the ancient and common tongue of this republic scholars possess 'a sound and ancient means of universal communication; and, if so, of general peace'.

And yet, even before Bentley went to Oxford, a writer in *Nouvelles de la république des lettres*[1] was observing that translations of the Classics into French were coming out all over the place, and that 'classical scholars are beginning to fear that Latin will be dispossessed of its ancient sovereignty'. As for peace and amity, Dr Wordsworth omitted to notice that scholarly fraternity was never further to seek than in the days when Richardus Bentleius began his letters with '*Eruditissime et amicissime*', and ended them '*Vale, et tuum ama RICH: BENTLEIUM*', adding a postscript: '*Doctissimum et integerrimum Dodwellum meo nomine saluta. . . .*' Even scholastic warfare may assume a certain politeness when veiled in the decent obscurity of a learned language.

---

[1] August 1684. Quoted by Paul Hazard, *The European Mind, 1680–1715*, p. 81.

5

Oxford Apprentice

Richardus Bentleius served his apprenticeship among the scholars of Oxford. Walking the ancient streets and haunting Bodley's library, he went with his head in the clouds of golden projects. Great things were expected of him by his fellows of the lodge, for did he not carry with him the credentials of that great and good man, the learned Bishop of Worcester? The learning and the virtues of his master lent him a passport to especial distinction. It was known that he was proposing to collect and edit all the fragments of the Greek poets: an enormous project which, for its satisfactory achievement would have required the full-time employment of an army of specialists. Nor were there wanting proposals for his scholarly endeavours from the learned around him. Dr William Lloyd, Bishop of St Asaph, proposed that he should set himself to the task of publishing the Greek lexicographers, Hesychius, Suidas, the Etymologicon Magnum, Julius Pollux, Erotianus, Phrynichus, and the rest, complete in four folio volumes, with polyglot[1] and appendix. Lloyd, himself a considerable scholar, had it on Stillingfleet's authority that his chaplain was a genius of immense potentialities for the cause of learning. None of these grandiose schemes, however, was destined to come to fruition in completed editions, although Bentley was, in course of time, to shore against these ruins certain single volumes, notably his Callimachus and his Suidas. They are of interest now only as a measure of the young man's estimate of his own powers and as evidence of the great expectations of the learned world around him. It was only on the eve of his return from Oxford to Westminster that he came upon the work that was to lay the foundation of his fame by the printed word.

It was a copy of a Greek chronicle of the sixth century AD

[1] Variorum.

among the Barrocian collection in the Bodleian Library, compiled by one John of Antioch or, more precisely, 'Joannes Malela Antiochenus'. One might have imagined that he had gone out of his way to select the dullest and most putid text that the Bodleian could offer. John of Antioch began with Adam and went on to the age of Justinian, sweeping into his rag-bag every item of gossip and fable that he could collect. It was indeed a particularly grisly example of that mixture of mythology and history which for centuries served, *faute de mieux*, as the material for historical chronology and lexicography. In its employment of the ancient poets as mere 'sources' of chronological knowledge, it was not less barbarous than it was credulous. Even Bentley, whose lively intelligence was not easily intimidated by the lucubrations of Dryasdust, at first found the egregious John of Antioch too intolerably boring for serious attention. But the truth is that he did not really select John of Antioch. Rather, John of Antioch's editors selected Bentley. He came in at a late stage of the labours of other scholars who sought him out.

The job of editing and publishing the chronicle of John of Antioch had been handed down among a succession of scholars for the better part of a century. Lexicographers and divines had awaited a definitive edition ever since ancient chronology had become a learned preoccupation. It was from such sources that the Greek lexicographers drew much of their material. For the historian, too, John of Antioch was a source-book. The establishment of a sound chronology, cleansed of the merely fabulous and legendary, is a prerequisite of historical science, and it was the work of chronologists like Dodwell and Gronovius, and of mocking publicists like Fontenelle and assiduous sceptics like Pierre Bayle, in the seventeenth century, who made straight the path for historians of the eighteenth century, from Voltaire to Hume and Gibbon. Bentley's contribution to the chronology of John of Antioch was a contribution to 'the history of history'. The edition was actually in the press, along with Edmund Chilmead's Latin translation and notes, and *prolegomena*, or introduction, by Humphrey Hody ('Hodius'), tutor of Wadham and a fellow chaplain with Bentley to the Bishop of Worcester; the whole under the supervision of Dr John Mill ('Millius'), principal of St Edmund's Hall. Likely enough it was the *prolegomena* supplied by Humphrey Hody that really brought Bentley into the enterprise. Was he perhaps spurred into a desire to participate by the prominent part taken by his brother chaplain? Dr Mill, who was a friend and admirer of the young scholar, gladly allowed Bentley to see the sheets of the great edition as they came from the press, at the same time exacting from him a promise to allow him to print his comments as an appendix. Since Bentley was on the point of leaving Oxford for Westminster, he took the relevant material for his commentary with him, and very soon the celebrated *Epistola ad Millium* was ready for printing. Such was the origin of Bentley's first essay in criticism.

The *Epistola* made up less than 100 pages of Dr Mill's octavo volume. Humphrey Hody's *prolegomena* consisted of sixty-four pages. The Greek and Latin versions, in parallel, of the venerable John's chronicle, came in between. Hody did his work with high scholastic competence. First of all, he did something that scholars love above all things to do. He proved that his text was not the work of its reputed author but of another man of the same name; that there had, in fact, been two Johns of Antioch, and that this was the wrong one; and that the author of the chronicle ought to be distinguished from his double by his nickname, which was 'Malela' (meaning, oddly enough, 'the eloquent'). Of slightly more importance, but not very much, Hody proved that the author of the chronicle had lived a trifle later than had previously been supposed, and wrote slightly more degenerate Greek. When Bentley wrote his *Epistola*, he resisted Hody's insistence on 'Malela' and maintained that the correct form was 'Malelas'. He could play the learned game as well as, and better than, Hodius. The spectacle of two chaplains of the bishop of Worcester kicking up the dust over a final 's' may appear slightly absurd, but the point had reference to a general principle of orthography: whether or not the latinizing of Greek words involved the retention of the Greek suffix 'as', or changed it to the declinable Latin 'a'. Bentley showed from analogy and example that 'Malelas' was the more likely form, and his usage has won the day. Hody, when he read Bentley's passage on the question, added four pages to his introductory note, upholding 'Malela', and concluding with a prayer against scholastic arrogance, presumption, and angry words.

Thus, in his very first printed venture into learned argument, Richard Bentley succeeded in raising the dust of controversy and in incurring the charges of arrogance, presumption and contentiousness. No doubt Hody was chagrined that his brother chaplain should have intervened in the affairs of John of Antioch at all. After all, the learned Hodius himself had made his reputation as a young man by a dissertation against Aristeas on the translators of the Septuagint, and was later to become professor of Greek. He could not know that he was in harness with a thoroughbred who was to out-prance many a higher stepper than Hody. Nor were his reproaches in the matter of arrogance and presumption justified by Bentley's manner. The younger man may have been feeling his oats, and a certain mettlesome manner is to be expected of genius when first in youth it is not only right but knows itself to be so. And, after all, Bentley's intervention had been invited by his friend Dr Mill, who was positively anxious that his edition should benefit by the comments of a man whose intellectual powers he admired and whose future career he was anxious to promote. Perfectly correctly, Mill showed Bentley's comments to Hody before the edition went into its final printing so that he might reply to any points with which he felt himself to be in disagreement. The proofs of the *Epistola* were also read by Bernardus, alias Dr Edward Bernard, who offered the author certain critical observations in a friendly spirit, points which Bentley met with firmness and a good-tempered confidence in his own judgment. They had also been seen by Henry Dodwell, who stood at that time as one of the greatest authorities on ancient chronology. By and large, therefore, Bentley had good reason for confidence in a favourable reception among competent judges.

In the event, *Epistola ad Millium* exceeded even the highest expectations of the learned. The 'new and already bright star' that had appeared in the firmament of letters was greeted with acclaim by both Graevius and Spanheim, the most notable scholars of the age. '*Ricardus Bentleius, novum sed splendidissimum Britanniæ lumen*', John George Graevius of Utrecht called him. Baron Ezechiel Spanheim referred to him as '*novum idemque jam lucidum litteratæ Britanniæ sidus, Ricardus Bentleius*'. And the chorus of acclaim for *Epistola ad Millium* has scarcely subsided from that day to this. Dr Monk speaks of its 'various and accurate learning, and the astonishing sagacity displayed. . . .' He likens the learning of the essay to 'the overflowing of an inexhaustible stream!' In short, 'the originality of Bentley's style, the boldness of his opinions, and his secure reliance upon unfailing stores of learning, all marked him out as a scholar to be ranked with Scaliger, Casaubon, and Gataker'. Professor Jebb, half a century later, calls it 'an extraordinary performance for a scholar of twenty-eight in the year 1690', and adds the tribute of David Ruhnken to Bentley's 'learned daring'. The occasion of Ruhnken's tribute was his review of the fortunes of Hesychius, the grammarian, at the hands of the critics. Such eminent scholars as Scaliger, Casaubon, and others, had never dared to say openly what they really thought about Hesychius. It was Bentley who 'first shook off the servile yoke' in his famous letter to Mill, 'a wonderful monument of genius and learning such as could have come only from the first critic of his time'. .

Bentley was to achieve many another masterly performance in the course of a long life, but *Epistola ad Millium*, his earliest hostage to fame and fortune, remains uniquely deserving of the attention of those who wish to arrive at an assessment of his qualities both as a man and a scholar. It is here, within rather less than a hundred pages, that are to be discerned all his primary characteristics in perfect embryo. In the first place there is the sheer weight of learning, his magnificent range of reference. Already he could show the profusion of the harvest of his years of apprenticeship both at Westminster and at Oxford. What Professor Jebb calls 'his discursive exuberance of learning' would imply that he had read everything, though he himself once said that a man needed to live to eighty to read everything worth reading. He never claimed to possess a phenomenal memory. He was a great maker of marginalia and indices in the books he read, and he undoubtedly possessed highly developed associative powers. He could always lay his hands promptly upon what he wanted. This enabled him to bring up his batteries and discharge overwhelming fire-power at the point of impact: for critical scholarship was, by its very nature, and gratefully, to Bentley, a battle. In *Epistola ad Millium* we find him citing, correcting and explaining more than sixty Greek and Latin writers, ranging over almost the whole field of ancient literature. Evidently, neither his project of publishing all the fragments of the Greek poets, nor the project of publishing a corrected edition of the principal lexicographers, had gone for nothing. His preliminary labours on these tasks furnished him with a large part of the resources which he employed in the *Epistola*. He already had at his disposal more than 5,000 corrections to the lexicon of Hesychius, and he was now able to establish the main causes of Hesychius's errors. His study of the Greek fragments likewise enabled him to correct many fallacious attributions in Attic drama and poetry, including attributions which had deceived Porphyry and Grotius. While working on the projected edition of the fragments, he had collated manuscript versions of the Greek *Handbook of Metres*, and he was now able to put forth his discovery of the *synaphea* in anapaestic verse, an early example of the intuitive genius that was later to produce his restoration of the *digamma*. All this may seem dry bones to a modern reader, but it affords ample evidence that the ambitious schemes that Bentley had harboured during his residence at Oxford had endued him with a phenomenal range of exact knowledge which he could already bring to bear upon a single, and not very promising, editorial task. A display of learned pyrotechnics, perhaps, but a wondrous augury of a young scholar's future achievements in the field of criticism. From *Epistola ad Millium*, any scholar concerned in the establishment of sound knowledge of Greek drama, metre and orthography must have thrilled to discern the shape of things to come in one of the noblest fields of humane letters.

Much of what Bentley achieved in the way of critical scholarship in the letter to Mill might have been achieved by another. There was a great deal of sheer beaver-work involved. But there is much more that belongs to Bentley alone. Weight of learning, breadth and range of reference, these are the commonplaces of high scholarship. What captured the mind and imagination of those in a position to assess his achievement was, as we have seen, his 'learned daring', his intuitive insight into a real world, his masterly *ordonnance*, and – inseparable from these things – his inimitable style. Not his Latinity. To be stately in Latin is a sufficiently commonplace achievement in a man of Bentley's formal training. The opening passage of the *Epistola ad Millium,* wherein he addresses his learned friend *O Milli jucundissime suavissime* etc., with the pleasantly reminiscent formality of a fellow scholar, recalling their walks and talks in learned debate at Oxford, and the promise he had given to set down his thoughts on the *Chronicle of Malelas,* all this is gracefully composed according to a familiar and conventional pattern. It is when he turns to examining the text that he becomes suddenly himself, Richard Bentley with his individual voice: a new voice in letters. The Latin tongue, so perfectly adapted to refinement upon the commonplace, loses anonymity and becomes the tongue of the robust and downright Yorkshireman, the man sounding through the toga in a unique triumph of plasticity over pattern. Already we know how this man will sound when he writes in English. Here is the identical timbre that will ring through the Boyle lectures and the dissertation on *Phalaris* before the century is out. With Richard Bentley the style was the man, no less in Latin than in English. To be oneself so unmistakably in a tongue worn smooth and thin by the tides of scholastic discourse over 2,000 years is a triumph in itself.

Bentley's manner in *Epistola ad Millium* is less that of a learned lecturer laying down the law than that of a good talker asking questions in order to elicit the meaning which, he suspects, lies hidden in the wretched text before him. What on earth, he asks, is the fellow trying to say? He says one thing here, and another thing there. No doubt he means something, if we can only get at it. Bentley's commentary is strewn with such interjections as *Quam turpiter autem hic se dedit!* . . . How vilely the fellow gives himself away, he makes me ashamed. . . . If Euripides ever said that, he must have said it in his sleep. . . . At this, everyone will say of me: *O juvenem confidentem et temerarium!* O bold and confident young man! . . . Yes, he is bold, brash, sardonic, even flippant in turn, but he is all the time keeping the reader wide awake with the keen and lively flourish of his scalpel, dividing sense from nonsense, salvaging meaning from plethoric unmeaning. Dr Monk thought he went too far on at least one occasion. This was when he seemed to address Dr John Mill as Johnny. Such indecorum to the dignified head of a house, Dr Monk considered, could be justified neither by the familiarity of friendship nor by the licence of a dead language. It turns out, however, that Bentley was addressing not the Principal of St Edmund's Hall but the old ass of Antioch himself. Dr Mill is *O Milli jucundissime, suavissime*. . . . Even Bentley drew the line at Johnny Mill.

6

The Christian Advocate – I

Bentley left Oxford in the winter of 1690–1. When *Epistola ad Millium* appeared in Dr Mill's edition of the *Chronicle of Malelas* at midsummer 1691, he was once more living at Stillingfleet's house in Park Street, Westminster. From this date until he moved into the Master's Lodge at Trinity, early in 1700, he was once more a Londoner. Oxford had been an interlude of two years, while the London years made up some sixteen of the eighteen years between his first and his last periods of residence at Cambridge. So much for Alexander Pope's jibe at the great doctor whose knowledge of his fellow men was confined to the groves of académe. During this, his second period of residence in London, Bentley was to become a familiar figure in the capital city of the Augustan age. He preached against infidelity, at St Martin's and other London churches. He routed the Oxford legions from afar in the Battle of the Books with the batteries of his *Phalaris*. He was elected a fellow of the Royal Society. He counted Wren and Evelyn, Pepys and John Locke, among his acquaintance, entertaining them – and others scarcely less distinguished – at informal parties at his lodging in St James' Palace, where he came to reside in 1694 as the king's librarian.

His first London triumph was as Boyle lecturer in 1692.

The afterglow of the *Epistola* was still bright in the eyes of the learned world when the Rev Mr Bentley rose up in the pulpit of St Martin's in the forenoon of Monday, March 7, 1692, to deliver the first of the Boyle lectures for proving the Christian religion against notorious infidels. The Hon Robert Boyle, 'youngest son of the first Earl of Cork, and the Father of Modern Chemistry', had died in the previous winter, leaving a bequest of £50 a year for the furtherance of this cause, upon which he had spent the greater part of his life and no inconsiderable part of his fortune. A man of great piety, as well as a great pioneer of modern chemistry, Boyle was distressed by the threats to Christian belief which seemed to flow from the philosophy of 'Thomas Hobbes, the Atheist', and from the mechanistic cosmology of 'that pleasant wit, Monsieur Des Cartes', and was deeply concerned to show 'the reconcilableness of reason and religion' – not only in the interests of religion, but in those of the 'New Philosophy' itself. To him, as to Newton, and to most of the great men of science of the century, the advances of natural science were calculated rather to strengthen than to weaken man's faith in their Great Original, the First Cause of all things in nature. To put up a preaching minister of the Christian religion to deliver eight discourses every year for this purpose in the churches of the metropolis, at a salary of £50, seemed to Robert Boyle a suitable way of continuing his life-work beyond the grave.

The trustees of the Boyle Lectureship included Thomas Tenison, Bishop of Lincoln, and John Evelyn, both of whom held a very high opinion of young Mr Bentley's promise as a Christian and a scholar. They had no difficulty whatever in securing his nomination as the first Boyle lecturer. 'We made choice of one Mr Bentley, chaplain to the Bishop of Worcester,' Evelyn records, *tout court*. Bentley always regarded it as the greatest honour of his life. He was only in deacon's orders. He had just celebrated his thirtieth birthday. He was yet unproved as a lecturer or a preacher. And here he was, taking upon him the mantle of Christian advocate before a metropolitan audience, following in the footsteps of his great patron and friend, Edward Stillingfleet, *Ecclesiæ Anglicanæ Defensor*. . . . We cannot doubt that the great *Defensor* had been consulted in the appointment. Nonetheless, even Richard Bentley must have felt the butterflies threshing around under his gown and bands as he rose up in St Martin's pulpit on that Monday morning in March 1692. That he permitted himself to give any outward sign of inward qualms, however, is extremely improbable. A tall, fresh-complexioned figure, lofty in manner, he must have made a sufficiently invigorating spectacle.

He took as his text (for, after a pleasant English habit, the lecture was also a sermon) the first verse of the 14th Psalm; 'the fool hath said in his heart, there is no God. . . .' He then launched into a pounding discourse in which atheists were informed that they were not only fools but knaves, foolish and corrupt in both will and understanding. They 'engage in that labyrinth of nonsense and folly out of an absurd and preposterous affectation of seeming wiser than their neighbours'. The preacher disavowed any intention of arguing with them on the authority of Holy Scripture, an authority which they did not accept anyway. Rather he would ground himself upon the mind of man and the 'mighty Volumes of Visible nature'. It was his intention to show them that the structure and working of the universe, even as they were revealed by the mighty Newton, 'should work with considering men for the belief of a deity' – as the great man himself had said. From the starry firmament on high, down to the lowliest insect, the universe proclaimed its divine original, an all wise, all good, and all powerful God.

Descending to a lower level of discourse, he would show them the *utility* of belief for a happy life here below and a happy inheritance hereafter. Unbelief was attended by shocking morals, ill-health, and death-bed terrors. Atheists lived corrupt and flagitious lives, counting it 'a greater advantage to take one's swing of sensuality, and have a glut of voluptuousness in this life' than to put up with commandments and rules which they consider contrary to human nature, in the delusive hope of future rewards at the hands of a God who did not exist. Likewise, atheism loosened the bonds of social life and undermined the state. 'No atheist, as such, can be a true friend, an affectionate relation, or a loyal subject,' the preacher concluded. As for a nation of atheists, 'farewell all government and society itself, all professions and arts and conveniences of life, all that is laudable and valuable in the world . . . religion is not only useful to civil society, but fundamentally necessary to its very birth and constitution. . . .'

Poor stuff, this, one might consider, to deliver in a metropolitan church in the Year of Grace, 1692 – ten years after Pierre Bayle's *Thoughts on the Comet* and two years before the birth of Voltaire. The bible of the Age of Reason, Locke's *Essay Concerning Human Understanding*, had been off the press for two years. The Cartesian revolution, with its emphasis on the primary obligation of philosophic doubt, had been on foot for half a century. Yet here was the white hope of Christian apologetics in Augustan London setting the tone of a course of lectures with the moralistic railing of a field-preacher; prepared to appeal to the necessity of a deity as a divine hypothesis, to the utility of a deity on grounds of personal hygiene and social stability; to appeal to both the highest and the lowest in human nature with equal alacrity and force. He produced no evidence whatever that atheists are necessarily immoral, or that they adopt atheism as a way of getting loose from moral restraints or as 'an absurd and preposterous affectation of seeming wiser than their neighbours'. Pierre Bayle's refutation of these aspersions was ignored, and even if the preacher had not read *Thoughts on the Comet*, it was – to say the least – surprising that he spoke as if they had never occurred to him. He was seemingly content to meet the atheist's objection that religion was 'first contrived and introduced by politicians' for the benefit of civil obedience by a simple avowal that 'no community ever was or can be begun or maintained, but upon the basis of religion'. As for his similitude between the foolishness of an unbeliever and that of an heir turning down a comfortable inheritance, it might seem to put a premium on intellectual dishonesty. The proof of a deity from the 'mighty volumes of visible nature' was as yet a promise. Its performance was postponed, along with much else. At present, the preacher contented himself with asserting the sottishness and wickedness of atheism and the gross folly and stupidity of atheists: 'no dotage so infatuate, no frenzy so extravagant as theirs'.

Whether the 'most honoured patrons, trustees', to whom Bentley owed his appointment, were present at this opening performance is uncertain. One of them, John Evelyn, certainly attended the second discourse a month later, when the preacher undertook to confute atheism from the faculties of the soul, under the proposition: 'Matter and Motion cannot think' – and was deeply impressed. 'One of the most learned and convincing discourses I had ever heard,' he recorded in his diary (April 4, 1692). Learned it certainly was. It displayed a thorough acquaintance with the work of Descartes and Locke, in addition to the ancient Sceptics. Convincing, no less certainly – to the already converted – and who, after all, among the congregation

69

of St Martin's, was not? The question whether matter can think had been treated by John Locke in a hypothetical way. Locke could not see why matter should not think, if God gave it the power to do so. He confessed that he could not conceive of its doing so, but all things were possible in God, and (as Dr Johnson might have said) 'there's an end on't'. For materialists, then and now, however, this was not the end on't, nor even the beginning on't. For them, matter generated thought by its own internal motion, and God didn't come into the question. This was, and is, a perfectly respectable position. Modern materialists, more especially of the dialectical kind, have for long been prepared to furnish forth the thesis without embarrassment, and in our time it has taken hold of a large part of mankind. In Bentley's day it was either, as in Locke, a hypothesis that had to be considered, even if it could not be tested; or it was an article of faith which had to be held in secret for safety's sake; or else it was a blasphemy to be repudiated with ridicule and horror. Bentley, like Descartes, prefers what has been called 'the ghost in the machine'. He undertakes to prove that 'there is an immaterial substance in us which we call soul and spirit, essentially distinct from our bodies; and that this spirit doth necessarily evince the existence of a spiritual Being'. He does not prove it. He states it. It is self-evident that there is something in our composition that thinks and apprehends. 'It is no less self-evident that these faculties proceed from something or other as their efficient cause . . . some cogitative substance (*res cogitans*, Descartes called it), some incorporeal inhabitant, within us, which we call spirit and and soul.' This 'incorporeal inhabitant', or ghost in the machine of the body, is the miniature man who was often represented as taking flight from the body in medieval pictures of death-bed scenes. This mixing up of ghosts with machines is the familiar category-error of talking about things different in kind, or category, as if they belonged to the same kind or category. It is confusion, or quite literally nonsense. Bentley was to go on like this when in subsequent lectures he came to the proof of a deity from the beautiful economy of the living bodies of men and animals. The argument from design, Paley's watch, God the clock-maker and winder, the well-ordered garden implying a Divine Gardener – all these irrelevant and confusing analogies of eighteenth-century thought, come into view with the Boyle lectures of 1692.

All the same, there was a marked improvement in the quality of the lectures as the series proceeded. The born controversialist, the hair-splitter, the clever scorer of debating points, gives place to the learned and patient expositor marshalling the discoveries of modern science as auxiliary to the cause of religion. The hammer of the atheists in their folly and unrighteousness gives place to the disciple of Isaac Newton and the naturalists intent upon employing man's new knowledge of nature as it 'might work with considering men for the belief of a deity'. The last three lectures stand under the general heading: 'A Confutation of Atheism from the Origin and Frame of the World', and they represent a brilliant improvisation on the Newtonian cosmology for the promotion of religious belief. They place Bentley in the foremost rank of Christian apologists in the long battle between science and religion. It was not a question of Bentley's 'getting up' the *Principia* in order to use it for religious propaganda. He possessed strong natural powers of logical ratiocination, and there seems to be little doubt that he attended Newton's lectures as Lucasian Professor of Mathematics while at Cambridge. We find him seeking, and receiving, instruction from the author of *Principia Mathematica* himself some months before the Boyle lectures were even founded, probably in consequence of his study of the ancient cosmologists, Lucretius and Epicurus. The *Principia* had been published some five years when Bentley turned to the composition of the Boyle lectures. Some acquaintance with its teaching was already a must among educated men. In the Boyle lectures, delivered before a mixed audience, he speaks as if it were possible to take for granted at least a working knowledge of the Newtonian system, and to refer his listeners to the book itself instead of retailing a detailed account of the Newtonian demonstrations. No doubt he took too much for granted. While the Newtonian conception of the universe was becoming a part of the outlook of educated men, it was not because they had read *Principia*. It was because men like Richard Bentley were interpreting it for them. Dr Monk went so far as to acclaim Bentley as 'the first to lay open these discoveries in a popular form'. To attempt to establish priorities in such a matter would be a difficult, and perhaps a rather profitless undertaking, but it may still be safely asserted that Bentley was the first to perform the task well.

It was certainly a task that made great demands upon the performer. Newton himself was well aware of this. Denis Diderot, himself one of the leading popularizers of science in the following century and the father of the great *Encyclopedia*, once said that Newton himself could have made his work perfectly intelligible to the common reader if he had troubled to spend another month on the job. He was apparently unaware of the fact that Newton had originally attempted to present his work in a simple and accessible form but had given up the attempt, daunted by the difficulties involved. When Bentley sought the master's instructions for proceeding with his own study of the work, he received Newton's advice: 'At ye first perusal of my Book, it's enough if you understand ye Propositions with some of ye Demonstrations which are easier than the rest. For when you understand ye easier, they will afterwards give you light unto ye harder.' Whatever procedure he adopted, it is certain that Bentley achieved a remarkable mastery of his subject. Before publishing the lectures, he consulted Newton again. Although he felt constrained to correct his pupil on one or two important points, the master was on the whole delighted. A few years later, when Bentley was at war with the scholars of Christ Church over *Phalaris*, his Boyle lectures were scrutinized by John Keill, his opposite number at Oxford in the propagation of the Newtonian system, in the hope of finding errors for his discomfiture. The vindictive proceeding proved fruitless, save in one particular. Bentley had pointed to the revolutions of the earth upon its own centre, and 'these useful vicissitudes of night and day' without which 'one half of it could never see the day, but must eternally be condemned to solitude and darkness', as an 'eminent token of the divine wisdom and goodness', contrasting this providential arrangement with the divine arrangements as regards the moon, 'not once wheeling upon her own centre', much to the detriment of that unfortunate orb. Keill pointed out that (as Newton had discovered) 'the moon does turn once, in the time of her period, about her own centre', and that it is just because she does so that the moon always shows the same face to us. This, he considered, should be evident 'to any one who thinks'. He concluded that 'it were to be wished that great critics would confine their labours to their lexicons'. Bentley omitted the words 'not once wheeling upon her own centre' in the edition of 1699.

7

The Christian Advocate - II

In undertaking to popularize Newton's system, Bentley was a pioneer in a venture that was to engage the intellectual energies of a succession of men of letters, especially in France, over the next fifty years and more. Voltaire produced his *Elements of the Philosophy of Newton* in 1738. Madame de Châtelet's translation of the *Principia* into French had already earned for her the soubriquet 'the Lady Newton'. By that time, there was even an Italian version, *Il Newtonianismo per la Dama*, the work of Count Algarotti. There were many others. But popularization was not the exclusive purpose of these labours. The predominant concern was generally to put Newton's system in place of the prevailing system of Descartes. The 'Vorticist' physics of Descartes left the deity on one side. Having created the universe out of matter and motion, God was supposed to have set the system off with a divine flip and left it to spin around to all eternity without further intervention. As Pascal said, he found it impossible to forgive Descartes for simply making use of a deity in order to give things a shove, and then having no further use for him. In place of this, the Newtonian system instituted a resident engineer, an ubiquitous, ever-present and active deity: a kind of celestial clock-maker and clock-minder. By 1738, Voltaire could discern two camps, two intellectual factions, in the intellectual life of France, using the names of Descartes and Newton as their rallying-cries. The faction-fight continued for many years. Even at Cambridge, Newton's own university, the Cartesian system was still being taught well into the eighteenth century. And as long as the great Fontenelle lived, the system of Descartes was never to lack a loyal advocate. Fontenelle lived until 1757, having been born in 1657, and almost his last work, *Theorie des Tourbillons cartesiens*, published when he was ninety-five, although composed a few years earlier, was to maintain the

Cartesian vorticist physics intact. He had been the first to popularize the system, in his *Entretiens sur la Pluralité des Mondes* (1686); it had gone into more than thirty editions; he may be said to have had a vested interest in vorticism. To say that it was easy to popularize the Cartesian version of the universe is not to detract from the exquisite skill, and the tactical *ordonnance*, of Fontenelle's wholly charming book. *Le Monde*, according to Descartes, was intensely satisfying to the aesthetic sense. *Le beau monde* of France took to it with delight. *'Ah, le beau monde! J'adore ses tourbillons!'* It left nothing mysterious. It answered all the questions.

Newton's system was difficult. It was shot through and through with mystery, and its comprehension was dependent upon knowledge of the higher mathematics. Newton never made any pretence to understand final causes, or to understand the nature of gravity. He had to point out to Bentley how dangerous it was to speak of gravity 'as essential and inherent to matter'. 'Pray,' he begged, 'do not ascribe that notion to me; for the cause of gravity is what I do not pretend to know. . . .' True, 'gravity put the planets into motion, but, without the divine power, it could never put them into such a circling motion as they have about the sun; and therefore, for this, as well as other reasons, I am impelled to ascribe the frame of this system to an intelligent Agent'. An 'arm' had to be postulated, the arm of a preceding and presiding God without whom the system could not be guaranteed to work in the way that it was observed to work, as a system of mighty gravitational forces. But suppose that gravity was a property inherent in matter, instead of a property 'put into' matter by a deity in varying quantities for the purposes of a preconceived equilibrium, then surely the universe as we know it might have evolved by chance? Newton's self-confessed ignorance about final causes sometimes led his critics – especially in France – to charge him with deliberately retaining an 'unknowable' element in his system out of an ultimate attachment to occultism or superstition. Far from making 'all things light', as Pope was to acclaim him, the great man had left many things wrapped in darkness. And of course this was true. Newton, a deeply religious man, was prepared to let God have His secrets. The mind of finite man could not know the ways and workings of the infinite. And least of all were such enquiries the province of scientists. He would have agreed with Diderot when he said: '*Qui sommes-nous, pour expliquer les fins de la nature?* . . . *Le physicien, dont la profession est d'instruire et non d'edifier, abandonnera donc le* pourquoi, *et ne s'occupera que du* comment.'

On the other hand, it was Diderot who grasped the fundamental inadequacy of Newtonian physics for the confutation of atheists. He recognised the validity of the materialist's argument that Newton had not by any means excluded the possibility of interpreting the universe as a 'fortuitous concourse of atoms', a chance formation of matter in motion. He saw the need to face this, the atheist's charge, '*que le monde resulte du jet fortuit des atomes*', and not merely to ridicule it, as Bentley had done. 'If a man should affirm that an ape, casually meeting with pen, ink and paper, and falling to scribble, did happen to write exactly the *Leviathan* of Thomas Hobbes, would an atheist believe such a story? . . . Can any credulity be comparable to this?' Thus Bentley, mocking and merely derisive. And again: supposing the letters of the alphabet 'thrown at random upon the ground', how many millions of millions of years must pass before a throw resulted in their settling down into the correct order of the alphabet? The odds against its happening are so enormous as to make the consideration negligible. When Diderot came to this consideration, however, he took it seriously, for so long as there remains one chance in no-matter-how-many million that the atheist may be right, the atheist has not been answered. It could not be denied, by a simple resort to ridicule, that in an infinite series of throws ('jets') the letters of the alphabet *might* settle down into a complete and accurate version of the *Iliad* or the *Henriade*. In other words, the presence of pattern or design in nature could never be a conclusive argument for a divine artist or architect. What was needed by the religious advocate, Diderot concluded, was not simply pattern or design but purpose, the evident adaptation of structure in living organisms to their function. '*La Divinité n'estelle pas aussi clairement empreinte dans l'oeil d'un ciron que la faculté de penser dans les ouvrages du grand Newton?*' It was this that turned Diderot's mind away from the mathematical and mechanistic sciences towards the study of anatomy, biology, insectology. From the gigantic structures of sidereal physics to the structure of living organisms. From the universe as a machine to the wing of a butterfly and the eye of a cheese-mite. From macrocosm to microcosm. From the telescope to the microscope. Bentley also brought in the biological sciences, but not because he doubted the complete efficacy of the mechanistic and mathematical sciences of Newton for the confutation of atheism. He brought them in as auxiliary, not as indispensable.

The history of science has greatly suffered in its perspectives by the historian's concentration for long periods upon the mechanical sciences at the expense of the sciences of living nature. The giant figure of Newton has often tended to overshadow the patient labours of microscopists, like Hooke and Leeuwenhoek, and (until recently) great botanists like John Ray. Bentley, however, did not make this mistake, perhaps because in the seventeenth century the work of these supposedly 'humbler' workers in the field of 'natural knowledge' were very much in the foreground of the picture of scientific advance, while Newton's gigantic predominance was not perceptible until its end. The order in which Bentley treats of the evidential value of the two types of scientific advance for religious advocacy is significant here. Newtonian science serves him principally in his last three lectures on the 'confutation of atheism from the origin and frame of the world' as the grand 'clincher' of the whole. But it is in the fourth lecture, nearly half-way through the course, that he treats of the biologists, the men of the microscope. This aspect of the lectures has received little attention, so firmly have later commentators concentrated their attention upon the Newtonian aspect. Yet it is here, more than half a century before Diderot's *Pensées sur l'interpretation de la Nature*, with its butterflies and cheese-mites, that we find Bentley citing Redi, Malpighi, Swammerdam and Leeuwenhoek in order to illustrate 'the fearful and wonderful' economy of living organisms, an economy that could only be ascribed to the work of an 'intelligent artist who had first in his comprehensive intellect a complete *idea* and model of the whole organical body before he entered upon the work'. The experiments of 'that sagacious and learned naturalist, Francisco Redi', 'the happy curiosity of Malpighi', and the observations of 'the most accurate Leeuwenhoek', had made untenable any theory of the spontaneous generation of organic life – a theory particularly attractive to materialists wishing to dispense with a divine act of creation, as became very evident from the interest it continued to evoke long into the eighteenth century. When Diderot declared in 1747 that *'les meditations sublimes de Malebranche et de Descartes étaient moins propres à ébranler le materialisme qu'une observation de Malpighi'*, and that it was in the work of such men *'qu'on a trouvé des preuves satisfaisantes de l'éxistence d'un être souverainement intelligent'*, he sometimes seems to be merely paraphrasing Bentley's fourth Boyle lecture of 1692. Diderot was thoroughly conversant with the works of his English contemporaries and predecessors (he at one time made a living by translating English works into French), and Bentley's *Confutation* had quickly won a reputation on the continent.

It must ever remain remarkable that this rising star of classical learning should have followed up the critical triumph of *Epistola ad Millium*, within a year, with a work so wide in its appeal, so 'modern' in its grasp upon the scientific achievements of the age. It bears all the marks of its author's bold and contentious character in its style and manner. Sometimes, notably in the opening lecture, Bentley the impatient litigant overwhelms Bentley the masterly advocate. Then the tone is shrill, bullying, almost abusive. Mostly, however, his manner is vigorous, balanced, serenely confident. The sardonic aside, the homely image, the avoidance of rhetoric in argument and its brief but happy indulgence when argument is over and the point well made: all the components of the inimitable Bentleian manner still preserve the *Confutation of Atheism* from the dusty death that has overtaken a hundred tracts and treatises on similar subjects composed in that age of religious apologetics. The book lives by its language, even when its arguments and its purpose have ceased to impress by their relevance to our world and its issues. A short anthology of passages from the *Confutation* might be made to reveal the prose style of Bentley as belonging to the plain and even homely tradition of Bunyan and Dryden rather than the gorgeous tradition of Hobbes and Sir Thomas Browne. It was the tradition leading to William Cobbett, a character with whom Bentley had many similarities.

Bentley on 'thinking matter', or motion as the begetter of thought:

> If, then, motion in general, or any degree of its velocity, can beget cogitation, surely a ship under sail must be a very intelligent creature, though while she lies at anchor those faculties must be asleep: some cold water or ice must be phlegmatic and senseless, but when it boils in a kettle it has wonderful heats of thinking and ebullitions of fancy.

Bentley on the divine wisdom in limiting the physical powers of the human body:

> And if mankind had had wings . . . all the world must have consented to clip them; or else the human race had been extinct before this time, nothing upon that supposition being safe from murder and rapine.

Bentley on the spontaneous generation of life:

> [The notions] of the astrological undertakers, that would raise men like vegetables out of some fat and slimy soil, well digested by the kindly heat of the sun, and impregnated with the influence of the stars upon some remarkable and periodical conjunctions; which opinion hath been vamped up of late by Cardan and Cesalpinus and other newsmongers from the skies; a pretence as groundless and silly as the dreaming oneiro-critics of Artemidorus and Astrampsychus, or the modern chiromancy and divinations of gipsies.

There is more than an echo of Thomas Browne in this. On the other hand, he is content to mock at Epicurus' account of free-will with a homely image from the bowling-green:

> 'Tis as if one should say that a bowl equally poised, and thrown upon a plain and smooth bowling-green, will run necessarily and fatally in a direct motion; but if it be made with a bias, that may decline it a little from a straight line, it may acquire by that motion a liberty of will, and so run spontaneously to the jack.

There is in these lectures every device, from the conversa-tional interjection to the sublime apostrophe, and all devised with conscious art to capture and retain the attention of a mixed audience. Like St Paul at Athens, he fitted his discourse pertinently to the persons he addressed. He was no babbler, or busy prating fellow. As he said of St Paul at the opening of the third lecture, 'he did not talk at random; but was thoroughly acquainted with the several humours and opinions of his auditors'. Perhaps, indeed, Bentley had cast himself for the role of the apostle, who was also, as he did not fail to point out, 'a great master in all the learning of the Greeks'. Unlike St Paul, however, who never presumed to measure the effect of his discourse when it was done, Bentley was very sure that he had nipped atheism in the bud. Looking back in later years, he was ready to declare, and apparently to believe, 'that the atheists had fallen silent since that time, and sheltered themselves under deism'. So Cobbett liked to think that his lectures in 1829–30 had brought about the Great Reform Bill of 1832. 'If you could have heard one of these, you would not wonder that the nation was roused, and that we now have that Reform, which the nation owes to those lectures more than to all other causes put together.'

Certainly the applause that met the Boyle lectures of 1692 was (to quote Dr Monk) 'loud and universal'. Only a certain Mr Henry Layton seems to have raised a note of protest. Mr Layton thought that the preacher's design to prove God's providence and creation from the immateriality of souls, under the heading 'Matter and Motion cannot think', was a mistake. 'I judge,' Mr Layton said, 'he hath taken the wrong sow by the ear.' But, as Dr Monk remarks, Bentley had little to fear from a person who expressed himself in such low, not to say vulgar language. It appears that Mr Layton was a Yorkshireman too.

The Trinity Pantheon. Statues of great Trinity men in the ante-Chapel.
Left to right: Bacon, Barrow, Newton, Macaulay, Tennyson, Whewell.

The Great Gate, and the Wren Library, Trinity College.

The statue of the Founder of Trinity, King Henry VIII, is shown bearing ball and sceptre (though see footnote on page 112). The name of Edward III, founder of King's Hall, a predecessor of Henry VIII's foundation, is to be seen below, along with the coats of arms of his sons. (Right) The Library, seen with

8

The Keeper

Christian advocacy, the hammering of atheists, the popularization of science might seem to be digressions from the field of
classical criticism. It is unlikely that Richard Bentley regarded
them as such. The world of learning was still one world, the
problem of 'The Two Cultures' scarcely conceivable as yet.
Bentley could preach science from the pulpit without self-
consciousness or apology, and he approached cosmology and
biology alike, not simply from his knowledge of the work of
Newton and Leeuwenhoek and Malpighi, but also from his
familiarity with Democritus and Lucretius and the *Astronomica*
of Manilius. He was unaware of any dichotomy between his
study of ancient literature and his study of modern science.
Hence it would be misleading to talk of his 'return' to his
classical studies after the Boyle lectures. He had never left them.
In the middle of the summer of 1692, when he was half-way
through the course, he entered upon a learned correspondence
with John George Graevius, the veteran classical scholar of the
age – a correspondence that was to continue in amity and mutual
regard until the death of Graevius in 1703. Graevius was to
admire *The Confutation of Atheism*, when it came out in book
form, and was to promote the publication of a Dutch translation.
But their discourse was not of Newton and Leeuwenhoek and
Malpighi, but of Manilius and Callimachus. Bentley was still
very much concerned with his Oxford project of publishing the
fragments of the poets.

There was nothing in the terms of the Boyle foundation for-
bidding the re-appointment of a lecturer for a second year, and
Bentley's patrons and friends were justified in expecting that a
man who had done so well would be invited to accept a second
term. One of the trustees, however, Sir John Rotheram, pressed
his preference for Dr Kidder, Bishop of Bath and Wells, so that

Bentley was passed over, somewhat to the chagrin of John Evelyn, his most ardent supporter. Bentley himself appears to have expressed neither disappointment nor resentment. He was thinking a great deal about Manilius.

Manilius held a special place in his affections, partly because he considered that he, and Ovid, were the only wits among the ancient poets, and partly because Manilius was the author of *Astronomica*. Manilius was capable of apostrophising the deity in terms that delighted the disciple of Newton:

> Wherefore do we see the stars arise in their seasons, and move, as at a word spoken, on the paths prescribed to them? Of whom there is none that hastens, neither is there any that tarries behind. Why are the nights beautiful with these that change not, and the nights of winter from of old? These things are not the work of chance, but the order of a God most high. . . .

Between the time he left Oxford and the delivery of the Boyle lectures, he had undertaken much research into what may be called 'the Manilian question'. Who was Manilius? Hardly anything was known of him excepting his name and that he had lived in the reign of Caesar Augustus. But what if, as Gaspar Gevärts had held so obstinately, he was really Flavius Theodorus Mallius, consul in AD 399, nearly four centuries later? Plainly it was the first duty of a scholar now proposing to edit and publish Manilius to check up on this question of chronology. It was precisely the kind of problem that had engaged the learned editors and commentators of the chronicle of John of Antioch.

Friends and admirers rallied round with the loan of scarce editions, manuscripts, and collations from foreign libraries. Sir Edward Sherburn, an old Cavalier scholar who had transcribed the first book of *Astronomica* and collected materials for a commentary, produced a box full of documents which he had bought in Antwerp. Its contents had once belonged to Gaspar Gevärts – the sole patentee of the opinion that Manilius was Mallius. It was the contents of this box that sent Bentley, in the summer of 1692, upon his course of learned correspondence with the great Graevius of Utrecht. For, among the Gevärtian documents he had discovered two letters from Graevius which appeared to endorse the Mallian hypothesis about the identity of Manilius. It turned out, upon enquiry, that Graevius had briefly endorsed the Mallian theory, but that he had since disclaimed it. Graevius had professed profound admiration for the author of *Epistola ad Millium* and was delighted at the inauguration of a correspondence with the younger man, whom he regarded as the scholar most likely, and worthy, to succeed him as king of classical criticism. Bentley finally enraptured him by sending over to Utrecht another of the contents of Sir Edward Sherburn's box – and with Sir Edward's leave, a treatise on the life of Flavius Theodorus Mallius by one Albertus Rubenius: a treatise designed by Rubenius to dissuade his friend Gevärts from continuing to make a fool of himself by persisting in the Mallian theory. This was the kind of document that Graevius would be delighted to receive. Bentley made it quite clear that it had come into his hands by the courtesy of Sherburn. Unfortunately Graevius acknowledged it with a panegyric upon the genius of Richard Bentley, and proceeded to publish it without reference to the name of old Sir Edward.

As often happens when a man enjoys a succession of scholastic triumphs, and more especially when those triumphs are in diverse fields of achievement – *Epistola ad Millium* and the *Confutation of Atheism* were successive triumphs of this kind – there are many who look for his stumbling. So it was now. Old Sir Edward Sherburn let it be known that, in his opinion, 'Dr Bentley had ungratefully robbed him of the honour of that publication'. This aspersion was to prove especially useful to Bentley's enemies after the publication of his *Dissertation on the Epistles of Phalaris* in 1697, that bombshell which set the learned world of Oxford licking its wounds and thirsting for revenge. Bentley secured from Graevius a transcription of that part of his letter wherein he had explicitly mentioned Sir Edward as the agency through which the treatise of Rubenius had come to light, and Graevius blamed himself for the oversight by which he had accredited Bentley with its discovery. But it was all to no avail. It was necessary to brand the author of the *Dissertation on Phalaris* as a thief of other men's laurels, an upstart, a brawler and a rascal.

Whatever may have been the case later, certainly at this stage

83

of his career Bentley was slow to anger. His treatment of Joshua Barnes shows that. Barnes, a Cambridge scholar 'whose peculiarities', to quote Dr Monk, 'have occasioned his name to be seldom mentioned without a smile', was working on an edition of Euripides. He was aware that Bentley believed the six 'Epistles' attributed to Euripides to be spurious, and wrote to ask why. Bentley told him, with suitable modesty and restraint. He did not venture to *assert* them to be false, only to *believe* it, citing some rather ludicrous examples of internal evidence. Barnes' sole acknowledgment of Bentley's assistance was to publish the Epistles intact among the works of Euripides, together with the comment that anyone who held them to be spurious must be either impudent or lacking in judgment – *perfrictae frontis, aut judicii imminuti.* And yet Bentley's communication of this opinion had been courteous, friendly, and even flattering to his correspondent, nor did he make any attempt to retaliate when Barnes came out with his offensive comment, a point at which most scholars might have been expected to deliver at least the retort courteous.

Manilius was ready for the printer early in the year 1694, along with a text of *Philostratus.* The War of the Grand Alliance, however, had brought about a rise in the cost of paper and printing which discouraged the publication of books for a limited market, and Bentley decided to get the work done at Leipzig. When the first sheets came to hand, the work proved to be of such inferior quality that he resolved to abandon the project. Olearius of Leipzig brought out part of the *Philostratus* in an edition of 1709. The *Manilius* came out with Henry Woodfall only in 1739. A handsome quarto volume, it was to be Bentley's last published work, and it had had to wait nearly half a century for its *imprimatur.* The editor's typographical conscience was responsible for the initial delay. Scholastic thirst for a long and rapid succession of published works could not overcome Bentley's devotion to the highest standard of typography and book production.

Bentley delivered his second course of Boyle lectures in 1694. This time his subject was the defence of Christianity against infidels. These lectures were never published, though he was talking of seeing them through the press as late as 1696, when he was busy preparing his *Dissertation on the Epistles of Phalaris* – 'a job for our friend Mr Wotton', as he called it in a letter to John Evelyn. Perhaps he was anxious to maintain a show of his good intentions, for Tenison, now archbishop of Canterbury, was urgent for their publication, as was Evelyn, and His Grace of Canterbury at any rate was not a patron whose wishes could be lightly disregarded. What happened to the text of this second course has never been discovered. It is very doubtful whether Bentley on the infidels would have added much to Bentley on the atheists. When he was invited to preach a still further course in 1695, he was glad to be excused, and to propose 'our friend, Mr Wotton', as a substitute. 'I am glad to be excused,' he told Evelyn; 'this year I shall find myself other work sufficient.' In the spring of 1694 he had been formally appointed by Royal Patent to the office of keeper of all the king's libraries in England, an appointment which had received the king's sign manual in the previous December. The appointment was for life. It carried with it a lodging in the Palace of St James, and a stipend of £200 per annum, although Bentley had to engage to pay £130 annually to a certain Mr Thynne, the gentleman to whom – in the course of the usual political scramble for 'places' in those days – it had originally been given at the death of Henry de Justel, the previous holder. Once again, Bentley owed much to the 'interest' exerted on his behalf by Edward Stillingfleet. Stillingfleet was deeply in the confidence of Queen Mary, to whom William III entrusted his ecclesiastical, academic and cultural patronage. Even before the completion of the original course of Boyle lectures, the great *Defensor* had secured his protégé a prebendal stall at Worcester. He also gave him the rectory of Hartlebury in Worcestershire to keep warm until young James Stillingfleet, Bentley's late pupil, was qualified to hold it. A chaplaincy to the king followed almost as a matter of course.

On taking up his duties as keeper of the royal libraries in the spring of 1694, Bentley left Park Street for his bachelor lodging in the Palace of St James, where he was to live until his installation at the Master's Lodge at Trinity in 1700. He was not lost to the company of Bishop Stillingfleet, however, for as prebend of Worcester he was engaged to reside at the bishop's palace when the bishop himself was in residence. The life of an ecclesiastical commuter suited him admirably. He was thirty-four years old, in robust health, and happily conscious of his own merits. The rewards of virtue and accomplishment were steadily coming his way. In the summer of 1696 he kept a Public Act at Cambridge for the degree of Doctor of Divinity, and preached at Public Commencement in defence of Revelation against the deists. He was already a fellow of the Royal Society, which brought him into the company of many of the most distinguished minds of his time. The new keeper was entertaining Newton and Locke, Evelyn and Wren, at an informal conversation-club which met twice a week at his lodging in St James's Palace. Launched into the most illustrious intellectual society of Augustan London, lodged in a royal palace and commuting with the palace of the Bishop of Worcester, admired and consulted on equal terms by the leading classical scholar of Europe in the person of John George Graevius, within five years of the publication of *Epistola ad Millium* the man from the north might have been forgiven a certain air of self-satisfaction. It was observed that he assumed some hauteur of manner at this time, an air of superiority which was certainly not to diminish with the years. His cast of countenance – a bold eye, a slightly tip-tilted nose, full lips which lent themselves easily to a sneer – contributed readily to this impression.

He had yet to crown his fame with the *Dissertation*. Fortune, in terms of hard cash, was to be postponed until he became Master of Trinity. As yet, the bachelor housekeeper of St James's was but decently equipped for plain living and high thinking. Not that he was ever a man of ostentatious personal tastes. In only one respect did he cultivate magnificence. He believed in doing himself well in the outward trappings of his office. His lodging at St James's greatly pleased him, for the rooms looked out upon the park, and he had the Princess Anne of Denmark and the Earl of Marlborough for neighbours. But the room which housed the books and manuscripts was utterly inadequate. Its contents were scattered about in the utmost confusion, and quite unfit to be shown to visiting scholars; as he said himself, 'not fit to be seen'. He at once took certain rare works – notably the Alexandrian manuscripts of the Greek bible – into safe keeping in his own apartments, so that persons wishing to see such treasure 'might see it without seeing the Library'. At the same time he resisted the efforts of Archbishop Tenison and others to have the manuscripts of the royal library included in the great *Catalogus librorum manuscriptorum Magnae Britannicae et Hiberniae* then printing at Oxford. He managed to persuade Queen Mary that their inclusion was inopportune – probably because the librarian himself was not yet perfectly acquainted with their description. He planned to get hold of certain 'closets' or small rooms on the floor above his own, as repositories for the housing and display of these treasures. However, his neighbour the Earl of Marlborough, having undertaken to solicit the queen on behalf of the librarian, got them annexed to his own apartments instead. Bentley, far from being chagrined by this, rather rejoiced, for, as he told Evelyn, 'by loss of them my Lord Marlborough thinks himself obliged . . . to obtain for me a new ground floor room to be built into the park, contiguous to my lodgings'. This was the more likely because his lordship would be able to extend his own quarters 'by raising a second story over this designed ground-room'. Indeed, Bentley envisaged nothing less than the building of a new library. The Treasury gave consent, and a bill was drawn up. 'Pressure of public business' put off its presentation to Parliament. At the end of the year 1694 the queen died, and Bentley's best chance of getting his plans carried out died with her.

It was at this time, in the year 1696, that Bentley redeemed a promise he had made to Graevius to contribute to an edition of *Callimachus*. The task of preparing the edition had been undertaken by Graevius' son, who had died before completing it. Bentley had promised to send Graevius more than double the number of Callimachan fragments than had been assembled by all preceding editors, together with manifold corrections. To Bentley this was one more instalment of the work he had projected while at Oxford: the great edition of all the fragments of the ancient poets. Actually he sent Graevius 420, and for good measure he included a rescension of the poet's epigrams and some notes on the Hymns. This was beaver-work, indeed, but as always with Bentley, it was a great deal more than that. He was not content to sweep together a heap of *disjecti membra poetae*, like the boffins of the learned world raking over their golden dust-heaps. He arranged the fragments of *Callimachus*, by a brilliant application of critical method, under the titles of the several works to which they must have originally belonged. The dry bones were made to live, the *disjecti membra poetae* were articulated in the form and substance of a body. The world of Greek scholarship could afford no example of such systematic, rigorous, and yet intuitive treatment of the literary ruins of old time. Bentley's *Callimachus*, as Richard Jebb put it, was not final. It could not be. Rather it was exemplary. It differed from the work of his predecessors as the work of a numismatist differs from that of a gold-digger. 'The first pattern of thorough treatment and the first model of critical method,' Jebb assures us, 'were furnished by Bentley's *Callimachus.*' Its pre-eminence shines the more brightly for the paste that surrounds it in the commentary supplied to Graevius' edition by the learned Baron Ezechiel Spanheim from his rich stores of antiquarian, philological and mythological learning. The difference between Bentley and Spanheim is the difference between genius and talent, between critical insight and laborious compilation. Bentley, in this work, set a new standard, established a new mode of classical criticism.

It was in this year, 1696, that Bentley added to his laurels certain bays that were to remain fresh and green long after the brightness of his name and fame had suffered tarnish under the blasts of academic warfare in his old university. He was to win the honourable title of 'Second Founder of the University Press', and to this day the London home of that proud institution bears the name of 'Bentley House'. Since the Charter of 1534 the press had been in the hands of tradesmen licensed to print and sell books in much the same way that innkeepers were licensed to brew and sell beer. Printing and book-production remained at a low level because they were at the mercy of the commercial fortunes of patent-holders. What was wanted at Cambridge was a printing house free from the commercial worries of publication and distribution, an institution – as the chancellor of the university envisaged it – which could print 'the great and excellent writings' of the learned members of the university free from the prejudiced hands of 'unskilful hordes of incorrect printers'. The Duke of Somerset, who was the chancellor at this time, had this matter very much at heart. He was writing to the university as 'servant of you all', as he put it, to advocate the setting up of such an institution under the direct control of the university as early as November 1695, within six months of the lapsing of the Licensing Act of 1662, though it was his letter to the university of June 29 following that is generally taken as the initiation of the great change that was to come. A grace was passed on January 21, 1698, setting up a governing body of thirty-seven members, to be known as 'The Curators of the Press'. Sixteen of them were heads of houses, nine were professors, and the remaining twelve were members of the senate. This body constituted the predecessor of 'The Syndics of the Press', temporarily appointed by grace in 1737, although the permanent syndicate was not established until 1782. It is this body which governs the press today. The management of the 'renovation of the Press' was entrusted to Bentley with the fullest possible power of attorney: *potestatem generalem et mandatum speciale.* . . . Fortunately for a man of his masterful energies, the grace which set up the thirty-seven curators provided for a quorum of five only.

A few years later, to be precise in 1712, Bentley was claiming that the public press at Cambridge was 'projected and founded solely by myself'. Dr Monk took his word for it, and Monk's avowal has been generally repeated by later writers. Whatever the literal truth, his care and devotion to the press at its birth has been freely acknowledged, notably by his friend John Evelyn. There is no need to doubt that his was the initial energy and imagination that set the infant on its way. He was now in his middle thirties, renowned as the author of *Epistola ad Millium* and as the first lecturer on the Boyle foundation, pre-eminent among bibliophiles as the keeper of the king's libraries. He was what we should now call a 'progressive', and there can be little doubt that he had grasped the full significance of the lapsing of the Licensing Act in May 1695. With typical promptitude he went to work setting up a new printing house in Queens' Lane and appointing an 'Inspector of the Press'. This office was filled by Cornelius Cronfelt (*anglice* Crownfield), a

Dutchman who had probably come to England with the forces of King William. This soldierly and 'very ingenious' man was to become University Printer in 1705. As 'Inspector' of the press, he received a salary of £25 p.a., and lived on the premises of the printing house in Queens Lane. He was a well-known and respected citizen of Cambridge in his day, and a loyal parishioner of St Botolph's Church, where he is commemorated. He died in 1743.

In July 1696 Crownfield set out for Holland to select and order types. The first consignment of types and printer's ink arrived in Queens Lane on October 25, 1697,[1] and the presses arrived by coach under Crownfield's personal supervision on November 19. By November 1698 the infant press was at work on its first substantial book, a Horace by James Talbot, the first of Jacob Tonson's splendid series of quarto classics. Its successors included editions of Virgil, Terence, Catullus, Tibullus and Propertius. The new press also produced a Cicero for Edmund Jeffery.

There had been some delay in getting the printing house finished. A grace had granted £1,000 for the purpose, other funds being contributed by the Duke of Somerset and his friends. The cost of the work, and of the printing of the earliest volumes, was high, for almost everything had to be bought in Holland, including the services of many of the workmen, and carried to England. Except a certain amount of Long Primer Hebrew, Brevier Greek and mathematical figures, all the sizeable type used at the press came from Holland. Nowhere else in Europe, and certainly not in England, could types of suitable quality be obtained. Even when English type-founders procured Dutch matrices they cast the type indifferently. As for the type-setters, or compositors, English workmen had no very high reputation for anything but the most commonplace English printing. 'Our English compositors are ignorant,' Bentley declared in 1708, 'and print Latin books as they are used to do English ones; if they are not set right by one used to observe the beauties of ye best printing abroad.' Cornelius Crownfield, we may be sure, 'set them right', and we may be no less sure that Richard

---

[1] The consignment weighed 45 cwt: without packing it comprised about 3,000 lb of type.

Bentley was at his shoulder. The first books to come from the press were printed in the finest types obtainable, and although the cost was high, with the additional expense of packing and transport, it was well worth it. There was nothing better to be had in Europe at that time, and for long after, than the van Dijk romans and italics from Amsterdam, for van Dijk was the most distinguished type-cutter in the Holland of the seventeenth century. Crownfield had been personally to the foundry in Amsterdam to do business with the widow of Jan Jacobsz, whose name was Schipper: in the books of the University Press, which have been preserved intact for two-and-a-half centuries, the names Schipper and Cleijburg stand, line after line, beside entries of supplies of two-line pica, roman and italic. Great Primer, and English of all types, were supplied from that source too. By 1699 the press was taking delivery of Paragon Greek, and in the following year some English Greek. The curators secured 100 lb of English Hebrew from Emanuel Althias of Amsterdam in 1709, and two years later were buying a small fount of English Hebrew from an English foundry run by Mrs Elizabeth Grover. Brevier Greek type was cast by Edward Head in 1714, and Saxon letters by James' foundry, both in London. So the English type-founders begin to come into the picture, but it was long before the fine Dutch types could be dispensed with when really impressive work was on the presses. Matthew Prior, at the British Embassy in Paris, conducted negotiations for the export of some of the beautiful French Greek types, but the negotiations petered out in consequence of the exacting demands for acknowledgments on the title-page of all books in which the type was employed.

His work at the University Press was perhaps the happiest of Bentley's labours in the service of the university, for his devotion to fine printing, and his taste for the aesthetic qualities of book production, were among the purest and most disinterested of his activities. When he came to reside at the Master's Lodge at Trinity, a year or two after his initial work on the 'renovation' of the press, he devoted himself to further, and no less fruitful endeavours on behalf of this his favourite avocation beyond his study-walls.[1]

[1] See below, p. 125.

9

Phalaris

Bentley's conduct as keeper of the royal libraries was to come in for much adverse criticism. Swift was to portray him, in *The Battle of the Books* (1704), as a spider gorged with flies, presiding over a cobwebby confusion, 'the avenues to his castle . . . guarded with turnpikes and palisadoes. . . . After you had passed several courts you came to the centre, wherein you might behold the constable himself in his own lodgings, which had windows fronting to every avenue, and ports to sally out upon all occasions of prey or defence.' This venomous and jealous creature was in the habit of carrying off the books of all the advocates of modern learning and lodging them in the fairest apartments, while he consigned works by the advocates of the Ancients to obscure corners, or even threatened to turn them out of doors altogether. It was complained that the keeper sat on certain manuscripts in his own lodging, so that it was difficult, if not impossible, for visiting scholars to make use of them. A certain foreign scholar, it was reported, applying to Dr Bentley for a sight of the Alexandrian MS, 'met with no other answer but that the Library was not fit to be seen'. To which complaint the keeper rejoined that he had constantly kept that MS in his own lodging for this very reason, 'that persons might see it without seeing the Library', and that there were at least a hundred in England who had seen it there. As for the library's not being fit to be seen, even after four years of his keepership, the librarian was being blamed 'if the room be too mean, and too little for the books; if it be much out of repair; if the situation be inconvenient; if the access to it be dishonourable . . .' was he to be expected to have erected a new library at his own expense? 'For the expenses and toils of a long war are but too just an excuse that the thoughts of a new library were not part of the public cares. . . .'

Part of the trouble was the keeper's absence for some months in every year when he was commuting to Worcester. This, at least in part, was responsible for his quarrel with the Hon Charles Boyle, of Christ Church in the University of Oxford. The dean of Christ Church, Dr Aldrich, had put this bright young scholar on to the task of producing an edition of the *Epistles of Phalaris*, a work which had a special interest to scholars in general since Sir William Temple had commended the letters of this ancient Sicilian tyrant as an unsurpassed example of the epistolary art, and a knock-down argument for the superiority of ancient over modern literature in general. Mr Boyle was in need of the collation of an epistle with a manuscript in the King's Library at St James's. Instead of approaching the keeper in person, or even by letter, he had commissioned his London bookseller (or, as we should now describe him, 'publisher'), Mr Thomas Bennett, to get the collation done for him. Mr Bennett, of the Sign of the Half Moon in St Paul's Churchyard, was both dilatory and careless in executing this commission. He mentioned it to Bentley early in 1694, before his formal institution as keeper, and Bentley had expressed himself as more than willing to do any service in his power for the kinsman of the great Robert Boyle, founder of the lectureship in which he had had the honour to serve the cause of Christianity. Bennett seems to have left the further discussion of the matter until he should run across the keeper either in the street or at his shop in St Paul's Churchyard. Then he asked Bentley what he thought of the Hon Charles Boyle's project of editing a new *Phalaris*, and Bentley told him perfectly frankly that it was not worth while, since the reputed epistles of Phalaris were spurious, adding – rather gratuitously – that he did not doubt, all the same, that the work would sell simply on account of the names of the persons concerned in the venture.

Thomas Bennett had no reason to love the new keeper. Bentley, with typical energy, had been concerned to enforce the claims of the King's Library, under the Licensing Act of 1662, to receive copies of all books published in England.[1] The Act lapsed in 1694, and was only formally renewed – as regards this particular – in 1709. But the keeper was intent at least on recovering arrears, for publishers had been slack in performing

[1] Copies were required also for the libraries of the two universities.

their legal obligation in the matter, an obligation which they had always resented. Thomas Bennett had shown himself particularly resentful. Why, he wanted to know, should publishers be saddled with this obligation to give away their property? Bentley, who procured about a thousand volumes for the royal library by his insistence upon its statutory rights, told Thomas Bennett that if he expected a favour from the royal library (such as the collation of a MS for Mr Boyle) 'he ought in justice to present to it some book of competent value'. He was perfectly willing to allow the collation for Mr Boyle, but he thought that Mr Bennett should fulfil his obligation to the library by a suitable *quid pro quo*. In the event the collator employed by Mr Bennett on behalf of Mr Boyle had more than a week for a job that Bentley always said should not have taken him more than about four hours. The fact that the MS had to be returned before the job was completed was entirely due to Mr Bennett's dilatory behaviour throughout, and the collator's snail-like pace. The deadline for the return of the MS was a Saturday night. No further time could be allowed because Bentley was due to leave London for Worcester by the 5 o'clock coach on the Monday morning. It was his duty to let no book go out of the King's Library without particular order, which meant by His Majesty's warrant. The keeper had already ventured beyond his power in lending the book privately and without such an order, in his wish to oblige Mr Boyle. If Mr Boyle was now incensed because the collation had not been completed in time, Bentley believed that he knew the true reason for his displeasure. 'I had the hard hap, in some private conversation, to say the Epistles were a spurious piece, and unworthy of a new edition. *Hinc illæ lacrymae.*' Thomas Bennett had seen to it that Mr Boyle, and the Oxford scholars in general, were appraised of the contemptuous opinions of the insolent keeper, not only about the *Epistles of Phalaris*, but about Oxford scholarship wasting its time on them. Was it to be tolerated that the Honourable Charles Boyle and the gentlemen-scholars of 'The House' should suffer such scurvy treatment from an upstart from Cambridge, a subsizar out of Yorkshire, amanuensis to a bishop, lately jumped into the office of library-keeper, and suffering from a head several sizes too big for him?

On New Year's Day 1695 the Hon Charles Boyle brought forth his edition of the *Epistles of Phalaris*.

On the 26th of the same month, Richard Bentley opened a copy of this work and read in the preface: *Collatas etiam curavi usque ad Epist. 40 cum MS in Bibliotheca Regia, cujus mihi copiam ulteriorem Bibliothecarius pro singulari sua humanitate negavit. . . .* 'I have attended to the collation of the letters with the MSS in the Royal Library as far as Epistle 40; the librarian, with that courtesy which distinguishes him, denied me further access.'

In still other words: the ill-conditioned watch-dog guarding access to the royal library at St James's had sat on a manuscript required by the Hon Charles Boyle for the proper editing of his book.

On reading this, the watch-dog raised a discreet bark. He wrote that same evening to the Hon Charles, giving his own account of what had happened. He expected that when he had been apprised of the facts, the Hon Charles would stop publication of the work until the offending passage had been altered. Instead, two posts later, he received a reply to the effect that Mr Bentley's account might be true, but the account he had received from his publisher was different, and that it was too late for him to interpose, since the work was on sale, and Mr Bentley might do himself right by whatever method he pleased.

There followed an ominous silence.

The keeper, in the intervals of keeping at St James's, commuting at Worcester, renovating the Cambridge Press, editing Manilius and supplying 420 fragments of Callimachus to John George Graevius, was quietly going about his 'job for Mr Wotton'. When the job was done, it appeared as an appendix to a second edition of William Wotton's 'Essay on the Ancient and Modern Learning', in 1697. It bore the title: *A Dissertation upon the Epistles of Phalaris, Themistocles, Socrates, Euripides and the Fables of Aesop*. It consisted of about one hundred pages of close argument, of which rather less than half were devoted to the *Epistles of Phalaris*, and about eight to the offensive behaviour of Charles Boyle. He apologised for bringing up the subject at all. He would have preferred to give it 'the neglect that is due to weak detraction'. But since he was engaged to write on Phalaris for

Mr Wotton, 'to omit to take notice of that slander would be tacitly to own it'.

He did not write his *Dissertation* in order to refute a libel on the king's keeper, but in order to expose 'that Sophist, whoever he was, that wrote a small book of letters in the name and character of Phalaris . . . to discover the ass under the skin of that lion'. This Phalaris was a Sicilian tyrant of the sixth century BC who made himself master of the hill-town of Agrigentum, a Greek colony. His name was a byword throughout Hellas, for abominable cruelties, one of his peculiar pleasures being to roast his enemies in the brazen image of a bull. Sir William Temple, in his *Essay on Ancient and Modern Learning* of 1692, had proclaimed a collection of some 150 letters, supposedly surviving from this gentleman's hand, 'to have more race, more spirit, more force of wit and genius, than any others I have ever seen, either ancient or modern'. Temple acknowledged that 'several learned men' had doubted their originality, attributing them to Politian or Lucian. Temple, himself a man of affairs, refused to believe them the work of 'the scholar or the sophist'. To him they breathed the genuine spirit of 'the tyrant and the commander', with their diversity of passion, their knowledge of life and contempt of death. In fact, one suspects that the letters of Phalaris were just the kind of letters that Sir William Temple would like to have written if he had been a man of affairs in the sixth century BC.

And now Richard Bentley had promised to demonstrate, for the benefit of Wotton's book, that the letters of Phalaris were spurious, and to expose whoever had imposed them as genuine upon the credulity of mankind as a sophist and an ass in one. (Incidentally, any scholar who could solemnly edit them as genuine in the year of Grace 1695 must be endowed with pretty long ears too. As for Sir William Temple, that eminent champion of the superiority of ancient letters over the work of all later authors, to whom the *Epistles of Phalaris* were a chief proof of his contention. . . .) And this is what he did. He did it from chronology and philology, from matter and manner, from an unrivalled knowledge of Greek language and literature. He proved forgery at the outset by showing Phalaris borrowing money from a certain city almost 300 years before it was named

The Master's Lodge, Trinity College.

Joanna Bentley Conjux:
Denavit Bentheius.

Joanna Bentley, the Master's wife.
This portrait also hangs in the Master's Lodge.

August 6. 1700.

Honoured Madam,

I shall always reflect on these Days, as some of the happiest of all my Life; when I valued my self to be beloved by You in some proportion to the Love I had for you. How that Affection came to be cast & defeated, I had rather forget then enquire. Providence, which governs all things, suffer'd it to be so & we must not be angry at it's Disposal. But it has pleased God, since that time, to make such alteration in my Circumstances, as gives me some hope that a Proposal of that kind may be now better entertain'd by You & your Relations, then formerly it was. I dare safely promise on my part, that you will be always as dear to Me, as if no manner of Breach had happen'd betwixt us; nay I trust in God that an Affection will be far more united for having been once parted; as a Limb becomes stronger for being broken, if it be well set again. If you please & permit me to make you a Visit upon this Errand, and so discourse further about particulars, as soon as I have notice of it, I shall wait upon you at Oxley, being

Hon. Madam, Your most affectionate
Humble Servant R Bentley.

Bentley's Letter of Proposal of Marriage.
Facsimile of original in the Wren Library. See page 119.

or even built, and presenting his physician with a set of drinking-cups that could not have been fashioned until more than a century after his own death. Thus he goes on, exposing forgery, anachronism and internal inconsistency, point by point, until the last judgment upon matter and manner. 'But, to let pass all further arguments from words and language, to me the very matter and business of the letters sufficiently discovers them to be an imposture. What force of wit and spirit in the style, what lively painting of humour, some fancy they discern there, I will not imagine or dispute. But methinks little sense and judgment is shown in the groundwork and subject of them.

'. . . For, take them in the whole bulk, if a great person would give me leave, I should say they are a fardle of commonplaces, without any life or spirit from action or circumstance. Do but cast your eye upon Cicero's letters, or any statesman's, as Phalaris was: what lively characters of men there! what descriptions of place! what notifications of time! what particularity of circumstances! what multiplicity of designs and events! When you return to these again, you feel, by the emptiness and deadness of them, that you converse with some dreaming pedant with his elbow on his desk; not with an active, ambitious tyrant, with his hand on his sword, commanding a million of subjects. . . .'
Meanwhile, at the head of this *reductio ad absurdam*, stood a quotation from 'a great person':

I think the *Epistles of Phalaris* to have more race, more spirit, more force of wit and genius, than any others I have ever seen, either ancient or modern. . . . Such diversity of passions, upon such variety of actions and passages of life and government; such freedom of thought, such boldness of expression; such bounty to his friends, such scorn of his enemies; such honour of learned men, such esteem of good; such knowledge of life, such contempt of death; with such fierceness of nature and cruelty of revenge, could never be represented but by him that possessed them. . . .

Sir William Temple:
Essay upon Ancient and Modern Learning.

10

The Battle of the Books

Richard Bentley had treated Sir William Temple 'not indecently, but with no great reverence', as Macaulay put it.

Sir William was now in his seventieth year. He had played a distinguished part in the government of Charles II, had maintained a dignified neutrality in the Revolution of 1688, and had for some years lived in retirement at Moor Park, with Jonathan Swift for a secretary. There he wrote his memoirs, several treatises (the best of them on *Gardening*), and a number of rather boring essays (the worst of them on *Heroic Virtue*). He was an elder statesman, rather vain, much accustomed to deference, and quite unaccustomed to 'rude collision'. The least wise thing he ever did was to publish his *Essay on Ancient and Modern Learning*. He went to school at Bishop's Stortford, and he knew a little less Greek than Shakespeare.[1] 'This Essay,' wrote Lord Macaulay, 'silly as it is, was exceedingly well received both in England and on the Continent.' It certainly put its author at the head of the intellectual faction which at this time were upholding the superiority of the ancient to the modern authors. It seems that the Ancients who were also classical scholars (for the terms were by no means synonymous) were prepared to turn a blind eye to its blunders, while the Moderns were too ignorant to notice them. No doubt Macaulay was exaggerating when he declared that none of the contestants took the trouble to read and understand the works they argued about, that few were even 'decently acquainted with either ancient or modern literature, and hardly one was acquainted with both'. Excellent Latinists abounded, but Greek was at this period ill-taught at both school and university. As G. M. Trevelyan puts it: 'the excellent Latinists of Christ Church had not enough Greek to be aware

[1] Nor does he appear to have remedied the situation when he proceeded to Emmanuel College, Cambridge.

that Bentley had proved them dunces over the *Letters of Phalaris.*'
When Addison produced his *Cato* in 1713, a writer in the
Guardian could venture the opinion that it 'exceeded any of the
dramatic pieces of the ancients'. This dictum could only mean
that it was as good as Seneca, since 'scarcely anyone in Europe
except Bentley was capable of reading the Greek drama with
ease and intelligence . . . !'

Had Sir William Temple been content to praise the *Letters of
Phalaris*, Aesop's *Fables*, and so on, on grounds of personal
taste, nobody could have been much concerned one way or the
other by the exuberance of an old man's fancy. He had, however,
praised them as evidence in support of a general thesis: that, as
he said, 'the oldest books we have are still in their kind the best'.
The champion of the ineluctable superiority of the Ancients was
prepared to go even further, and to maintain the superiority of
the Ancients in all departments whatsoever, not only literary,
moral and intellectual, but physical, scientific and mechanical:
the lot. On the whole, the history of mankind was one of decay
and degeneration, or at the very least of vain efforts to keep up
with the Ancients. Anyone who ventured to think otherwise was
guilty of 'sufficiency, the worst composition out of the pride and
ignorance of mankind'. Progress was a myth born of pride and
complacency. William Wotton in his *Reflections on the Ancient
and Modern Learning* had made no attempt to explode this stuff
for the nonsense it was. He gently and firmly strove to rectify
the balance. Calmly, cautiously, candidly, he discriminates
between the claims of Ancients and Moderns in various departments of achievement. He examines the actual achievements of
the belauded heroes on either side. He points out highly
pertinent omissions. Temple, for instance, had had nothing to say
of Dante, Pascal, Molière, Chaucer, Milton and Shakespeare.
But such mild chiding was to indulge merely in the childish
game of team-picking. The radical answer to the asininity of
Sir William Temple was to be a patient exercise in chronology:
not to prove that the most ancient authors were not the best, but
to prove that they were not the most ancient. This was what
Richard Bentley did. By showing that our texts of the *Epistles of
Phalaris*, of Aesop's *Fables*, and many other ancient authors –
including Socrates and Euripides – were very far from being the

99

most ancient works of European literature, pure and undefiled, he knocked a very large hole in the bottom of Sir William's Ark of the Covenant of ancient pre-eminence. Only a man of Bentley's enormous erudition, philological expertise and unrivalled critical method, could have carried through this exploit with complete success. As it was, the veil of the temple was not only rent, it was ripped to pieces and the fragments cast upon the wind. This was more than 'rude collision'. It was annihilation. And the Honourable Charles Boyle, and the gentlemen-scholars of Christ Church, knew far too little Greek even to realize the fact. Within a very few months they came back for more.

Sir William himself complained bitterly in private, but he declined to enter into public argument with 'such a mean, dull, unmannerly pedant'. In this he was wise. Had he done so, as Macaulay observes, it 'would certainly have been a most extraordinary performance'. He contented himself with composing a reply, full of wrath and indignation, to William Wotton.[1] He had reason to believe that he could safely leave Richard Bentley to other hands. For the gentlemen-scholars of Christ Church rallied around the doyen of the Ancients like the Greeks when Hector fell. And, after all, they had wounds of their own to avenge as friends of the Hon Charles Boyle, the latest editor of Phalaris. They sprang to arms, not only in defence of Sir William, but to vindicate the honour of 'The House'. The Cambridge Goth was at the gate. There was a subdued sound of sharpening spears in Oxford town. Light cavalry was mustering. Something terrible was coming to Richard Bentley.

It came in 1698. It turned out to be what Lord Macaulay was to call: 'the best book ever written by any man on the wrong side of a question of which he was profoundly ignorant'. It was decked out with the learning of a schoolboy spread out as thin leaf, and sprinkled with disgraceful blunders for which old Busby would have flogged them all round. Thus, again, Macaulay with typical abandon. It bore the title: *Dr Bentley's*

[1] Temple's *Some Thoughts upon Reviewing the Essay of Ancient and Modern Learning* was left unfinished at his death in 1699. It appeared in the third part of his *Miscellanea* in 1701. In it he speaks of 'young barbarous Goths and Vandals, breaking or defacing the statues of those ancient heroes. . . . '

Dissertations on the Epistles of Phalaris, and the Fables of Aesop, Examin'd by the Honourable Charles Boyle, Esq. It consisted of nearly 300 pages of 'Examination', a preface, and an index entitled 'Account of Dr Bentley' with such intriguing headings as 'His clean and gentle metaphors', and 'His modesty and decency in contradicting great men. . . .' Although given out under the name of Charles Boyle, that gentleman had very little to do with it. More than half of it was written by Francis Atterbury, lately Mr Boyle's tutor. Other contributors were Smalridge (who provided an excellent parody of Bentley's style in a pretended proof that Bentley could not have written the *Dissertation* anyway), R. and J. Freind, and Anthony Alsop. In fact, the book was generally ascribed to the 'associated wits' of Christ Church, a confederacy said to be dedicated to putting down Bentley. For The House was at that time 'widely and justly celebrated as a place where the lighter parts of classical learning were cultivated with success', although 'with the deeper mysteries of philology neither the instructors nor the pupils had the smallest acquaintance'. No academical society, however, possessed a greater array of orators, wits, politicians, bustling adventurers, men who 'united the superficial accomplishments of the scholar with the manners and arts of the man of the world'. This formidable body was resolved 'to try how far smart repartees, well-turned sentences, confidence, puffing and intrigue could, on the question of whether a Greek book was or was not genuine, supply the place of a little learning'.

Macaulay's delineation of the classical society of Christ Church, composed exactly 140 years after the great flare-up of Bentley v. Boyle, owes something no doubt to his celebrated hindsight and his notorious passion for antithesis. When he wrote, in 1838, the battle was long over, Bentley's triumph was accepted historical fact, classical scholarship – and not only at Trinity – had long acquired that 'peculiar character which may be called Bentleian'. As Macaulay's great kinsman has put it: 'the typical English scholar was equally at home with Aristophanes and with Horace'.[1] It was far otherwise in 1698. The work

[1] G. M. Trevelyan, in his *England under Queen Anne*, Vol. II, p. 34, and in his *Illustrated English Social History*, Vol. III, p. 17.

of the 'associated wits' of Christ Church was at once hailed as having said the last word on Bentley and *Phalaris*. Boyle's *Examination* (to use its popular short-title) went into a second edition at once. Additional matter was included as edition followed edition. The demand for the book brought a fourth edition in 1745. Bentley himself spoke of the work as consisting merely of 'banter and grimace'. It was in truth much more than that. It remains still one of the liveliest and most entertaining works of controversy ever written, rivalling in these respects the *Dissertation* that called it forth. It was especially popular with readers who knew enough to understand what it was all about and were insufficiently instructed to reach an informed judgment upon the intellectual and scholarly issues which underlay the conflict of personalities. Many rejoiced in it as a long-overdue effort to take Dr Bentley down a peg. Samuel Pepys, President of the Royal Society, was one of these. While he valued Bentley's learning, he said, he thought it needed 'a little filing'. He did not doubt that 'a few such strokes as this will do it and him good'. Perhaps it did, for it has often been observed that the rumpus raised by the Oxford wits, in which fashionable and political society, not to mention thousands who didn't know whether Phalaris had ruled in Sicily or Siam, joined with alacrity and glee, seemed to have shocked him into wariness and sobriety when he produced his counterblast in the second *Dissertation* in 1699: 'for the first and last time', Macaulay thought.

In the meantime, while Bentley was supposed to have been left for dead, or at any rate licking his mortal wounds in some dark corner of the King's Library at St James's, the watchers on the side-lines of the field of battle set to work with the customary showers of missiles, *Views, Free but Modest Censures, Short Reflections, Answers, Vindications*, etc, etc. A fellow Johnian, John Milner – one of the non-jurors tucked away in the old college – took a judicious *View* of both Bentley's *Dissertation* and Boyle's *Examination*, 'in order to the Manifesting of the Incertitude of Heathen Chronology'. A certain 'F.B.' who preferred to describe himself as an 'M.A. of Cambridge', came out with *A Free but Modest Censure on the late Controversial Writing and Debates*. Thomas Rymer, signing himself simply 'T.R.', censured the Christ Church wits in some *Short Reflections*, which met with an *Answer* on behalf of that society, which he countered with a *Vindication*. These, and many more, have long settled into the dust which lies at the feet of the great peaks of literature. The great peak known as Bentley's *Dissertation on Phalaris* appeared in the firmament of letters in 1699. It looms there still, vast, abiding, and 'awful'.

This second *Dissertation* is about four times the first one in length. It reduces the earlier work to the scope of a mere synopsis. The heads of argument are now transformed. Argument becomes expatiation. Every nail is knocked in. What had previously been paragraphs now become essays. Now we have not merely Phalaris, but *The Age of Phalaris*, and *The Age of Pythagoras*, *The Age of Comedy*, *The Age of Tragedy*, *Attic Dialect*, *New Attic*, *Sicilian Money*, and much else. The Hon Charles Boyle and the Christ Church wits fade from sight under the shadow of this tremendous monument. Their insults and aspersions are playfully but finally brushed aside in a preface of more than a hundred pages, as a lion might brush aside a colony of mice with imperious paw. There is nothing left to be said. Bentley told them what they must say – if they hoped to be heard on the subject again – and he leaves the reader in no doubt that they are incapable of saying it. Bentley matches them in wit and raillery. He out-distances them beyond sight in scholarship. The thunderbolt had fallen, and the trumpets of the enemy were stricken into silence. *Immortalis ista Dissertatio* were Porson's words for it. Few in these later ages of the world have read it, and fewer are likely to read it in the future. Those who may still wish to sample a great masterpiece of criticism will content themselves with the first dissertation, its miniature prototype. Thereby they may at least savour the greatness of an imperial intellect in its finest hour.

Perhaps it was fortunate for the self-esteem of the confederated wits that their knowledge of Greek did not suffice to apprise them of the overwhelming character of their defeat. And, after all, their quarrel with Dr Bentley remained, whatever might have happened to the fortunes of Phalaris. The lance of learning, couched so rashly in defence of Sir William Temple and the cause of the Ancients, had been struck from

103

their hands. But there still remained a lance to break with 'Dr Bentley's Humanity and Justice to those authors who have written before him'. It was still necessary to correct his 'misrepresentation of all Matters of Fact wherein he is concerned', and to show up 'the D's Advantageous Character of himself, at full length'. Even before Bentley's second *Dissertation* was out, the wits had prepared *A Short Account* of his flagitious conduct in these respects. An appendix of Dr Bentley's misrepresentation of facts was supplied by Dr William King, an old member of The House and a pleasant wit, who claimed to have overheard some of the doctor's animadversions upon Mr Boyle's project for an edition of Phalaris, at Thomas Bennett's shop in St Paul's Churchyard. King was celebrated for a *jeu d'esprit* called *The Journey to London* wherein he had made some play with the slang-names of certain liquors, such as *Humtiedumtie, Three-threads, Old Pharoah, Knockdown,* etc. Bentley mocked him for his peculiar knowledge of the subject. 'We must not expect from the Dr that he should know the worth of books: for he is better skilled in the catalogue of ales, his *Humtydumty, Hugmatee, Three-threads,* and the rest of that glorious list, than in the catalogues of MSS.' Apart from the appendix to *A Short Account,* Dr King was to take his revenge for this in his *Dialogues of the Dead* before the year was out. Meanwhile, Francis Atterbury, the principal author of Boyle's *Examination,* was preparing to come back, not with a rival work of scholarship – of that he was incapable – but with a further commentary upon Bentley's conduct and character. This purported to be 'A Short Review of the Controversy between Mr Boyle and Dr Bentley. With Reflections upon it'. The latter part of its very long title gave away its true purpose, however. It was concerned with 'the D's Advantageous Character of himself, at full length'. And the whole thing was 'Recommended to the serious perusal of such as propose to be considered for their Fairness, Modesty, and good temper in Writing'. By the time this sorry performance appeared, Bentley was Master of Trinity.

Of all the ammunition fired off against the author of the *Dissertation* in these years, only one survives as a living work. It came out in 1740. It was called *A Tale of a Tub,* and it contained 'An Account of a Battle between the Ancient and Modern

Books in St James's Library'. It had been written during the life-
time of Jonathan Swift's master and patron at Moor Park. It
included a dedication to Prince Posterity, the only patron that
the great satirist could wholly trust. There Captain Bentley,
'the most deformed of all the moderns', clanks into battle in
patched and rusty armour, armed with a flail and a chamber-
pot, under the command of the generals who made use of him
'for his talent of Railing', and prepared at a moment's notice to
turn upon them like a wounded elephant and to inform them
that 'they were all a pack of rogues, and fools and sons of whores,
and d – d cowards, and confounded loggerheads, and illiterate
whelps, and nonsensical scoundrels; that, if himself had been
constituted general, those presumptuous dogs, the ancients,
would long before have been beaten out of the field'. Scaliger is
made to address him as a 'Miscreant prater! . . . All arts of
civilising others render thee rude and intractable; courts have
taught thee ill manners, and polite conversation has finished
thee a pedant.' Minded to perform some mighty exploit to
redeem himself, he joins forces with his friend Wotton to slay
Phalaris and Aesop while they sleep. The two friends are slain
by the brave Boyle, skewered side by side with one lance.

   To portray Bentley as a champion of the Moderns, and to
interpret the quarrel of Bentley v. Boyle as an episode in the
Battle of the Books, would be seriously to misread his interests
and intentions. The Battle of the Books, of Ancients v. Moderns,
was in some respects a mean and trivial contest over literary
tastes or fashions, an intellectual dog-fight in which a learned
man might intervene in order to pull out a bone of reputation.
To read Macaulay's slight, and slighting, remarks on the subject in his *Essay on Temple* (1838), one might imagine that the
whole contest had been fore-ordained in order to reveal the
superiority of the future Master of Trinity to the federated
scholars of Oxford in general, and those of Christ Church in
particular. This 'most idle and contemptible controversy', he
tells us, began in France, where – as was only to be expected –
it was fought with all the flippant ferocity of the Fronde.
Presently, 'this childish controversy spread to England', and in
that great age of party politics it was hardly likely that the
question would be tried according to large and philosophical

principles of criticism. Temple and Boyle on the one hand; Wotton and Bentley on the other; between them they contrived to maintain and increase the triviality of the contest. Only Bentley rose above the dust of contending factions with the masterpiece which settled the question foreover, and established his claim to the first place amongst classical scholars, then and for all time.

In fact, however, the so-called Battle of the Books was concerned with much else than books. The name itself is misleading as a description of the intellectual dispute that was proceeding at that time. Jonathan Swift's use of it was perfectly legitimate, for he was concerned with a fantasy in which the books in the King's Library actually fought each other 'last Friday'. The contest of 'Ancients v. Moderns', however, had been going on for many years in France, and had been alive in Italy at the time of the Renaissance. It might in some sense be said to have gone on all through western history. As Bentley pointed out, the claim that the oldest books were the best in their kind had been made by the Ancients themselves. All through the Middle Ages scholars had been looking back at the work of the pre-Christian poets and prose-writers as the best there had ever been or that there was ever likely to be. At the time of the Italian Renaissance, ancient models were cherished almost super-stitiously. To imitate the work of the Ancients was generally regarded as the best that man could do. To aspire to the second-best was the limit of human achievement. But, as usually happens when men aspire to rival the past, they are later seen to have been making the future. New needs, new interests, the opening up of fresh fields of inquiry, generate a new attitude to the past. The limitations, as well as the glories, of the Ancients become apparent. The discovery of new worlds that the Ancients had never known, the increasing awareness of the possibilities of experimental science for man's control of his environment, for the conquest of pain and distance and unhappiness, these things evoke a theory of progress and a tendency to dwell on the limitations of our predecessors and the possibility of ever-increasing freedom. The Ancients shrink in stature, and the Moderns rise in self-respect, if not in self-conceit.

This kind of 'progress' was bound to become a self-conscious concept in those departments where the Ancients had so evidently fallen short: notably in the field of applied science. It was not so evidently legitimate in literature, the fine arts, and philosophy. Great works of art are not produced by accumulated knowledge and the lapse of time. The media of art are the human soul and its activities. These things do not evidently grow more complex, more rich, more rarified, with the passing generations, although man's capacity for dealing with them in terms of creative and interpretative activity may do so. Thus the concept of progress, the whole notion of modern 'superiority', may have far more relevance in some fields of human activity than in others. But in the age of the rising conflict between the Ancients and the Moderns (roughly from 1600 to 1700), the contest spread into almost every field. It agitated the world not only of literature, but that of science, philosophy, the fine arts, and even religion. An argument about taste could never have achieved such longevity or involved so many and varied personalities – men as differently distinguished as Pascal, Fontenelle, Swift and Bentley, to mention but a few.

Bentley was concerned only in the literary controversy, and even here he was reluctant to be labelled as a contestant under the banner of either Ancient or Modern. The subject, he said, was 'so nice and delicate, and of so mixed and diffused a nature, that he was content to make the best use he could of both ancients and moderns without venturing . . . upon the hazard of a wrong comparison, or the envy of a true one'. The only question that interested him was this: who were the Ancients, and what was the quality of their work? When the champions of the Ancients claimed superiority for the oldest books, did they mean Homer and Archilochus, or Phalaris and Aesop? If they upheld the work of Phalaris and Aesop as 'inimitable originals', they were indulging in 'a piece of criticism of peculiar complexion, which must proceed from a singularity of palate and judgment'. He had no axe to grind in the great quarrel, unless a prejudice in favour of sound learning and critical method amounted to axe-grinding.

Dr William King, when he brought out his *Dialogues of the Dead* in 1699, invested Bentley with the name 'Bentivoglio' – a soubriquet which stuck to him for the rest of his life. He intended to label him as a ferocious pedant. This 'great Bentivoglio' was 'so exact a man at the original of a Sicilian city . . . that he can tell you the man who laid the first stone of it. There was not a potter in Athens, or a brazier in Corinth, but he knows when he set up. . . .' He knows when the first weathercock was set up on the tomb of Zethys and Calais, who invented yellow starch, lavender cakes and rose-cakes to preserve clothing from moth, and how Sardanapalus invented cushions. 'Perhaps never man came to the same pitch of chronology as the much esteemed Bentivoglio.' He can tell you the time a man lived by reading a single page of his book. Let him get a sentence of Greek in his mouth, and he can tell you the growth of it as a vintner can tell Burgundy from Madeira.

This 'tribute' to the author of the *Dissertation on the Epistles of Phalaris* was intended to be a form of banter. Banter was all that was left to the doctor's enemies by this time. The general impression was that the man was a magician. There was only one thing to do with him now. The six prelates who had charge of the ecclesiastical and academic patronage of King William III unanimously recommended Richard Bentley to the vacant headship of Trinity College in Cambridge. There was no holding the man.

11

Trinity

When Thomas de Quincey wrote his review of Dr Monk's life of Bentley in the 'thirties of the last century, he opened with a fable of rural peace destroyed by neighbourly spleen. Walking with his friend Robert Southey, in the lonely valleys of Cumberland, he came upon a remote cranny in the hills where a tiny hamlet consisting of seven cottages reposed in what appeared to be 'an absolute and perpetual Sabbath'. It turned out, however, that 'not one of these seven households will now speak to any of the other six'. Reading Monk's *Bentley*, de Quincey found himself constantly reminded of this sad state of affairs. For where else, he asked, might one expect to find peace and concord if not in 'the privileged haunts of meditation . . . the cloistral solitudes of Oxford and Cambridge'? And yet, in the quiet groves beside the Cam, where still echoed the footsteps and the voices of Bacon and Milton, of Barrow and Newton, 'immortal hatreds' were to be nourished for forty years, young men were to grow old and grey in contest, and some were to die while imperishable passions still raged within them. De Quincey's astonishment and dismay at this discovery probably owed a good deal to his love of dramatic antithesis and the necessities of a rhetorical style. He cannot have been so amazed as all that on discovering the intensity of the feuds that may from time to time shatter the putative peace of the academic world. Dons, even classical dons, are but men.

No one any longer disputes whether at Trinity Bentley came upon a nest of turtle-doves and set it in a roar, or whether he walked into a snake-pit and drew upon himself its venom. Such crude alternatives survive only in ill-founded gossip. Nor is it likely that Edward Stillingfleet ever declared 'we must send Bentley to rule over the turbulent fellows of Trinity College: if anybody can do it, he is the person. . . .' The bishop was dead when the vacancy at Trinity occurred. Nor were the fellows of Trinity turbulent until the master's conduct provoked them to resistance after some eight years of long-suffering patience. The worst that can be said of Trinity when the new master arrived is that, like Cambridge colleges in general, a certain amount of deterioration in the standards of fellowship had been caused by the exclusion and imposition of fellows for party and political reasons during the seventeenth century. Of course there must have been a certain amount of trepidation in some quarters when it was learnt that the celebrated Bentivoglio, scourge of the Christ Church wits, the expert on Phalaris and ancient tyrannies, was at the gate.

Bentley took the customary oaths[1] on February 1, 1700, swearing to maintain inviolate the college statutes and to consult the common benefit rather than his private interests. Beyond the high wall, a few yards to the north-east, the neighbouring House of St John the Evangelist flanked the chapel of Trinity College where her son, now a man of thirty-eight, had come to the magisterial seat. When someone offered the new Master of Trinity congratulations on such an achievement by a Johnian, he is said to have quoted the Psalmist: 'By the help of my God, I have leaped over the wall.'

He was only the third Master of Trinity out of twenty to come from outside the college, and the fact that he came from St John's is unlikely to have enhanced the warmth of his welcome. Trinity men were in the habit of referring to the members of the neighbouring college as 'Johnian pigs'. The Rev Mr Alex Scott, rector of a Lincolnshire parish, was to write in 1710 when he heard of the broils within his college: 'When I first heard of that man's being placed over you, I pity'd your condition. I did think that that noble society would never be happy under the government of a sordid[2] Jonian.' It was a cross set upon Trinity by providence, Mr Scott decided. There was no remedy but to bear it with patience 'until such time as it shall please God to rid you of him'. The Johnians were in the habit of

[1] The present-day custom of literally 'knocking on the Gate' seems to be little more than one hundred years old. The first master recorded as doing so was Whewell.

[2] The word 'sordid' at this time did not simply denote materialistic but poor and dirty, what the Victorians were to call 'low'.

returning these compliments by recalling Roger Ascham's reference to Trinity as a *'Colonia deducta* from the suburbs of St
John's', the intellectual offspring of a 'pitying mother' who had
undertaken to 'supply all other inferior foundations' defects by
her sons sent forth for their enlightenment'. A hundred years
before Bentley went to Trinity, Thomas Nashe, writing his
preface to Robert Greene's *Menaphon*, had called their college
'an university within itself', and the prime foundation of learning in England. It had been the privilege of St John's, said
Nashe, to establish true scholarship at Cambridge; and certainly
the sixteenth century had seen Lady Margaret's foundation,
under statutes framed by the great Renaissance humanist
John Fisher, and with her readerships in Greek and Hebrew,
rise to unrivalled pre-eminence in Tudor Cambridge. Under the
mastership of Nicholas Metcalfe (1518–37), St John's had
flourished not only in learning but in substance: to the extent
of a five-fold increase in income, it is said. And all this some
few years before King Henry set up his college of the Holy
and Undivided Trinity next door. With his proud Johnian background, Bentley may well have felt that he was condescending,
an attitude that came easily to him at all times. Certainly he
was not long in giving the impression of coming as a light unto
the Gentiles, a posture difficult to forgive by the members of a
colonia deducta. His high-handed and energetic 'reforms' were
unlikely to come the more gratefully because they came at the
hands of a Johnian.

At the time of his accession, the mastership of Trinity had not
yet come to rank as one of some half-dozen of the more magnificent offices in church and state. It was in no small degree the
work of Richard Bentley to make it such. Of course, as a royal
foundation, Trinity had 'great expectations' and great responsi-
bilities. Her master, as steward of a royal house, enjoyed the
privilege of entertaining the sovereign on visits to the university,
of educating the royal princes (or its share of them), and of
lodging the king's judges of assize. These, and other prerogatives, meant that the master, along with some few others –
like the Provost of King's – must combine the humble mien of a
scholar with the politic pride of a vicegerent. Richard Bentley
possessed the necessary qualifications for at any rate part per-

formance of the role. As vicegerent he was magnificent. His duties and prerogatives were ever present to his mind. There have been masters who required to be reminded of their precise and delicate status. When William Whewell, entertaining Queen Victoria, proposed that his sovereign should retire to his house in order to rest a while, he is said to have received the royal reminder: '*My* house, Mr Whewell.' Bentley would never have needed to be reminded. Within a very short time of his accession, he entertained Queen Anne, who invested Isaac Newton with the Order of Knighthood in his drawing room. He was assiduous in preparing to receive the heir to the throne into the lodge as an undergraduate, though the weakly child was to die, like all the queen's children, in its infancy. The visit of King George II was to see the elderly master standing by the royal chair like a proud and yet humble servitor. One of the initial causes of his quarrel with the fellows was his determination to transform the Master's Lodge from an antique manor-house into a suitably regal setting for the master of a royal foundation who must walk with kings and yet keep the common touch. He was never in any difficulty about the latter.

The image of the founder of the house of the Holy and Undivided Trinity stands in its niche above the Great Gate; there the great Harry straddles in majesty, sceptre in hand[1], and flanked by the emblems of empire. Whether or not Dr Monk was justified in his statement that the king had endowed it with revenues taken from the dissolved monasteries, he was not far wrong when he called it 'the first-fruits of the Reformation'. The old king died a few weeks after his transformation of old Michael-house[2] into new Trinity College, and his foundation did not receive its printed statutes until the reign of Queen Elizabeth I. The king had dedicated the house to the promotion of 'Divine Learning and all kinds of good letters', among more general purposes like the amplification of the Christian faith and the education of youth in piety, virtue, learning and science.

---

[1] On closer inspection, the sceptre is plainly seen to be a chair-leg, and no less plainly an investiture of undergraduate origin. As the distinguished fellow whose rooms are over the Great Gate likes to remark: 'They think we don't know. . . . '

[2] Henry VIII's foundation also embraced a sister establishment, King's Hall.

So comprehensive were the king's intentions – 'a College of literature, the sciences, philosophy, good arts and sacred Theology' – that Trinity was evidently intended to be what Nashe called St John's, 'a University in itself', a magnificent conception which her latest master took to heart and was to attempt vigorously to realise. Bentley's ambitions for Trinity are only to be understood in the light of his zealous grasp of the founder's intentions. It is important to understand that his limitless ambitions for his college had their root in much more than his personal cult of glory.[1]

Trinity's first great age of prosperity and fame was the age of Queen Elizabeth I and King James I. Thomas Nevile, who was master in the reign of King James, could recall a time when Trinity filled both archbishoprics, seven bishoprics, eleven deaneries and ten professorships. Six of the translators of King James's bible were resident fellows of Trinity, and the heads of most of the other colleges at Cambridge were of the same vintage. Sir Francis Bacon and Sir Edward Coke, both Trinity men, had been the twin lights of law and learning in those days. With the troubles which followed upon the accession of King Charles I there succeeded a period of decline. During the Commonwealth all the Royalist fellows were expelled. With the Restoration, and down to the Revolution of 1688, fellows were frequently excluded by tests and others intruded into the college by royal mandate, often regardless of intellectual merit. By the end of the century, Dr Monk concludes, the Trinity fellowship 'was more destitute of distinguished names than at any preceding or subsequent period'. There were, indeed, notable, even illustrious exceptions, like Pearson and Barrow and Newton. Some fine building was done, notably Nevile's Court and Wren's Library. But the number of scholars declined, the general level of scholarship fell, and the qualification of merit was no longer required for entry upon the foundation. Something must also be accounted to the fact that this was a transitional

---

[1] George Peacock was to write, almost exactly a century after Bentley's death, that at Trinity College a man could get an education 'not merely co-extensive with that which had been provided by the Statutes of the University . . . but likewise that left no deficiency to be supplied even by the lectures of the ordinary readers'. (*Observations on the Statutes of the University of Cambridge*, London 1841.)

period in academical studies, between dissatisfaction with the old scholastic learning and the rejuvenated intellectual life of the first age of modern science: what Monk called 'the intermediate state of torpor'.

It would be a mistake, however, to imagine that this depressed state of things was either very serious in itself or peculiar to Trinity. Bentley's poor opinion of the fellows of Trinity when he came among them was retrospective, coloured by the ever darkening dyes of malice and contempt as the civil war proceeded. In fact they were as decent a set of men as any college in the university could show at that time. There were distinguished intellects among them, very few were roisterers, all were more inclined to peaceable living than to faction-fighting, until their domineering master stirred them at last to resistance by his persistent acts of tyranny. The worst that Bentley could say of them was only rendered true, if it were ever true at all, by his own intolerable conduct towards them. Their principal weaknesses when he stepped into the place of Dr Montagu in 1700 were almost wholly the consequence of the fact that for some forty years they had had masters but no master. Dr Pearson (1662–1672) had been a mouse, unwilling to accept even fresh table-linen at college expense. His successor, Isaac Barrow, reigned for only four years, and after him came John North, son of Lord North, who for half his short reign (1677–83) was physically incapacitated by apoplexy. John Montagu (master 1683–99), the nervous, easy-going and amiable son of the first Earl of Sandwich, had been prepared to amble along the easy path of preferment[1] until it led him to a deanery at Durham.[2] It is fairly clear that what Trinity needed by 1700 was shock-treatment. Whether that was what the Royal Commissioners intended for Trinity when they recommended Richard Bentley, that is what she got.

The first thing he did was to claim £170, the previous master's share of the college dividend payable at Michaelmas. He was under the impression that this sum represented profits

[1] The phrase is Jebb's (R. C. Jebb, *Bentley*, p. 95).
[2] That Dr Monk regarded this move as 'promotion' was to lead Thomas De Quincey to take him severely to task: which serves to show what enhancement of dignity was to come to the Mastership of Trinity after Richard Bentley's reign.

114

accruing during the vacancy. He got his way by threatening the bursar with a suit at Canterbury. The second thing he did was to demand £110 payable in dues on St Thomas's Day. He was nearly £300 to the good within a few weeks of his admission as master. He then turned to the reformation of morals and learning, sending down an undergraduate for frequenting a bawdy-house (a single-handed sentence, and therefore contrary to statute),[1] opening the library to the undergraduate members of the college, and instituting a reformed mode of election to fellowships and scholarships. 'Start as you intend to go on' is a rough and ready maxim for the newly-appointed man in authority. Bentley's start at Trinity was certainly a portent, with its combination of attention to his own financial interest, indifference to statutory limitations, and energetic concern for the intellectual well-being of the college.

Before the new master could proceed upon a suitably magisterial course, however, he deemed it necessary to install himself in a lodge suitably appointed to the dignity of his office. Nothing much had been done to the Master's Lodge for more than half a century. It resembled a gothic manor house, with its long, low rooms, its leaded windows, its brick and stone hearths and its tapestried walls. When he put the question of its renovation and re-decoration at college expense to the Seniority, they agreed with alacrity. The dignity and amenity of the Master's Lodge must after all redound to the pride and credit of the whole society. Besides, it was known that the lodge was shortly to receive the heir apparent, the young Duke of Gloucester, at the special behest of the Princess Anne, where he was to live his undergraduate days in the household of the Rev Doctor Bentley. On no account were the fellows of Trinity prepared to stint themselves in preparing a suitable lodging for their future sovereign. When Dr Bentley offered to contribute £100 towards the cost from his private purse, his generous offer was only accepted with reluctance. He appears to have estimated the cost of the whole work at £300, a ridiculously low figure, but no figure at all was entered in the record of the

---

[1] By statute, such disciplinary action required a full hearing of the accused and sentence after consent of five out of the eight members of the Seniority.

decision in the college Register, which the master entered with his own hand and caused to be counter-signed by the eight members of the Seniority. Nor was there entered in the record any precise specification of the amount of work to be done. Mention was made of new ceiling, wainscot, flooring and 'other convenient improvements', a vague term which obviously could be made to cover just as much, or as little, as the master himself might consider 'convenient'. The master, of course, had his own ideas about this. He proceeded not only to have the tapestries replaced by wainscot, the floors and ceilings improved by good timbers and plaster; he had the old leaded lights replaced with sash-windows after the latest fashion, and the old hearths set into handsome marble chimney-pieces. The cost of the work turned out to be not £300 but near £1,600.

The vainglory of sash-windows, wainscot, and plaster ceilings was to be thrown in the master's face for many years to come. Especially the sash-windows, for these were visible from the outside and were denounced not only as a fashionable extravagance but as an offence against the Gothic tradition of the Great Court. Bentley, however, was a 'modern' just as much as he was professionally an 'ancient'. Only the medieval repelled him. He made no more bones about the preservation of 'Gothic barbarism' on grounds of historic sentiment than did the itinerant lady, Celia Fiennes, who at that time was touring England on a side-saddle, noting down modern improvements and marking ancient monuments which required removal in the interests of amenity. Richard Bentley shared this wholly unsentimental – or possibly unhistorical – attitude to the litter which infested the world he lived in. It was the dawn of the eighteenth century, and the new Master of Trinity was never behind the spirit of his age. He was now briskly engaged in making the Master's Lodge at Trinity a fit habitation for a gentleman; and a gentleman of the eighteenth century.

Also, one might add, for an eighteenth-century lady.

In a little notebook entitled *Ephemeris*, Bentley wrote against the date January 4, 1701:

'I married Mrs Joanna Bernard, daughter of Sr John Bernard, Baronet.'

Two days later there occurs the entry:

116

'I brought my wife to St James's – '

For he was still the keeper of the king's libraries, and his lodging at the palace was still his best abode. Near the end of the month of January, 1701, he wrote in his notebook:

'I returned to ye College.'

Presumably Joanna went with him. Thus in *Ephemeris* he recorded the celebration of a marriage that was to last happily for forty years.

12

Vice-Chancellor in Love

After you were sworn and admitted Master, why did you
marry and bring your wife into College, there to reside and
inhabit; when by the said College statutes, which you are
sworn to observe, if the Master marries, immediately after it is
certainly known, *Collegium penitus amittat*; and by the
University charters and statutes, confirmed by Act of
Parliament, you are forbid to bring your wife, or any woman
into College, upon pain of forfeiting your mastership?

Ninth Article exhibited against Dr Bentley by
the Fellows of Trinity College, 1710.

Richard Bentley had a way all his own with statutes. He once
said of a statute that annoyed him, that it should 'be broken in
order to be kept'. In this particular case, as regards wives or
women in college, however, the question did not arise, for he
had taken the precaution of securing a royal dispensation under
the Great Seal. So much for the charge of illegality. For the rest,
the answer to Article Nine is at once evident to anyone who
looks at the portrait of Mrs Bentley which still hangs in the
Master's Lodge, the house which she made sweet with her
presence through so many years of storm and strife.

Joanna was a local girl, a daughter of Sir John Bernard of
Brampton, near Huntingdon, whence came also the family of
Samuel Pepys. As with so many of the best things in his life,
Bentley owed his wife to Edward Stillingfleet in whose house-
hold he had first made her acquaintance. How long the acquain-
tance lasted before it ripened into affection we do not know, but
it is unlikely that Dr Bentley entered into the state of Holy
Matrimony without due deliberation. He was nearly forty. He
had never had less than a lively concern for his career. The lady
was well-connected, being kinswoman to Henry St John,
Viscount Bolingbroke. She was also connected with Abigail
Masham, who was to replace Sarah, Duchess of Marlborough,

as the favourite of Queen Anne. The Princess Anne, now within a year of succeeding to the throne, held Dr Bentley in high esteem, but it was nonetheless valuable to him to have second strings to pull among her advisers and favourites. The Bernard family, however, does not appear to have welcomed the man from the north, for all his scholarship and his brilliant academic prospects, with open arms, and the course of true love by no means ran smooth even for the Master of Trinity and the Vice-Chancellor of the University of Cambridge. His letter proposing marriage to Joanna still exists, and it more than hints at the obstacles that had impeded him. It is dated August 6, 1700.

> I shall always reflect on those Dayes, as some of the happiest of all my Life; when I believed myself to be loved by You in some proportion to the Love I had for you. How that Affection came to be cross'd and defeated, I had rather forget than enquire. Providence, which governs all things, suffer'd it to be so, and we must not be angry at it's disposal. But it has pleased God, since that time, to make such alteration in my Circumstances, as give me some hope that a proposal of that kind may be now better entertained by You and your Relations, than formerly it was. I dare safely promise on my part, that you will be always as dear to Me, as if no manner of Breach had happened betwixt us; nay, I trust in God that our Affections will be for ever more united for having been once parted: as a Limb becomes stronger for being broken, if it be well set again. If you please to permit me to make a Visit upon this Errand, and to discourse further about particulars; as soon as I have notice of it, I shall wait upon you at Arlsey, being
> Hon'ed Madam,
> Your most affectionate
> Humble Servant
> R. Bentley.

Dr Monk in his somewhat cold references to Bentley's marriage simply tells his readers that the doctor had long cherished an attachment for Joanna Bernard, and that 'being now raised to a station of dignity and consequence, he succeeded in obtaining the object of his affections'. The object, once obtained, proved entirely satisfactory. To this there is abundant testimony, especially in the writings of the doctor's enemies, who were fond of contrasting in sympathetic fashion the virtues of Mrs Bentley with the horrid defects of her spouse.

So far as can be known, Joanna was the only woman in Richard Bentley's life. To judge from the few letters that have survived from his courtship in the later months of 1700, Bentivoglio in love was never less than himself in assurance and self-esteem. His forms of address to the lady proceed from 'Honoured Madam' in September to 'my dearest friend' in November. By mid-November he is assuring his 'dearest' that his happiness and quiet is absolutely in her power, and that her absence 'makes every week seem a month'. All the same, he expresses the opinion that the course they are pursuing 'appears to me to be the greatest advantage for you as well as, and even more than, for myself'. Of course it was for the lady to name the day, but the doctor made it clear that he preferred the first day of January. Besides, January 1 was the anniversary of his entry into the household of Dr Stillingfleet, and the first day of his own natal month. 'For God's sake then, my sweetest love, comply with me in this.' He was suffering embarrassment at having to travel up and down to town for so long. 'It does not become my character and station,' he reminds the coy one, 'to fly thus backwards and forwards without concluding my great affair.' After all, he had recently been made archdeacon of Ely, and had entered into the office of vice-chancellor of the university. 'My station as Vice-Chancellor,' he wrote, 'makes all my motions so public.' People were talking. Let Joanna be governed by particular occasions, not by 'the common rule that it's decent for the lady to be as backward as she can make excuses for'. After all, she did not need to be reminded that she was affianced to no ordinary man. It is not every day that mankind is privileged to witness a vice-chancellor in love.

Joanna seems to have had some reservations. Her side of the pre-marital correspondence is lost, but we find Bentley protesting gently against some condition put forward by his 'sweetest love'. He feels sure that she will rescind this upon further consideration, or else she will look like a very hard-hearted mother. The exact meaning of this is beyond conjecture. The notion that Joanna was vexed by suspicions that the doctor was not entirely sound on the Old Testament, however, is not quite so 'exceedingly impossible' as Dr Monk was inclined to think. For Joanna appears to have been a bible Christian in a peculiarly fundamentalist sense of the term, and likely to be easily upset by any hint of textual criticism, a field in which Bentley was already famous. After all, she was a daughter of the East Anglian Cromwellian connection, 'in some degree tinctured with hereditary reserve and the primitive cast of character' says her grandson, Richard Cumberland, who claimed, writing in 1804–5, to have a perfect recollection of her manners and habits, 'although she was entirely free from the hypocritical cant and affected sanctity of the Oliverians'. Cumberland was born in the Master's Lodge at Trinity, and recalled to the end of his life how his grandmother, 'one of the best of women', puzzled and bewildered him with texts and passages from the Scriptures, and especially by the holy apophthegm 'The eyes of the Lord are in every place, beholding the evil and the good.'

What upset Joanna at the time of her courtship was Richard Bentley's objection to the dimensions of the golden image of Nebuchadnezzar as stated in VI Daniel. We owe the story to William Whiston's *Memoirs*.

> When Dr Bentley was courting his lady, who was a most excellent Christian woman, he had like to have lost her by stating to her an objection to the Book of Daniel, as if its author . . . knew no better than that men's height were ten times their breadth, whereas it is well known to be not more than six times.

Daniel had described Nebuchadnezzar's image of gold to be sixty cubits high and but six cubits broad. Dr Bentley, no doubt applying the critical method by which he had demolished Phalaris, seemed to be on his way to demolishing Daniel, 'which made the good lady weep', as Whiston puts it. Whiston tells us that the doctor also 'tried to run down the apocalypse as not written by the prophet John', and indeed he goes so far as to assert 'Dr Bentley's scepticism as to both the Old and New Testament'. Joanna may, or may not, have found comfort in Whiston's suggestion that when Daniel said sixty cubits he was including the pedestal, or pillar, on which the golden image may have rested. At any rate, she went to the altar at Eton College Chapel with Richard Bentley on January 4, 1701. This was three days later than the vice-chancellor had hoped and wished. The nuptials were celebrated by Dr Richardson, a fellow of Eton and Master of Peterhouse. Bentley had hoped to be married by a bishop.

Nevertheless the marriage was a wholly happy one. Throughout their married life the noise of battle rolled around the Master's Lodge, but the family scene within the walls was one of idyllic peace. When he closed the door of his lodge upon the Great Court, the embattled master of the college, the senate, and the law courts, became at once the loving husband and the fond father of the domestic hearth. The strait-laced lady whom he had first addressed in courtship as 'Honoured Madam', signing himself as her 'faithful and affectionate servant', was to remain his 'sweetest love'. Mrs Bentley presented three pledges of affection to her lord. First there was Elizabeth, who inherited the virtues and benignity of her mother, 'with habits more adapted to the fashions of the world'. Then came the beautiful Joanna II, who combined the vivacity and intellectual fibre of her father with a strong sense of the ridiculous, which her son, Richard Cumberland, confessed that 'she made rather too frequent use of'. Richard Bentley II turned out a gentleman and a wit, in the circle of Horace Walpole, 'a projector of Gothic embellishment for Strawberry Hill and humble designer of drawings to ornament a thin folio of a meagre collection of Odes by Gray, the most costive of poets'. His father, the great champion of merit, got him a fellowship at Trinity at the age of fifteen, but he remained a dilettante. 'A certain eccentricity and want of worldly prudence in my uncle's character,' Cumberland goes on to say, 'involved him in distresses and reduced him to situations uncongenial with his feelings and unpropitious to the cultivation and encouragement of his talents.'

Bentley, father and grandfather, loved to have children about him, and the lodge in his time became a paradise for the young. He slept in a room adjoining his study. The mightiest scholar of the age was never one to silence the sound of children at play, or to refuse them his attention with their young importuning. With the years he became more and more a home-keeping man. He preferred to dine at home rather than in hall, a preference which appears to have been both one of the causes as well as one of the effects of college warfare.

13

The Wind of Change

The office of vice-chancellor of the university came to Bentley, even before he had taken up residence in the Master's Lodge, because he was senior by degree among the heads of houses who had not held it before: an arrangement which – as in this instance – might land the university with a vice-chancellor quite inexperienced in its business or its modes of administration. Bentley had been away from Cambridge for twenty years. He was literally an outsider. His lodge was under renovation, and his best address was still St James's Palace. Vice-chancellerial hospitality in his college was hardly a possibility, even if he had been much concerned to dispense it, which it seemed he was not. This meant that from the start he could be accused of stinginess, a charge which pursued him henceforth, especially when he proceeded to cut down on college feasts and put up the price of claret. After the open-handed régime of his amiable predecessor, Dr Montagu, these penurious habits on the part of a master who never hesitated to come down on the college for lavish expenditure on the garnishing of his lodge, and who exacted every penny of his own dues from the moment he took office, created a somewhat painful impression.

As vice-chancellor, during the first year of his mastership, Bentley had a brush with the mayor and corporation in the perennial warfare between town and gown. It was within the jurisdiction of the vice-chancellor to regulate theatrical performances in the town, and vice-chancellor and mayor were jointly responsible for the good order of the great Sturbridge Fair on Midsummer Common. When it came to Bentley's notice that the town authorities had granted permission for a band of players to entertain the populace without reference to the vice-chancellor, he at once put a grace through the senate peremptorily re-asserting the rights of the university and investing no less than sixty-two Masters of Arts with proctorial authority to enforce discipline.

Not only the mayor of Cambridge, but the king of France required reproof towards the end of that year, 1701. The vice-chancellor undertook the pleasant duty of informing King William of the university's detestation of the action of the king of France in recognising Charles Edward Stuart, 'pretended Prince of Wales, as king of these realms'. The university's 'just detestation of the indignity offered to your sacred Majesty', and its cheerful and affectionate readiness to contribute its utmost to the defence of the Protestant succession and the threatened liberties of Europe, were expressed by the vice-chancellor in the name of the university, but in the unmistakable and downright style of Richard Bentley.

The most memorable activity of Richard Bentley during his year as vice-chancellor, however, concerned neither the mayor of Cambridge nor the king of France, but his old love, the University Press. As we have seen, five years earlier he had earned the soubriquet 'Second Founder of the Press',[1] and had been instrumental in procuring the work of some of the finest type-founders of Europe for its use. The handsome series of quarto classics for Tonson had gone on apace. Now, as vice-chancellor, Bentley was not only the head of the curators of the press but presided over, or at least served upon, the numerous committees which conducted its business in a period of intense building and housing activity. He was greatly concerned with the financing and production of Ludolf Kuster's edition of the Suidas Lexicon, a project that had interested him since his Oxford days. Kuster, in haste to return to his post at Berlin, responded to Bentley's welcome and encouragement at Cambridge by producing the substance of the three massive folios with a frantic energy and speed which seemed to ensure that the task would require to be done again, or at least greatly amended, before many years had passed. Bentley had engaged the university to bear the expense and risk of the enterprise, which involved severe financial loss. More happily remembered from his early years of renewed residence at Cambridge are the press's work on his own edition of *Horace* (1711) and his

[1] See above, pp. 88–91.

devoted work on getting out a second edition of Newton's *Principia* (1713).

It was at the end of 1701 that the last parliament of King William III's reign was chosen and the Whigs came in, including in their ranks the greatest of the sons of Trinity, Isaac Newton, at whose election as one of the Cambridge representatives, the vice-chancellor had been honoured and delighted to assist. King William died next year and the Princess Anne came to preside over a spell of Whig rule that was to last for ten years: the decade of Blenheim, Ramillies, Oudenarde and Malplaquet, and of the Act of Union with Scotland. These years were to see the great Whig lord of Trinity in the ascendant. It was only in the year 1710, when the Tories came back, that he was to receive his first check. Twelve months after that, his old neighbour at St James's Palace, John Churchill, duke of Marlborough, was dismissed. Whether the ascendancy of the Whigs in the nation's affairs served to embolden him in his high-handed career at Trinity during these years is a matter for speculation. Certainly he liked his own undertakings to chime with the mutations of the national destiny. The wind of change which began to blow across the Great Court of Trinity, and the first fights in which he indulged with the fellows, took place when the world was loud with the thunder of Blenheim. Almost at the moment when Marlborough and Prince Eugène were driving the allied forces of Louis XIV into the marshes of the Danube, Bentley was confronting the fellows of Trinity on the steps of Trinity Chapel, red as a forked radish, hand on thigh, demanding to know whether they had forgotten his rusty sword? And all over a bill for £350 for building a new staircase.

Beneficial reforms, incessant demands for money, high-handed methods of getting his way: all these make the story of Bentley's early years at Trinity a perplexing one. Never perhaps has an academic reformer muddied the issue of reformation with such a mixture of lofty motives and rebarbative manners. Passionately devoted to his vision of the great college of the founder's dream, he found present reality staring at him from the faces of half a hundred dull and comfortable fellows. It sickened him and aroused his contempt. He made it clear to them that a man of wider vision had come among them, a man of metropolitan outlook. He shouted his qualifications for his enlivening activity in their reluctant and startled ears, boasting – as they were to complain – 'of your great interest and acquaintance, and that you were the genius of the age, and what great things you would do for the college in general, and every member of it in particular . . . .' And while he boasted, he rode them, with whip and spur, shouting unseemly objurgations.

Perhaps it was contempt for the fellowship that set the master at once upon the task of improving the mode of its recruitment. By instituting a more rigorous examination system, he commenced a process of reformation that was to make a fellowship at Trinity one of the most highly-prized distinctions of the academic world. Traditionally, fellowships were, throughout the university, awarded on merit adjudged in terms of examination results, so that an undergraduate who distinguished himself in university examinations could regard election into a fellowship of his college almost as a matter of course. He might therefore expect to enter into the highest level of college society and government, perhaps for the rest of his life, on the sole qualification of a final undergraduate examination taken at an early age. Trinity, however, elected its fellows on tests of its own and not on places gained on graduation in the university. Before Bentley's mastership, these tests were not particularly exacting: a *viva voce* examination in the college chapel, conducted by the master and the eight senior fellows – which very often meant that an individual examiner's part in the process might be merely nominal. Bentley insisted that candidates should be examined by each elector in his (the elector's) own rooms, thus affording means for written examination if required, and adequate time for consultation between the examiners as a body before coming to conclusions. The new system transformed fellowship-elections at Trinity from a possibly perfunctory 'act' in chapel to a thorough examination enabling each of the electors to form a considered opinion of the candidate's merits. Of course there was objection to this new rigour, but the system was to prevail until an even more elaborate system was brought in towards the end of the century.

Similarly with scholarships, which in those days were not

awarded before entering the college but as awards of merit and for encouragement during the undergraduate's career there, and then only after two years. Bentley made them annual so that a freshman might benefit by them also. At the same time he ended the practice of electing to scholarships men who, on graduation, did not intend to continue in residence. This latter provision was ill-considered, since a man might wish to return after a lapse of time in order to compete for a fellowship, and, since only scholars were qualified for election, might find himself ineligible. A case of this kind cropped up almost at once, and of course Bentley came under fire . . . the way of the enlightened despot who stumbles is hard. Bentley had undertaken these reforms single-handed, without consulting the Seniority. The blame fell upon him alone when they proved defective in any particular. He might have saved himself from the charge of statute-breaking in a number of instances by taking the senior fellows into his confidence and counsel, had he been minded to do so: notably in the case of that young Mr Henson, alleged frequenter of bawdy-houses, whom he had sent down without summons, hearing or proof. But he was not minded to do so.

Nor, in most cases, was he blameworthy in terms of results. His reforms in the matter of elections to fellowships and scholarships were to involve a more arduous life for his colleagues, more frequent and meticulous labour as examiners. This was what he intended. It was part and parcel of his design to make Trinity a 'working College'. Besides, where he did over-step the mark by taking arbitrary and personal decisions, he was intent on showing the little world under his jurisdiction that he was not a man to be trifled with, something that needed to be shown *ab initio*. The wind of change might be keen, but it was wholesome. The bones of the 'old gentlemen', as he called the senior fellows, might shrink before the blast, but it was refreshing to the younger men whose interests he sought whole-heartedly to serve.

One of his earliest endeavours on behalf of the undergraduates was to get the new library opened for their use. This magnificent building, lining the river bank and closing Nevile's Court to the west, had been designed by Christopher Wren and erected at a cost of £18,000. The accumulation of certain chamber-rents, arising from the repair – at the expense of a benefactor – of the Bishop's Hostel, or Garret's Hostel, and amounting to some £360, were at Bentley's insistence expended in the purchase of books, despite the wish of the Seniority that the sum should be used to defray the cost of furniture and fittings. Either purpose was in accord with the terms of the benefaction. Bentley accused the fellows of misappropriating the funds and lining their own pockets, a wild charge, and totally without foundation. He also instituted a graduated charge for the privilege of using the library, thus building up a book-fund. The junior members greatly benefited by the master's library policy, but the seniors were much aggrieved by his aspersions. Nor did they love him the more for his edict permitting the juniors to leave hall freely before Grace after meat had been said. He did not openly accuse the seniors of prolonged guzzling, but he could see no reason why the young should be required to remain seated when they had eaten their supper simply because the seniors chose to sit long over their victuals, even if Chapter 17 of the statutes did require it. And why was supper not served in hall on Fridays? The master instituted meat-suppers on that ancient fast-day, partly perhaps to discourage tavern-parties in the town on Friday nights, partly no doubt to disclaim any truck with popish superstitions.

As for attendance at chapel, which was universally compulsory at that time, and for long after (except in so far as university statute might exempt men over forty from full disciplinary rigour), the master required attendance by junior fellows and rescinded the privilege of exemption enjoyed by noblemen and fellow commoners. These last were now also required to take their turn in the Latin 'declamations' which the statutes of Trinity enjoined upon all students after 6 o'clock supper on Saturday nights. He changed the appointed hour by ordering declamations to be delivered after evening service in chapel. Some thought it inappropriate for a surpliced congregation to listen to recitals from pagan poets immediately after Christian worship, but Bentley hoped by this amendment to secure larger audiences, and it is hardly likely that a man of his classical devotion would appreciate the distinction. He also tightened up the imposition of the statutory fines upon college lecturers who neglected the duty of holding forth daily in hall upon the works of Aristotle. However irritating might be the revival of these multitudinous fines and penalties, mostly fallen into obsolescence, Bentley made it fairly certain that no one should leave the house, *par excellence*, of 'Divine learning and all kinds of good letters' without undergoing a fair dosage of the Latin tongue.

'Divine learning' was certainly in good keeping under a master who was not only a doctor of Divinity but recently installed as archdeacon of Ely and very soon to carry off the chair of regius professor of Divinity. Statute did not require a fellow of Trinity to proceed beyond the degree of master of Arts, but certain privileges concerning stipends, preferment to college livings, and rooms in college, were annexed to the possessors of the higher degrees of bachelor and doctor of Divinity. For fellows to graduate in theology had been rare for some years before Bentley became master. In 1701, two graduated BD, and next year another four, and soon there was a great deal of controversy in the college about the relative standing of masters of Arts and bachelors of Divinity. Bentley, when asked to arbitrate, came down firmly, as might have been expected, in favour of the priority of the bachelors of Divinity. For the next seventy years almost every fellow of Trinity proceeded to a degree in Divinity. His decision of 1702 was intended to promote the pursuit of 'Divine learning' in accordance with the original purposes of the college. It also had the effect of promoting the superior dignity of doctors of Divinity. There were five DDs among the thirty-six signatories of the articles exhibited by the fellows of Trinity against Dr Bentley in 1710.

14

The Staircase,
and Some Other Matters

*Why did you of your own head pull down a good staircase in
your lodge, and give orders and directions for building a new
one, and that too fine for common use?*

Article XII against Dr Bentley, 1710.

This was the last and most unkindest cut of all in Dr Bentley's
plan of campaign for the repair and adornment of his lodge. The
cost of the work already undertaken had exceeded by at least five
times the amount of the original estimate. No sooner were the
bills paid, not without difficulty and dispute, than the insatiable
master decided that he must have a new staircase. The existing
staircase was in good repair and was sufficiently commodious to
accommodate four persons abreast, but Bentley had concluded
that it was inadequate to the dignity and importance of a master
of Trinity. The seniors promptly and unanimously refused. The
master went ahead with his plans, and the exceedingly beautiful
staircase which still adorns the lodge was constructed at a cost
of between £300 and £400. While the demolition of the old
staircase was proceeding, the bursar and certain of the seniors
entered the lodge and ordered the work to be halted. At this,
the master threatened to send the bursar into the country to
feed his turkeys: a Bentleian mode of identifying a bursar with
a menial. When he came back to the seniors with the bill he was
informed that it was up to him to meet the unauthorised
expenditure from his private purse. The master thereupon
reviewed his armoury of disciplinary powers, intending a
cannonade that should rival the guns then sounding at Blenheim.
Most of his weapons were rusty from long disuse. He could
refuse to allow fellows to absent themselves from college. In
other words, he could 'keep them in' until they came to a better

131

frame of mind. Indeed he could cripple them with penalties for past delinquencies in the matter of residence. He asked them plainly whether they had forgotten his 'rusty sword' – i.e. these long disused statutory powers of a master of Trinity? This was the occasion when he came upon them as they left chapel on a summer evening, all clothed in surplices and piety. Perhaps he imagined that at such a time and place they might mistake their master for the loved one. He was mistaken. As he broached the bill for the staircase they adopted an attitude of *noli me tangere* and passed on. His face grew very red and his voice rose shrill in objurgations upon the evening air. As they retreated, he brandished his 'rusty sword' at their retreating backs. . . .

He kept his word, devising for them a peculiarly injurious form of detention. According to statute, only fellows holding one of the sixteen college preacherships were permitted to accept preferment in the church. The master made it known that there would be no further elections to preacherships until his staircase was paid for out of the college account. Any fellow offered preferment would be obliged to decline it. The bill was paid, but only after two years. For his part, the master undertook to supply the junior bursar with an inventory of all furniture in the lodge that was college property. He appears to have forgotten to do this.

Bentley's building operations at Trinity were by no means confined to his lodge, or to the indulgence of the master's vainglory. The early years of the century were indeed the period of his noblest endeavours for the glory of Trinity as a house of various learning, and more especially for the promotion of the college as the home of the sciences, or – as the term went in those days – of Natural Philosophy at Cambridge. When, in the spring of 1705, Queen Anne, being at Newmarket, spent a day with her court at Cambridge, she knighted Isaac Newton in the drawing-room of the Master's Lodge. The splendid setting in which the Master received his sovereign on this auspicious occasion must have seemed even to the most grudging of the Seniority to justify the long and obdurate campaign he had fought for wainscoting, plaster ceilings, sash-windows, marble fire-places, staircase and all. The royal company were feasted in the hall at a cost of about £1,000, half of which had to be borrowed for the occasion. Evening service, however, was attended in King's College Chapel. Not only was King's College a royal foundation senior even to Trinity; the chapel at Trinity was in a bad state of repair and its decoration hardly fit for the devotions of the queen. Bentley was delighted that the royal seal should have been set upon Isaac Newton in his house, but he was no doubt somewhat chagrined to part with his royal mistress and her court for Divine Service in another place. Within a very short time of the queen's departure he set about the repair and redecoration of Trinity Chapel, resolved that Trinity should have at any rate the second finest chapel in the world. This enterprise must be considered his greatest contribution to the adornment of the college.

But first he wished to do honour to the cause which by this time was identified with the name and fame of Newton, the cause with which he had identified himself as the first Boyle lecturer, and from which he himself had a reflected glory. He secured the election to a fellowship at Trinity of the most brilliant young mathematician and natural philosopher of the age, Roger Cotes; and with the enthusiastic support of Newton got him appointed to the newly-founded Plumian Chair of Astronomy and Experimental Philosophy. Then, by raising subscriptions in both college and university, he proceeded to build an observatory over the Great Gate, high above the founder's effigy, and to furnish it with the finest astronomical equipment, and persuaded the college to assign the adjoining gateway-rooms to the use of the professor of Astronomy and his assistant for ever. Roger Cotes lived and worked there for the remaining ten years of his tragically short life. 'If Cotes had lived,' said Newton, 'we should have known something.' Indeed, much was learnt from his brilliant lectures and observations. More important, a tradition was founded which it was Bentley's purpose to promote: the traditional association of Trinity College with the cause of Natural Science. From the beginning Bentley had cherished the vision of Newton's college as the historic home of natural philosophy, the focal point of Cambridge science. Nor was this noble 'nobbling' of the Plumian Chair of Astronomy, with the attachment of Cotes to Trinity College, and Cotes' installation on the premises with all the instruments of his craft, Bentley's sole claim to be remembered as the first, and perhaps the greatest, pioneer of the natural sciences, as a distinctive glory of Cambridge. He did scarcely less for the establishment of chemistry when he brought John Francis Vigani of Verona, who had been elected Professor of Chemistry in the university in 1702, to enhance the glory of Trinity, fitting him up with a chemical laboratory made out of an old lumber-room near the Master's Lodge, whither he drew large audiences to his lectures. Vigani's room is now labelled as such in the passage-way leading off from the north-east corner of the Great Court, beneath the clock tower. But chemistry failed to flourish after Vigani's death and was to prove something of a Cinderella among Cambridge scientific studies in the eighteenth century.

Of course Bentley's transactions in these matters did not fail to produce some friction, and a certain amount of unfavourable comment. For example, he coolly diverted certain monies set aside for the library to the equipment of Cotes' observatory. Nor was the transformation of the lumber-room for Vigani's laboratory wholly beyond suspicion of ulterior motives. It was suspected that the master had one eye on the chemical laboratory as a future greenhouse for his garden, and when the fellows passed the plans for the conversion of the lumber-room into a laboratory (already carried out, by the way, as so often was the case when the master sought permission for his projects) they annexed a clause to their agreement stipulating that the laboratory should never be turned to any other use. The fellows also suspected that the master had an eye on their bowling-green as a suitable extension of his garden, not least because their recreative activities under his study windows disturbed his learned meditations. On a Saturday evening in July 1701, he had recorded in his *Ephemeris* notebook that certain of the fellows had 'played bowls in the College bowling-green all Chapel-time, in the evening service: seen out of my windows by me (who was then lame and could not be at Chapel). . . .' These suspicions were to be proved neither unworthy nor unjustified in the course of time. 'Why did you endeavour to take away from the College, and apply to your own use, the College bowling-green and summer-house . . .?' they asked him in their Articles of Complaint in 1710. By that time they were concerned also to ask him the same question about their Combination Room.

The repair and decoration of the chapel was a project to which the fellows responded with alacrity and generosity. It was not simply a matter of chagrin after the queen's visit in 1705. More immediately, when the task was undertaken in 1707, the incentive came from the presentation of a fine organ for the chapel by the master's friend, 'Father Smith', the most celebrated organ builder of the age. The organ could not be installed in the chapel until the structure had been repaired and the setting made appropriate to its reception. Certain monies in the shape of donations and benefactions had been in hand for several years past, and the master now instituted a subscription fund, himself leading off with a gift of £200. His idea was that each fellow should sacrifice his share of the college dividend for the current year, which meant that every senior would contribute £50 and every junior £25. This mode of subscription would obviously weigh heavily upon those whose financial resources depended solely, or in very large part, upon their fellowship dividend, and it did in fact cripple some of the fellows for years to come. One and all, however, appear to have risen generously and cheerfully to the occasion, but their initial alacrity was not sustained to any great degree by the master's somewhat heartless, and even flippant, comments upon their distresses, nor by his dog-in-the-manger mode of managing the details of the work as it proceeded. Subscribers wishing to know about this and that were told that they should have their answer 'when it was done'. Their tempers were not improved by the measures he took, on his own initiative, to retrench college expenditure – a very necessary policy at this time, partly at least because of his own calls upon the finances of the society during recent years, and partly because the cost of his latest undertaking (as with all Bentley's building projects) proved greatly in excess of the original estimate. The total cost of the chapel scheme was somewhat more than £6,000. Fellows' subscriptions produced rather less than one half of this amount. The master lent the college £1,000 at 5 per cent from Mrs Bentley's fortune, for which he was later to receive the thanks of the college in the form of a charge of profiting by usury. It should, of course, be remembered that these war-years were a time of generally rising costs, and all college bursars are well acquainted with this kind of financial problem in the course of building which, by its very nature, may last over a number of years of inflation.

Bentley's policy of retrenchment and reform at this time was to lay up an immense amount of criticism for him in the future. It was all too readily assumed that whenever he succeeded in saving money for the college, the proceeds were destined for the master's privy purse or for the luxurious living of his household. The Articles of Complaint brought against him in 1710 contain numerous clauses which begin with the words: 'Why did you waste great quantities of' this and that: 10,000 quarters of college corn, the same amount of malt, 500 chaldrons of coals. Why had he caused the said malt, etc. to be taken away from the college brewer and delivered to one of his own choosing, arbitrarily turning college servants out of their offices? Ditto, ditto with regard to college wheat and college bakers? . . . The imputation was always that he put in new brewers or bakers in order to palm off his own tithe-corn or malt on the college at above the market price (or some such higgling of the market for his own profit). In fact what he did was to overhaul the whole system of college buying and selling in order to put an end to the fraudulent waste or cheating by the college servants and tradesmen, who made a good thing out of collusion over prices. These excellent measures of economy came home to the fellows in his abolition of the 'Pandoxator's Dividend' and in several other painful ways. The Pandoxator was a college office held by a senior fellow who had the overseeing of the bake-house and brew-house, each employing several bakers and brewers and a clerk to supervise the buying of wheat and malt. These servants, Bentley discovered, were negligent and out of control. He asserted that they had not bought a single bushel of wheat or of malt in the open market for more than twenty years. The Pandoxator, too, 'had carved well for himself', enjoying a rake-off of one thirty-second part of the annual profit. Bentley promptly sacked the supervising clerk, or buyer, and four bakers and brewers, took on *one* baker and *one* brewer, and saw to it that all corn was bought in the market: thus saving the college some hundred pounds a year while securing to the college the best bread and beer to be had in the university. So much the master claimed to his own credit.

One might have expected his measures in this sort to have been received with applause. Unfortunately it was the custom, in years of financial stringency, to issue the fellows a small dividend based on the Pandoxator's surplus stock: £20 to the master, £10 to each senior fellow, and £5 to each junior. At the college audit of 1707, Bentley announced that the Pandoxator's dividend was an abuse and would cease forthwith. At the same time, the master took it upon himself to economise by reducing expenditure on college hospitality. Church festivals, Audit Days, Founder's Day and Trinity Sunday, all normally saw large gatherings sumptuously entertained in hall. Bentley, horrified to discover that these occasions sometimes involved the expenditure of no less than 30s *per capita*, clamped down on invitations, so that fellows were obliged to pay for their own guests. And when he discovered that Mr Jordan, the steward ('a fellow who is stated to have been sometimes affected in his intellects'), had been expending £50 more than usual on wine, he dismissed him in disgrace, only remitting the sentence when Mr Jordan undertook to subscribe £30 towards the Chapel Building Fund. The offices of junior bursar and steward – for which the master consistently expressed a certain contempt in a society of learned men – were in future to be confined to fellows of junior standing and their stipends cut to £4 and £3 per annum respectively. Nor was the master above the cheese-paring economy of stopping the service of the fellows' commons in their rooms instead of in hall. These various measures, some of them distinctly humiliating, caused much murmuring, and were frequently and not unnaturally blamed upon the financial stringency necessitated by the master's profusion in matters arising out of his cult of personal power, or 'vainglory'.

It would not have been so bad had Bentley avoided creating the impression that his economies were imposed at his personal fiat, and if he had stood consistently by the spirit of his own reforms. For example, during several years he vigorously maintained the practice of admission to the foundation solely on merit. In 1707, however, he began the practice of pre-election to fellowships, i.e. the election of candidates in advance of

vacancies occurring. The first case was that of young Edmund
Stubbe, nephew and heir of Dr Wolfran Stubbe, the vice-
master. Edmund turned out to be totally unworthy of the
honour. Indeed, Bentley himself was later to call him 'the worst
character that ever entered a College'. It seems that Edmund
Stubbe had been paying attentions to the master's niece, and
that Uncle Wolfran proposed to settle his fortune of £10,000
on the young couple. Young Stubbe ultimately married the
daughter of a Newmarket publican. It was this affair which
William Whiston described as the doctor's first lapse from integrity. 'Having made this deviation from the path of justice, he
never afterwards returned to it.' Certainly, he permitted two
further pre-elections to fellowships in the following year. At the
same time, he took it upon himself to make examples of two
fellows whose moral deficiencies, he declared, were 'dangerous
to the society . . . infecting and ruining all the youth'. Mr John
Wyvill, a fellow of four years' standing, was expelled for
cutting up pieces of the college silver. Mr John Breval, son of a
prebendary of Westminster, was expelled for committing
adultery in Berkshire. Mr Wyvill's was a temporary lapse. He
later became chaplain to the bishop of London. Mr Breval beat
the lady's husband and ran away to volunteer with Marlborough
in Flanders, where the duke took notice of him and gave him
employment. He was later known as a wit and a man-about-
town. He always said that Dr Bentley expelled him out of
personal pique because he voted on the wrong side at an election,
but the master said that he had been winning money at cards
from the undergraduates. Mr Wyvill never bore the master any
ill-will and wrote thanking him for the justice with which he
had been treated. The fellows of Trinity continued to cite both
cases as examples of their master's high-handed and unstatutable conduct. It is evident that he failed to secure the
lawfully required consent of the seniors, or to carry through his
judgment in the proper form of citation, hearing and proof.

By the year 1708, when these events took place, Bentley's
mastership was becoming intolerable to the fellows. They had
good reason to cabal against him, for they believed themselves
to have been robbed and insulted, and no one knew what further
injuries he might still have in store for them, nor upon whom his

next act of tyranny might fall. He seemed perfectly indifferent to their complaints and wholly without concern about their possible mode of retaliation. He proceeded upon his arrogant course with an air of insufferable majesty. He was heard to justify his disposal of a piece of the cook's kitchen-garden with the assertion that he was 'lord of the soil'. When Mr Eden, the junior bursar, declined to meet a bill of £15 for the unauthorised erection of a hen-house, the master discommuned him, i.e. deprived him of his statutory allowances of bread and ale. He would not be kicked by an ass, he said. Mr Barwell suffered the same penalty for persistently criticising the master's conduct, and so did several others. To put a member of a college 'out of commons' was a punishment normally reserved for undergraduates, and in any case the infliction of penalties or punishments upon a fellow needed the consent of his peers. Bentley's only reply to such objections was that he was 'not warm yet' – *lusus jocusque*. At length, when cavilling against his rule appears to have reached the proportions of conspiracy, he decided to break up the nest of traitors by depriving the fellows of the use of their Combination room. He was compelled to desist from this outrage, but the threat was never forgotten or forgiven.

15

'Farewell Peace to Trinity College'

When he came to the College, it was easy to perceive in their countenances that most of the Fellows were terrified . . . they scarcely spoke to one another, but looked like so many prisoners, which were uncertain whether to expect military execution or the favour of decimation.

EDMUND MILLER *Remarks.*

Edmund Miller was a lay fellow of Trinity College, that is to say he was one of the two fellows exempt from the obligation to enter into Holy Orders upon engaging in the study of either Civil Law or Medicine; in effect he was a barrister, whose avocations necessarily took him into a wider and more secular society than that of a Cambridge college. His arrival at Christmas 1710, to spend the festive season among his brethren of the Holy Trinity, brought among them a man of affairs capable of giving them the stiffening they so badly needed at that time. Edmund Miller was bold, brash, bustling, and ready for a fight. No doubt he was genuinely shocked at the cowed and fearful aspect of the reverend gentlemen. There can be as little doubt that he relished the prospect of conducting a case during vacation. The Christmas vacation of 1710 was to prove singularly barren of peace and good-will.

The situation at Trinity had been worsened of late by certain proposals of the master for a recasting of the system of college dividends, or the annual distribution of the surplus revenues among the master and fellows. Dividends had become the normal way of augmenting fellows' incomes with the fall in the value of money since the sixteenth century when the original provision for their maintenance had amounted to free board and lodging together with a small cash stipend ranging according to academical degrees, from £5 for doctors of Divinity to £2 13s 4d for masters of Arts. Since 1660 the apportionment of the college surplus had been roughly according to seniority, the master receiving £150, senior fellows £50, and so on down to £25 for mere masters of Arts. Thus there was a discrepancy between stipends (according to degrees) and dividends (according to seniority). In Bentley's view, dividends should be exactly proportionate to stipends, if only because this would promote one of his major objectives – the taking of higher degrees. His proposal now was to determine dividends by multiplying stipends by ten, thus placing dividends in direct ratio to stipends, or to eminence in terms of degrees. It was a reasonable proposal so long as provision were made for existing seniors who were too old to proceed to higher degrees, and would obviously encourage academic distinction. There was only one insuperable objection. The master's stipend by statute was £100, and when multiplied by ten would shoot up to £1,000. Even Bentley shrank from proposing that. Instead, he proposed to work on a basis of £85, giving him a dividend of £850. Later he was to propose £400, and finally £300. And yet he still met with opposition, for his proposals always included an additional sum by way of composition for his allowances, which he estimated at about £700. His servants, horses, fuel, lighting and victualling were supplied by the college, not as a statutory obligation but as a matter of grace, and the notion of compounding in a sum of £700 for these favours raised visions of the master living independently of the college, and possibly elsewhere than in the lodge. Moreover, Bentley had himself computed the money value of his allowances, and everybody knew that he had exceeded the maintenance costs of previous masters by several hundreds of pounds a year. All told, the master would be costing the college at least £1,000 a year.

There was a vast amount of haggling and debate, and the master resorted to many and varied kinds of pressure in order to secure acceptance of his scheme. He was prepared to discuss a number of changes in financial detail, but it was remarked that whatever the details they always added up to the same total as far as concerned the master's income. He used threats and promises, even hinting at blackmail in one or two cases of individuals of doubtful moral reputation. He incited the juniors, among whom he had lately been building up a party, with the assistance of his bullying ally, a certain Dr Ashenhurst, to petition the seniors in favour of his scheme, an example of the policy of *divide et impera* which his recent conduct in general had made fairly easy. He never wavered in his confidence of final success, such was his contempt for the flabbiness of the seniors, who, he believed, would always give way to any real threat to their peace and comfort. In this particular instance, he planned to bring them to surrender by threatening to hold up the issue of any further dividend unless it were based on his proposals. None had been paid for two years past, and two were due for payment in this present year 1709. The fellows were hard-pressed, for the last dividend issued had been taken up in subscriptions for the chapel. Bentley was prepared to conduct this financial siege-warfare until they came to their senses.

A number of conferences, or 'closetings', with the seniors took place in the Master's Lodge during the late autumn of 1709, culminating in a session on December 21 at which it seems that his dividend scheme would have reached acceptance had he been prepared to drop the matter of compensation for his allowances. The meeting had been adjourned to the following morning, when he had high hopes of final victory. Edmund Miller attended this meeting with the rest.

The master was ready for him. He always had a keen nose for an enemy. As soon as the meeting assembled, he took up the college statutes and read out the chapters concerning the qualifications for holding lay-fellowships. One of these was that the holders should be doctors in their faculties. Was Mr Miller a Doctor of Physic?

Mr Miller replied that the question was unnecessary, since the master knew perfectly well what he was.

The master then told Mr Miller that if he were not doctor of Physic by next Lady Day, he would declare his fellowship void.

Mr Miller said that this was not worth talking about. He had come to the meeting for a quite different purpose, which was to give his opinion on the master's latest financial proposals.

The master interrupted him several times during this brief

and pointed speech. He afterwards said that never in the long
history of the university had a master been addressed to his face,
and in the presence of the fellows, in such an insolent fashion.

Mr Miller denied incivility.

The fact was, of course, that Dr Bentley – like Edward
Gibbon when young Mr Pitt dared to differ from him – was
not accustomed to this style of conversation, or indeed to free
speech of any kind. A few days later he told the seniors that he
would bring the matter before the queen in Council unless they
agreed on the spot to accept his proposals. They had seen him
braved by Mr Miller, and now they were prepared to brave him
themselves. At this final refusal he broke out into abuse of the
race of lawyers. Were they going to allow themselves to be led
by the nose by a lawyer? 'Lawyers were the most ignominious
people in the nation.' He laid before them the choice between
good and evil, between life and death. He then turned upon
them in detail, addressing Mr Rashleigh as 'the College Dog',
and prophesying that Mr Cock would die in his shoes – presumably at the end of a rope. He then left the room with the farewell
message: 'From henceforth, farewell peace to Trinity College.'
In a few minutes he was on his horse, heading down the
London road.

If the doctor's swift departure meant that he was going to
appeal to allies in town, or to the queen in Council, it was important for the fellows to strike first. They consulted Mr Miller
about their next move. 'Leave it to me,' said Mr Miller, and
at once drew up a formal letter of complaint to be laid before
Counsel, which was forthwith signed by sixteen seniors and
eight juniors, comprising rather less than half of the fellows of
the college. It was a very concise letter, stating their disapproval of the master's financial project and the 'unworthy
and unstatutable methods' he had employed to secure its acceptance, and covering a multitude of sins with a brief reference
to 'many other things by him done since he became our master'.
Their request was that their griefs be 'represented to those who
are the proper judges thereof and in such manner as Counsel
doth advise, humbly craving such determination and sentence
"as appropriate judges in the matter should in their wisdom
and justice think meet"'. Already in this brief document is to

be detected uncertainty upon the question that was to exercise many minds and occupy a great deal of time in the years to come: 'Who, on earth, is the judge of a master of Trinity?'

Bentley seems to have been unimpressed by this proceeding. He came back to college, as Dr Monk shrewdly puts it, like 'a General who hears of a mutiny among his troops during his absence and resolves to arrest its progress by making a summary example of its ringleader'. He immediately summoned the seniors and declared Edmund Miller's fellowship void by his own fiat as executor of the statutes, nominating his creature Ashenhurst in his place, on condition that he proceed Professor of Medicine when he was of standing to do so. He wrote these decisions into the Conclusion Book with his own hand, and commanded the college butler to remove Mr Miller's name from the college boards. Mr Miller at once appealed to the vice-master, whose office by statute it was to compose differences that might arise between the master and any fellow. Dr Wolfran Stubbe summoned the master to a meeting of the seniors in his rooms on the following morning. The master failed to appear, and the seniors recorded their unanimous opinion that Mr Miller had been wrongly expelled from his fellowship and that his name ought to be restored to the buttery board. Bentley remained fuming in his lodge. It was, he held, 'a new and unparallel'd thing for a Master to be summoned to the Vice-Master's rooms, without first inquiring whether he designed to come or would rather wish them to come to him'. And anyway, 'they knew that I was indisposed of a great cold and confin'd at home'.

A fellowship is a freehold. For a master to deprive a man of his freehold without trial or hearing and by his own absolute authority, was not only contrary to statute but contrary to elementary principles of both Common Law and natural justice. It bore a painful resemblance to the arbitrary practices of King James II, and to the conduct of the deposed house of Stuart in general. Who could feel secure in his rights and property in future? Reflection upon this universal menace was sufficient to turn Bentley's critics and complainants at Trinity College into enemies and plaintiffs. It was from this time onwards that they were resolved to dislodge their master. Edmund Miller, his name once more restored to the boards, was instructed to press on with measures for the prosecution, and on 20 January he set out for London. Four days later, having once more cut out the offensive name from the boards, Dr Bentley followed.

16

Death Comes for the Bishop

'How it ended both to the Complainers and the Visitor
himself shall be buried in silence, since he lost his life in it.'
Bentley at the end of his trial before Bishop Moore.

Four years were to elapse before, in the month of May 1714,
the Master of Trinity appeared before the bishop of Ely in his
court at Ely House, Westminster. Much of the intervening
time had been spent in deciding whether the bishop of Ely was
empowered as 'Visitor' to entertain and to judge upon the complaints of the fellows of Trinity against their master. Bentley did
everything in his power to deny it, and, when it became evident
that he must face proceedings before the bishop, contrived to
delay the opening of those proceedings until the last possible
moment. His tactics in this prolonged delaying action were a
mixture of legalistic wrangling on the basis of the Trinity
statutes, strategic use of scholarship, and copious personal abuse.

The somewhat bucolic countenance of John Moore, Lord
Bishop of Ely 1707–14, greets the visitor to the university
library in Cambridge from his portrait hanging beside the left-
hand flight of stairs in the entrance-hall. It is partnered by the
portrait of the periwigged Charles, Second Viscount Town-
shend (better remembered as 'Turnip'), and it looks diagonally
across to the portrait of King George I. Bishop, king and
minister are all three properly represented in that place, for the
bishop's books were bought by the king at his death, and
presented to the university on the advice of the viscount. The
bishop's eyes are bright, his chin and upper lip wear a faint
blue 'five o'clock shadow', and his hair is plainly his own,
making a pleasant change from the normal wiggery of the
Augustan episcopate. Indeed John Moore's hair actually streams
back from his broad, clear brow, and, together with the fresh
tints in his cheeks, lends him the aspect of a man who has just

146

come back from a fenland walk in gown and lawn-sleeves on a windy afternoon. It is an aspect appropriate to the son of an ironmonger of Market Harborough, a suitable man to sit in judgment upon the grandson of a Yorkshire stonemason. Comparing them, one would imagine that it was not the bishop but the archdeacon who would be the more likely to perish in the encounter. Yet, at the end of the day – indeed, at the end of many days – the bishop it was who died. Not that Bentley came through the ordeal wholly without anxiety. There was a point in the proceedings when, at an unfavourable word from the bishop, he fainted. On the other hand, the bishop caught an everlasting cold.

The fellows of Trinity, or somewhat less than half of them, opened the engagement with an extremely general petition of complaint drawn up by Edmund Miller, addressed to the bishop of Ely as Visitor of Trinity College under Chapter 40 of the college statutes. It was framed as the humble complaint of long-suffering men against the master's malversation and waste of college property, of his unstatutable, violent and unworthy methods, and in especial of his latest attempt to alter the system of dividends. It concluded with a promise to lay before the bishop, 'within a convenient time', the several particulars which would make the truth of these general allegations manifest.

The bishop sent a copy of this letter to the master, and Bentley at once took the offensive. One of the reasons for a college having a Visitor is to enable dirty linen to be washed in private. *Si res exigat*, Chapter 40 of the Elizabethan Statutes of Trinity College runs – if the matter require it – appeal may be made to the Visitor to mediate and judge. Thus, so to speak, the matter may be settled between gentlemen. Bentley, however, had other views. For one thing, he was not persuaded that he was dealing with gentlemen, and certainly not with equals, but with a gaggle of mutinous subordinates, poor-spirited and low-minded fellows, incapable of rising to the level of their master's visionary ideals for the intellectual life of the college, petty grumblers and viewless sots. He would denounce them, and their impertinent petition, to the world at large. In the full fury of his wrath he sat down and wrote *A Letter to the Bishop of Ely*. It purported to be 'published for general information by a gentleman of the Temple' from a copy given by the Master of Trinity to this gentleman who thought that its publication was a debt he owed to the public. All of which sounds very like an admission that the master was well enough aware that he was doing something indecorous, quite apart from the fact that he was prejudging his own cause.

The *Letter* was in the tradition of Bentley's *Phalaris* style, but more so. It marks an unmistakable turning-point in his career: the point at which he ceased, as Master of Trinity, to be a great scholar engaged in domestic controversy with his colleagues, and became an embattled figure waging war with personal enemies on the national stage. There was to be no private washing of dirty linen in future. What was going on at Cambridge was to be everybody's business, an aspect of party politics, a battle in which men took sides in the world of public affairs, far removed from the fields of scholarship and letters. Bentley, evidently, would have it so. The tone, the language, the frame of reference he adopted in the celebrated *Letter*, made sure of it. Lord Carteret, some twenty years after the crisis of 1714, when Bentley was facing another and greater crisis in the university, expressed his astonishment that any man of 'tolerable sense or learning' could even admonish the man without 'the censure of dullness and incapacity, and the amazement of mankind'. He dismissed the anti-Bentley movement as 'the distempered frenzies of cloistered bigots'. Bentley was a Whig, and most of the 'cloistered bigots' were Tories, and, he declared in the *Letter*, 'Had I been of their party, had I herded and sotted with them, had I suffered them to play their cheats in their several offices; I might have done what I would, I might have devoured and destroyed the College and yet come away with their applauses for a great and good Master.' It remains more than doubtful, however, whether even the most satisfactorily Tory master could have got away with Bentley's style at any time. Anyway, he resigned himself to the party whip. It was an age of faction-fighting, and if they disliked him on party lines, he said, ''tis impossible to help it'. This is the only trace of the tone of martyrdom in the *Letter*.

For the rest, his tone was of outraged legalism and aggressive superiority. His legalism is often trivial or irrelevant: for example, his complaint that he should, by statute, have received admonishment by the vice-master before petition to the Visitor was resorted to, or that Miller was disqualified as either a petitioner or an intermediary by his ejection from his fellowship, or that only the eight seniors had any right to subscribe to the petition, and that the signatures of the rest therefore invalidated it. The aggressive nature of his riposte to the fellows is best exemplified by his assertion that their animosity against their master arose from their dislike of his reforms. It was, he asserted, 'the last struggle and effort of vice and idleness against virtue, learning and good discipline'. In other words, as he had put it when he dressed them down at the Master's Lodge on the occasion of their contumacy about Edmund Miller and his fellowship: he had offered them the choice between good and evil, between life and death: and they had chosen darkness and death. But then, as he hastened to add, the commendations of such wretches would have been more scandalous than their railings. 'No one could have favour of these if he is not like them in his vices.' The root of their complaint, he declared, was fear for their financial disadvantage. They said that their master's reforms had reduced, or threatened to reduce, some of them to 'great necessity'. But what they really feared was a rise in the price of claret by a shilling a bottle. For this is 'the grand article in their expenses, far above all other charges, of clothes, or (what are now forgot by them) books'. Whatever other debts they maybe have, they had none to the stationers.

Dr Monk, when he came to write his *Life of Bentley* in 1830, found it 'even now disgusting to see such invectives against persons whose station demanded the character of wisdom, gravity and piety'. There may have been scandal in particular cases, but neither provocation nor resentment could justify his injuring the credit and interests of his society by publicly vilifying its governors. The distinguished son of another corporate and learned body which had suffered by the same vitriolic pen expressed his sympathy. Dr Atterbury, formerly the patron of the Christ Church wits, and now dean of Carlisle, wrote to Dr Colbatch, one of the most eminent of the seniors of Trinity, offering his sympathy and good offices in 'this quarrel and the dirty way of managing it, which both sides, I find, equally fall into'. The consequence, as Colbatch had hinted, might very well be a royal visitation, or a general and public inquiry into the state of affairs not only at Trinity but throughout the university. Than which, to fellows of colleges, nothing could, in any age, be more dire. The general public had certainly been intrigued and excited by the mud-slinging and general scandal created by Bentley's *Letter* and the numerous replies it had evoked. Among these last, some of the most animated and condemnatory came from the pens of junior fellows of Trinity, amongst whom the master had sought to acquire a following. Thomas Blomer's *Full view of Dr Bentley's Letter* was probably the funniest and the most disparaging, while the *True State of Trinity College* by White and Paris was charged with the venom of personal resentment. For sheer information or ammunition, for satirists and publicists alike, Edmund Miller provided an armoury of detailed fact culled from college books and accounts, much of which was put to effective use by Dr King, one of the doctor's old enemies in the *Phalaris* campaign, in his *Horace in Trinity College*. In this spirit, Dr King took the poet to the Master's Lodge and regaled him on victuals supplied at college expense to the enormous enlargement of his carcase.

Bentley had brought this down upon himself by his scurrilous *Letter*, and many thought that he had done his cause much injury. His tone had scarcely been that of injured innocence but rather that of a man who knew himself to be in the wrong but thought to brave it out by taking the offensive (in every sense of the word) and carrying the war into the enemy's camp. No one who entered into combat with him, however, could possibly have expected him to pull his punches. Bentley was always Voltaire's *animal méchant qui, quand on le bat, se défend.* Moreover he was a superb strategist. His *Letter* was no puerile exercise in bandying incivilities, nor was it an attempt to bludgeon his adversaries into silence by contempt. It was directed to disposing of the right of the fellows of Trinity to cite him before the Bishop of Ely, whether by legalistic objection in detail or by successfully contesting the standing of the Bishop as Visitor, or judge in any issue concerning the master. The original statutes of Trinity certainly named the bishop of Ely as Visitor in all cases concerning the master, although in point of fact the bishop's visitatorial power had never been used. The Elizabethan statutes lodged general visitatorial authority in the crown, and Bentley consistently stood by the case for the crown as his only judge. Was it conceivable that any lesser authority than the crown could sit in judgment upon a master of Trinity? As soon as it was clear that the Bishop of Ely was prepared to entertain the petition of the fellows against him, Bentley petitioned the Queen's Most Excellent Majesty for her protection against the bishop's pretensions to exercise visitatorial authority in the affairs of her royal foundation and especially the masters thereof.

This was in December 1710. The queen submitted the petition to her law officers and, pending their opinion, the bishop was required to take no action. The attorney-general and the solicitor-general reported in the following May. They held that by the original statutes of Trinity College, the Bishop of Ely was Visitor in matters concerning the master, although there was room for dispute on the matter, since the bishop had never exercised this authority, and indeed 'general' visitatorial power had been lodged in the crown by the statutes of Queen Elizabeth. Here was the historical loop-hole by which further contention could delay proceedings. But Bentley was not content simply to exploit this, and thereby to keep the pot of controversy boiling. In July he approached the Lord Treasurer, Robert Harley, Earl of Oxford, the effective prime minister of the day. Harley was a kinsman of Mrs Bentley. There had recently been an attempt on his life. He was a scholar and a bibliophile. Bentley wrote to his lordship, congratulating him upon his heaven-sent escape, and informing him that he had an edition of *Horace* almost ready for dedication to his lordship. Harley, of course, could not serve him directly in his own person, but he could, and did, submit the law officers' opinion to queen's counsel. Seven of them were for the crown as Visitor, and one for the Bishop of Ely. This resulted in a further delay during which the bishop was commanded to 'stop further proceedings according to her Majesty's direction'. Another year passed during which unavailing attempts were made to bring the fellows to accept the crown as visitor for the consideration of their petition, what time Bentley kept up the pressure by withholding college dividends. In the event, it was

not the fellows who had to submit. In April 1713, Lord Bolingbroke, Secretary of State, gave the Bishop of Ely authority to
proceed with the trial of the case of Dr Bentley.

The articles exhibited against Dr Bentley in 1713 afford a
tolerably accurate, if somewhat biased, history of the first ten
years of his mastership. Every article takes the form of a leading
question: 'Why did you . . . ?' or 'Why have you . . . ?' Wherever
possible the master's conduct is described as contrary to statute.
Wherever the master's impolite language was on record, it was
quoted verbatim.[1] There were fifty-four articles, ranging from
charges of wasting the college substance and extravagance in
beautifying the lodge and chapel, to despotic behaviour towards
fellows and undergraduates, not forgetting attempts to steal the
bowling-green and combination-room. The articles were subscribed by thirty-six fellows, headed by the vice-master and the
five seniors. Among the rest were Dr Colbatch, Edmund Miller,
and Conyers Middleton.

'I have rubbed through many a worse business than this,' was
the master's comment when, on a somewhat later occasion, he
was deprived of his degrees by the senate. No doubt he was
thinking of the glorious summer of 1714 when he escaped
deprivation of his mastership by the skin of his teeth. It came
about by a fortunate concatenation of events. Not for the first
time, or the last, a crisis in his personal fortunes chimed with a
crisis in the affairs of the nation. His skill in the tactics of evasion,
practised over the four years since 1710, was now to give him
the victory by one day. Many a cause was lost and won by the

---

[1] e.g. Article XXXII: 'Why did you use scurrilous words and language
to several of the Fellows, particularly by calling Mr Eden *an ass*, and
Mr Rashleigh the *college dog*, by telling Mr Cock *he would die in his shoes*,
and calling many others *fools* and *sots*, and other scurrilous names? . . . '
Article XXIX required to know why the master had insolently called
some of the statutes 'your rusty sword, which you would draw only upon
occasion'? and why he had called others 'your club, which you would use
as you thought fit'? Article XXXIII asked 'Why did you profanely and
blasphemously use and apply several expressions in Scripture? As "he
that honours me, I will honour. I set life or death before you; choose you
whether", or to that effect?' Article XXXII made mention of 'several
other expressions contrary to the 20th chapter of the said College statutes,
as "Farewell peace to Trinity College", and many others of the like
nature. . . . '

death of Queen Anne on August 1, 1714. It clinched the reprieve of the Master of Trinity. But it was the death of John Moore, Bishop of Ely, on the previous day that must have seemed to Richard Bentley like the hand of Providence.

For he had almost overreached himself at the last. The bishop's authority to try the case had been given in April 1713. The trial did not open until May 1714. Bentley had tried to secure that the case should come on at Cambridge, on his home ground, so to speak, conveniently for the accessibility of the books and papers required for his defence. The bishop, however, had insisted upon the case being heard at Ely House, his London residence. The great hall at Ely House was a draughty place, and the bishop was sixty-eight. He caught a severe chill during the six weeks of the proceedings and died on July 31, several weeks after the trial was over, and while both sides still awaited the promulgation of his judgment. His undelivered judgment was found among his private papers. 'By this our definitive sentence, we remove Richard Bentley from the office of Master of the College. . . .'

On personal grounds, Bentley might well have expected favourable treatment at the hands of John Moore, a Whig and a low churchman of his own *genre*. The two men were indeed very much akin in social origins and career. Like Bentley, Moore was of comparatively lowly birth, a grammar-school boy who had won his way by means of a sizarship to a Cambridge college (Clare Hall), and thence by his own abilities and the patronage of Heneage Finch, earl of Nottingham, to the bench of bishops – a parallel example of the career open to talent in the great age of patronage. Similarly, too, John Moore had a passion for building and book-collecting. The ironmonger's son did as much for the repair and rebuilding of the bishop's palace at Ely as the stone-mason's grandson did for the Master's Lodge at Trinity College, Cambridge. His library was, at his death, the finest in private hands in the kingdom, and worth £8,000 – though the king bought it for £6,000. The bishop had placed the great treasure of some 30,000 volumes and many priceless manuscripts at the disposal of scholars like Strype and Burnet, and Bentley himself. The bishop was also interested in medicine. In 1709 he had been among those who were prepared to back Bentley for the see of

Chichester. In short, the two men can hardly have faced each other in the hall of Ely Place in an attitude of either social or personal estrangement. Perhaps it was the shock of surprise that caused Bentley to faint at the bishop's severity in speaking of the Archdeacon of Ely's conduct as Master of Trinity. And after all, opinion in general – apart from the plaintiffs – had all along been on Bentley's side. The eminence of the great scholar served to protect him in face of charges concerning bushels of wheat and chaldrons of coal. Such charges must have appeared somewhat incredible to minds which, not unnaturally perhaps, tended to take for granted the synonymity of the scholar and the gentleman. It was the scandalous career of Richard Bentley that served to bring such synonymity under serious suspicion.

Ingenuas didicisse fideliter artes,
Emollit mores nec sinit esse feros.[1]

Horace's apophthegm, said Hartley Coleridge, displayed the value of classical learning in the clearest light. The only objection to it, he added, is that it is not true. He was writing in the 1830s.

---

[1] The choicest fruit of liberal learning is to make a clown or a brute into a gentleman.

17

Pudding-Time

When George in pudding-time came o'er
And moderate men look'd big, sir,
I turned a cat-in-the-pan once more
And so became a Whig, sir.

Bentley's dedication of his *Horace* to Robert Harley at the crisis of his fight with the fellows of Trinity in 1711 is an excellent example of what has been called his strategic use of scholarship. It is also a valuable reminder that the life of the great scholar, although perpetually noisy with warfare of one kind or another, remained always a scholar's life. There were indeed some two years at the beginning of his reign at Trinity when he absented himself almost completely from felicity. 'You must know that for the last two years I have hardly had two days free for literature,' he wrote to John George Graevius in August 1702. Not that he ever ceased to read his classical authors, for he was one of those rare men who can, so to speak, switch off their minds from attending to urgent and immediate difficulties of active life in order to concentrate on a purely intellectual problem. He might have said, with his contemporary, Montesquieu: 'There is no sorrow in life that an hour with a book could not cure.' And, in all probability, the same book; for, again like Montesquieu, when he read the ancients he took health and strength from the sense that he was himself one of them. Not that he was lost to his life-giving avocations unless he was actually engaged in reading and writing. He found invigoration in promoting the activities of other, generally younger, men in his own field.

Bentley's *Horace* came out near the end of 1711. He has told us why he turned his hand to this task at this time. It was, he said, 'a work that could be done bit by bit at odd hours, and would brook a thousand interruptions without serious loss'. For, on the whole, the text of Quintus Horatius Flaccus has been transmitted to the modern world with singularly few obvious corruptions, and it was a text that the eighteenth century may be said to have known backwards. Augustan England accepted the Roman Augustan as a poet and a gentleman of their own kith and kin. To have made use of him as a subject for the celebrated 'conjectural Criticism' which had displayed itself so brilliantly upon the fragments of Callimachus or the anachronistic misuse of the *Epistles of Phalaris* would have been both frivolous and pointless. What was needed, and what had never been satisfactorily done, for *Horace*, was to draw the reader's attention to the problems of interpretation presented by a remarkably pure text. This is what Bentley did, working at break-neck speed, piling up nearly 500 pages of small type in double-column, which he boasted had been 'thrown off' between July and November, 1711. He needed to hurry if his dedication to the Tory minister were to serve his cause. Like almost all his major works, the *Horace* was not only a *pièce d'occasion* but a *tour de force*. At the same time, it remains one of the greatest works of English scholarship, some would say the greatest.

Macaulay spoke of its 'perverted ingenuity', of its representing a genius gone wrong, the post-Phalaris Bentley in all his 'besotted reliance on his own powers and on his own luck'. It is true that the *Horace* sometimes supplies us with a fore-taste of the gay perversities of the *Paradise Lost* of some twenty years later. 'To the rescue, ye sportsmen, rustics and naturalists!' he shouts when he comes to Horace's use of the fable of the fox, thin enough to creep into a granary and stuff himself with corn, and too fat to creep out again. Foxes can't eat corn. They have neither the right teeth nor the right digestive organs. He would change the fox into a field-mouse in the interests of accuracy, reason, and common-sense, just as he was to correct Milton's natural history by pointing out that Leviathan could not 'stretch out huge in length', because the whale cannot contract any of his joints. 'The Giant,' as Professor Fraenkel has put it in referring to Bentley's treatment of *Satire* I, 10, 27–30, 'was often in a hurry and resorts to some violent expedient when a moment's pause might have enabled him to finish the job.'[1] All

[1] E. Fraenkel. *Horace*, p. 133.

the same, he has struck his finger (that 'arrowy finger', as
Housman called it) to the heart of the difficulty. Take, for
example, his speedy perception that *sic placet* in 1.23 of *Epode*
XVI refers to the formulas used in the Roman Senate (*placet
mihi si vobis placet*). Perhaps it was not a deeply perceptive
remark coming from one who was familiar with the proceedings
of the senate at Cambridge, but again to quote Fraenkel 'had
his remark been followed up, we might have been spared many
errors in the interpretation of the epode'. Inspired common
sense? Perverse ingenuity? It is always something fruitful,
something pregnant for further illumination. For this 'critical
genius in all its power' Fraenkel would recommend his treatment
of *Odes*, i, 32. Genius in criticism lies not in supplying the right
answers but in raising the right difficulties.

It was *à propos* of Bentley's *Horace* that Richard Johnson
released his little time-bomb, *Aristarchus Anti-Bentleianus*,
some five years later. Johnson seems to have borne a grudge
against Bentley since their undergraduate days at St John's.[1] In
the intervening years he had acquired a certain reputation as a
Latin grammarian with his *Grammatical Commentaries*. Now he
was master of Nottingham School, and seems to have been lying
in wait for his eminent contemporary with a good deal of malice
and a certain rude wit which (as Dr Monk remarks) proves him
to have been 'a vulgar fellow'. In *Aristarchus Anti-Bentleianus*
he takes the great doctor to task for what he calls 'shameful
blunders' as if he is correcting a schoolboy's exercise after an
unsatisfactory lunch. He finds forty-six errors in Bentley's
edition of Book I of Horace's Odes, and ninety mistakes in the
Latinity of his notes. Sometimes he is right, for Bentley's work
had been done in great haste and contains some obvious slips.
Nothing, however, can excuse Johnson's arrogantly abusive
tone, although he himself tries to excuse it by reference to the
doctor's treatment of his own learned victims. His diatribe
would scarcely deserve mention were it not for a comic interlude
in which he parodies Bentley's style of conjectural criticism or
boldness of emendation, offering what purports to be a Bentleian
treatment of the old English ballad of *Tom Bostock*. The skit
would have been more apposite fifteen years later, after the

[1] See above, p. 47.

master had done his worst for Milton's *Paradise Lost*. Why 'old' Tom Bostock, the doctor wants to know? Why not read 'bold'? Why, 'n'er be afraid of being too bold, no, rather boldly read *bold* Tom, I'll bear thee out; in Latin, *me vide*. But you'll say, neither edition, nor manuscript hath this reading; I thought as much. What of that . . . ? One grain of sense (and God be thanked I don't want that) weighs more with me, than a tun of their papers.'

Bentley does not appear to have noticed Johnson's performance, and it is doubtful whether he ever saw it. This part, at any rate, he could scarcely have failed to appreciate and forgive. Poor schoolmaster Johnson suffered from some mental illness, and three years after the appearance of *Aristarchus Anti-Bentleianus* he drowned himself in the Nottingham watermeadows.

Anyone but Bentley, after escaping from Ely House, might have been expected to seek peace and ensue it, thankful to have been spared the worst consequences of his misdeeds, content to count his blessings. Not so the Master of Trinity. Within three years he was celebrating his restoration to power and glory at Cambridge by the most daring act of brigandage in his career. At the age of fifty-five he carried off the Regius chair of Divinity, the most valuable in the university, by a *coup* which could scarcely have been more brazen if he had carried off that venerable seat on a hand-cart with the aid of a file of soldiers. From the moment when it became evident that Dr James, the president of Queens', was likely to die, the Master of Trinity made no secret of his pretensions, despite the fact that statute prohibited a Master of Trinity from election. He was resolved not only to have the Regius chair of Divinity, but to have it according to at least the forms of law.

The obstacles in his way might well have daunted a less sanguine and resourceful – not to say daring – character. The foundation statute, while it gave preference to fellows of Trinity, explicitly prohibited the holder of any office either in that college or indeed in the university.[1] Besides, the same statute

---

[1] *Nemo prædictorum Lectorum, durante tempore Lecturæ suæ, ullum officium, Magistratum aut Lecturam aliam vel in dicto Collegio, vel in Academia habeat, sub poena praedicta.*

underlined the prohibition of a master of Trinity by making that dignitary responsible for the admission of a regius professor of Divinity after election, and for acting as his judge, or 'Visitor', should the need arise. It was true that two previous masters had occupied the chair, though both cases had been quite exceptional. One had occurred during the Interregnum, a precedent which no respectable person would have wished to quote. In the other case, the professor had only become Master of Trinity some years after his election to the chair. The electors, by statute, were the vice-chancellor, the Master of Trinity, the Provost of King's, the Masters of St John's and Christ's, and the two senior fellows of Trinity. The vice-chancellor at this time was Mr Grigg, Master of Clare Hall, who shared the view of the Provost of King's and the Masters of St John's and Christ's – and almost everyone else – that Bentley was neither a desirable nor a statutable candidate. As for the two senior fellows of Trinity, they were still licking their wounds after the failure at Ely House. The only person on whom Bentley could rely for whole-hearted support was the Master of Trinity.

With the eye of a corps-commander for 'ground', Bentley at once seized upon the key-position. Statute required that on the day after a vacancy becoming known, the vice-chancellor should convene a meeting of the electors. When Dr James died, the vice-chancellor was in London.[1] His deputy, Dr Lany, approached the Master of Trinity at the late professor's funeral. He could scarcely have been quicker off the mark. Bentley at once asked Dr Lany whether he had received his authority under the hand and seal of the absent vice-chancellor? Dr Lany was unable to say precisely that he had, whereupon the Master of Trinity told him that in that case the matter was none of his business. Obviously no meeting of the electors could be convened that day. Indeed, Bentley was prepared to argue that there need be none the next day, or the day after, for [now that the statute had been broken] the office of Regius professor of Divinity had lapsed to the crown, which in effect meant the king's ministers. Did he think perhaps of rededicating his *Horace* to Robert Harley's

[1] He had gone to London to present an address to the king congratulating him on his safe return from Hanover, and on the foiling of a Jacobite invasion in league with the Swedes.

successors? Or did he hope to solicit the office from the duke of Somerset, chancellor of the university, that same 'proud Duke' who had initiated the renovation of the University Press, in which Bentley had played so notable a part?

The duke had certainly a part to play in Bentley's strategy. He was the most likely agent for the disarming of Mr Grigg, the vice-chancellor, whose patron he was. Somerset had appointed Grigg Master of Clare Hall after appeal to the Visitor in a deadlock between the fellows. When it became evident that he was not going to gain his objective by solicitation, since no one, least of all the king's ministers, was prepared to accept his argument that the delay in convening the electors by reason of the absence of the vice-chancellor, was sufficient to throw the office into the hands of the king, Bentley took steps to see to it that the vice-chancellor should go away again. Pressure was brought to bear upon Mr Grigg, presumably through his patron the chancellor, whose influence he could scarcely withstand, to absent himself from felicity a while, and not only to absent himself but to leave the Master of Trinity as his deputy in his absence. As deputy vice-chancellor, Bentley immediately convened the electors with his own consent as Master of Trinity. Another statutory provision added to his growing party. If any other elector happened to be vice-chancellor at the time of an election, it was provided that the president of Queens' should supply his place, and the president of Queens' at this moment was Dr John Davies, a loyal supporter of the doctor both before and after this event.[1] The two effective senior fellows of Trinity were George Modd and Edward Bathurst, since neither Wolfran Stubbe nor Mr Cock was able to be present,[2] and Bentley could manage them both. The other electors, the Provost of King's, and the Masters of St John's and Christ's, stayed away in a

[1] Davies had prefaced his edition of Cicero's *De Natura Deorum* (1717) with a highly laudatory dedication to the doctor. He was the only head of a house to vote in Bentley's favour when the Grace was passed depriving the doctor of his degrees in 1718. After his death in 1732 his papers were lost in a fire at Thomas Bentley's lodgings in the Strand. (See below, p. 203.)

[2] The name of Dr Stubbe had headed the signatories of the first petition against the master in 1709, when he was vice-master. Mr Cock was the senior who, the master had once predicted, would 'die in his shoes'. His name was there too. By this time he was too infirm to leave his rooms.

mistaken apprehension that their absence was the best way of expressing their disapproval, always an unwise supposition in university, or college, proceedings.

When Dr Bentley appeared at the schools along with his faithful followers, Davies, Modd and Bathurst, they waited for an hour for the rest to appear. Then Bentley offered himself as a candidate, and a day was fixed when he should deliver a probationary lecture, an examination of the candidate having been waived. A week later the doctor lectured before a large audience on the disputed text of I St John v.7, a question on which he was at that time much exercised in connection with a proposed new edition of the New Testament.[1] Next day he was elected regius professor of Divinity by the majority of four votes out of seven: his own, and those of Davies, Modd and Bathurst. The remaining three electors were still absent, nor, from beginning to end had any other candidate presented himself. Could the absentees have brought themselves to attend a meeting convened by the obstreperous Master of Trinity, they would almost certainly have put forward Dr Charles Ashton, Master of Jesus College, a learned and highly qualified gentleman whose mind Bentley once likened to a muddy fluid.

Such is the story of how Dr Bentley carried off the Regius chair of Divinity in the University of Cambridge, and as Dr Monk was to put it, it was to be hoped that 'the remembrance of the manner in which he possessed himself of the chair, might have been effaced by the applause that followed the execution of its duties'. For the doctor was now 'invested with increased sanctity of character'. For the moment, however, he was content to add insult to injury by delivering an inaugural lecture in which he thanked the gentlemen who had chosen him to be professor and gently mocked the other gentlemen whose absence from the election had given him a majority of the votes. Seldom, if ever, can an inaugural lecture, more especially by a Regius professor of Divinity, have given such evidence of victorious high spirits,

---

[1] See below, Ch. XIX. The text of the Praelection has not survived, but Dr Monk assembled a good deal of evidence from a number of sources in order to determine what were Bentley's views on the question of the disputed verse. (See Ch. XIII of the *Life*.) It seems certain that Bentley rejected the verse, while maintaining the orthodox doctrine of the Trinity which, in his opinion, 'did not stand in need of a false support'.

such gaiety of heart, such disrespect for so many among his audience. He had, we may remind ourselves, calculated that the chair ('believe those who have tried it – no bench is so hard') would enhance his income by another £600 per annum. Having survived the contest with his college, he was about to enter the lists with his university.

When the master returned to Cambridge in the summer of 1714 he had judged correctly that his enemies were wearying of the fight. Six of the fellows of Trinity had died since the opening of the attack in 1710. Others he understood to be irresolute, ageing, prepared for peace at almost any price. The 'cloistered zealots', as Lord Carteret was to call them, felt that they had done enough for honour and would be justified in accepting any overtures the master might be ready to make for a settlement. The new Bishop of Ely, Dr Fleetwood, lately translated from the see of St Asaph, encouraged them by making it clear that he would not entertain another petition against the master but would, if called upon, act as *general* visitor to the college, pronouncing upon the defects of master and fellows alike. Certain fellows had reason to be alarmed at the prospect of censure, and all felt the desirability of avoiding external interferences in the affairs of the college. Now was the time to close the ranks with a general pacification. Nor was Bentley averse from some such course, *pro tem*, and strictly without prejudice to such future action as he might decide upon. He gave up his stipends and dividends scheme, but he could not reconcile himself to the continued fellowship of Edmund Miller. He secured at any rate the prospect of Miller's removal by citing against him a property disqualification in the college statutes, and by agreeing with the Seniority to the pre-election of one David Humphreys in his place when his fellowship should be declared vacant. Miller at once petitioned the crown for redress and sought support for a petition to the Bishop of Ely against the master. The bishop declined to take cognizance.

Bentley was now recovering lost ground in the university. In particular he was cashing in on the fact that he had, even while the proceedings at Ely House were pending, 'done eminent service to the Christian religion and the clergy of England by refuting the objections and exposing the ignorance of an impious set of writers that call themselves Free-thinkers'. His *Remarks on the Discourse on Free-Thinking* in reply to Anthony Collins[1] (published under a pseudonym) really amounted to a further instalment of his Boyle lectures, and now his friends in the university[2] promoted a grace before the senate that he be offered the public thanks of the university. In 1715, too, at the time of the Jacobite rising, he preached his celebrated sermon on popery from the pulpit of Great St Mary's. This, when printed, was to remain the best-known of the doctor's works among the generality of folk who neither knew nor cared for things Latin or Greek. It was to survive for later generations through the genius of the Rev Laurence Sterne, a fellow Johnian, who embodied some of its choicest passages on the tortures of the Inquisition in the sermon which Corporal Trim reads to Mr Shandy, Uncle Toby and Dr Slop in the seventeenth chapter of Book II of the immortal *Life and Opinions*. Archdeacon Bentley falls a good deal short of James Joyce in the Jesuit preacher's sermon in *The Portrait of the Artist as a Young Man*, but in the eighteenth century it may be presumed that men had supped less full of horrors than they have in the twentieth. Corporal Trim protested that he had 'been in many a battle, a' please your Honour, but never in so melancholy a one as this. . . .' He swears that nothing in the world would induce him to read another line of it. Of course, the archdeacon was an authority on roasting alive in the belly of the brazen bull of Phalaris, and he never lacked for ferocity of imagination where the crimes of popery were concerned.

Bentley may be said to have had a vested interest in the House of Hanover and the Protestant Succession. The dynastic change of 1715, the defeat of the Roman Catholic cause, the subsequent triumph of the 'Whig Oligarchy', established once and for all the framework within which he was to live out his days. The big Whigs looked down, the men of the high chevelure and the low-

---

[1] Collins' *Discourse of Free-Thinking* was published in 1713. Its full title was *A Discourse of Free-Thinking Occasioned by the Rise and Growth of a Sect called Free-Thinkers*.

[2] Among them, in the lead, were Thomas Sherlock, Master of St Catherine's, Daniel Waterland of Magdalene and Professor Cotes, Plumian Professor: on the whole, young and forward-looking men.

church principles, Walpole, Hardwicke, Newcastle – and he was of their line, as may be seen at a glance at Thornhill's portrait of the master, a type-portrait in the tradition of Sir Godfrey Kneller and the Kit-Kat Club. In its intellectual aspect, indeed, the age that opened with George and Pudding-time might be called the age of Bentley. He had many a crisis to 'rub through' yet. He was to lose his degrees, and recover them. He was to stand a second trial at Ely House, and to kill a second Bishop of Ely. He was to be deprived of his mastership, suffering the fury of Dr Colbatch and the malice of the pope who raved at Twickenham. He was to live and die as the man in possession at Trinity Lodge, only to retire from the scene in the same year that Sir Robert Walpole retired from the House of Commons.

There can be little doubt that when he talked of 'rubbing through' he was talking from strength, the ultimate security of the big Whigs. In 1715, there appeared a pamphlet called *University Loyalty Considered; in a Letter to a Gentleman at Cambridge*, and subscribed *Philo-Georgius et Philo-Bentleius*, by which title the author seems to attribute himself to the joint-loins of the king and Master of Trinity. The master is said to be at least the equal of Sir Isaac Newton in genius, a man who knows 'as much as it is morally possible for any one man to know of every thing'. This ardent Whig makes the monarch and the master the twin gods of his idolatry, and asks if anything in 'such good times' (meaning 'pudding-time') could possibly obstruct the limitless promotion of a man of such great soul, of such innate authority, and of so majestic an air. But, he concludes, 'many have therefore taken an antipathy against him as a man that's high-minded'. No one has yet suggested that Bentley wrote this exordium himself, but it certainly expresses his sentiments, more especially in the matter of the antipathy of many in the university for a man who had changed sides since the great Tory débâcle of Queen Anne's last year. Not that Cambridge was at this time, as is sometimes assumed, a Whig stronghold. The Tory members for the university were returned again in 1715, and Toryism maintained a two-to-one majority in university politics for many years to come. Cambridge Toryism, however, was in these times, outside undergraduate circles, Hanoverian Toryism. Undergraduates might throw stones and

shout 'No Hanover!' and their seniors regarded these things as
evidence of nothing but 'juvenile licence', and dealt with them
leniently. Cambridge, from her 'quiet courts dedicated to poetry
and common-sense', looked with some disdain upon the senior
university whose chancellor, the Duke of Ormond, went off to
serve the Pretender, and whose proctors had to be reinforced
with a troop of horse to deal with undergraduate disorders.

The house of Hanover, taking its cue from moderate men,
bestowed its benefactions with special grace upon the university
of Sir Robert Walpole. Soon after his accession, King George I
responded to the senate's expressions of fervent zeal and attachment to His Majesty's person and government with the princely
gift of the late Bishop Moore's library,[1] a benefaction which gave
rise to the celebrated epigram:

> King George observing with judicious eyes
> The state of both his Universities,
> To Oxford sent a troop of Horse; and why?
> That learned body wanted loyalty.
> To Cambridge books he sent, as well discerning
> How much that loyal body wanted learning.

To which Cambridge returned the retort courteous:

> The King to Oxford sent a troop of Horse,
> For Tories own no argument but force;
> With equal skill to Cambridge books he sent,
> For Whigs admit no force but argument.

In the autumn of 1717, the king and his court being at
Newmarket, the vice-chancellor, heads of houses, and others
drove out to offer him their thanks in person and to invite him to
honour the university with a visit. The day was a Friday, the
4th day of October, and the king was graciously pleased to
reply that he would come on the following Sunday. Bentley was
at once involved in the ceremonial of the occasion as Master of
Trinity and Regius professor of Divinity. It was for him to

[1] These books, known as 'royal' at the University Library, never belonged to the King's Library. They are known as 'royal' simply because
they came to the library by royal benefaction.

receive the king at the lodge of his college, and to confer the degree of DD upon so many as the king was pleased to nominate at a *comitia regia*. The chancellor, the Duke of Somerset, was a member of Trinity College, and his Grace was pleased to announce that he would come down on Sunday in order to receive the king at the head of the university. When the chancellor visits the university it is the duty of his deputy, the vice-chancellor, to meet and accompany him. The king was to arrive at eleven of the forenoon. The chancellor therefore arranged to arrive at Trinity College at nine. The vice-chancellor, Dr William Grigg, Master of Clare Hall, accompanied by other heads of houses, would greet the chancellor at Trinity upon his arrival. Dr Grigg who had been made a cat's paw by Bentley over the election to the chair of Divinity, would gladly connive at any discomfiture arising from this rather tight schedule. Thus, when the vice-chancellor and heads arrived unexpectedly at the Master's Lodge early on Sunday morning, the master was considerably put out. He told Dr Grigg that the lodge was prepared for the reception of the king, and not for the meeting of chancellor and vice-chancellor. Whereupon the little party of heads dissolved, though the vice-chancellor himself, with the senior proctor and the esquire-bedells, hung on in the housekeeper's room to await the arrival of the duke. When the duke turned up, Dr Grigg met him in the middle of Great Court and conducted him to the lodge, where the master found himself surprised in his bed-gown and without his robes. Bentley seems to have preserved sufficient composure to greet his illustrious guests with all the dignity and courtesy proper to a Regius professor and Master of the Royal College, even when caught in his bed-gown and slippers.

Another contretemps – again brought about by Dr Grigg, the vice-chancellor – must have tried his temper even more severely. After the king had been conducted to the Regent House, the conferring of honorary degrees, and divine service in King's College Chapel, the procession set out once more for Trinity, where His Majesty and the whole company were to sit down to a banquet. Dr Grigg, anxious that the royal gaze should fall, if only for a passing moment, upon the beauties of his own college while *en route* for the royal foundation, led the party

from King's to Trinity by Trinity Lane, in those days a somewhat insalubrious thoroughfare, instead of by Trinity Street.
This meant that the king arrived at the back-gate, more properly
the Queen's Gate, instead of at the Great Gate, where the master,
fellows and scholars of his royal foundation were awaiting him,
together with the greater part of the population of Cambridge
and the surrounding countryside. To make the situation worse,
the Queen's Gate was locked and barred, a precaution against
the loyal *hoi-polloi's* crowding into the college by a back door, and
His Majesty had to wait for some minutes in the lane until someone could inform the porter at the Great Gate of his arrival on
the other side of the college, and until the porter could get
across to admit him to the house of his royal ancestors. At the
Great Gate, the master and his welcoming company were
obliged to do a sharp right-about-turn, and proceed to the
Queen's Gate in what haste was suited to their dignity. Halfway
across the Great Court, the master met His Majesty and made
him free at last of the college that was, after all, his own.

So, after all, the king dined amid the glories of the Master's
Lodge so expensively renovated in recent years, and later went
to service amidst the glories of the master's scarcely less
expensively redecorated chapel. All the bells rang from the
steeples of the Cambridge churches, and the air thundered to the
cry of *King George for ever!* or *Vivat Rex!* as the wee German
Georgie showed himself freely to his people. It is said that he
gave every sign of understanding every word that was addressed
to him by the Orator and Dr Bentley who, after all, delivered
their speeches in Latin. Everyone was pleased that he expressed
himself as so graciously pleased with his kind reception. 'What
will the sister university say to this?' wrote Dr Wilkins to the
Bishop of Carlisle. What indeed? What Dr Bentley said would
be even more interesting. We need hardly doubt that among his
happy reflections on the king's reception among the rightful
splendours that the Master of Trinity had prepared for him,
there figured also certain others pertaining to the egregious
Dr Grigg of Clare Hall, who had not only surprised the
Master of Trinity at 9 o'clock of a Sunday morning but had
kept the king waiting in the mud outside the back gate of his
college.

When the congregation of Sunday, 6 October, was resumed on Monday morning, after the king had returned to Newmarket, it was the duty of the regius professor to create a number of doctors of Divinity, for which he was to receive from each a customary broad-piece as a complimentary fee. His two predecessors in the regius chair had charged in the one case two, and in the other case, four guineas for this service. Some charge, in addition to the complimentary broad-piece, was not unreasonable, since it had become the practice for the professor to serve as an opponent[1] when candidates for theological degrees 'kept an Act', or went through the required exercise of Disputation. Bentley at once required a fee of four guineas from each candidate, cash down. A few promptly paid, but most refused. His demand, they said, was unwarrantable, unreasonable and extortionate. Very well, the professor retorted, they must go without their degrees. After a good deal of warm and unseemly argument, he undertook to refund the fee if, upon investigation, the point should be later decided against him. But he made it clear that he must have his four guineas before he would perform, and that if there were any more obduracy he would require ten. After all, he reminded them, he was the king's professor, and they were getting their degrees cheap, for doctorates in Divinity normally cost no less than £100, and the present line was being offered at the cut-price of £20 only because the recipients had been nominated by the king's favour on the occasion of his gracious visit to the university.[2] Most of the candidates would have had to take their DDs anyway, paying the professor his normal fee, and it was hardly just that he should be the loser simply because of the royal visit, which should not work to the loss or detriment of anyone, least of all to the king's professor of Divinity. . . . Some other professors expressed wonder at the greed of the Regius professor of Divinity, not simply because of the sacred subject he professed, but because his was the most profitable chair in the university. The Regius

---

[1] The respondent, or candidate, was supposed to undergo three 'opponencies'. However, provided his opponent was a doctor of Divinity he was exempt from two of these and so the professor who was testing him often voluntarily acted simultaneously as both 'moderater', or examiner, and opponent. Hence Bentley's demand for a fee.

[2] Or, as we should say, they were 'honorary degrees'.

professors of Law and of Physics had only the miserable annual stipend of £40 each, and might be forgiven for adding to it by whatever fees and perquisites they could acquire; which they certainly did, to the tune of £14 a time for creating doctors in their faculties. Bentley, however, refused to budge. He had undertaken to refund the four guineas in the event of the case being decided against him, and his IOU ought to be sufficient.

There were some, however, who rejected this as postponement to the Greek Kalends. One of them, Conyers Middleton, decided to sue the Regius professor for debt, in the sum of four guineas, in the vice-chancellor's court. The professor refused to appear before the court, which brought him into head-on collision with Dr Thomas Gooch, Master of Gonville and Caius. On October 17, 1718, Vice-chancellor Gooch brought a grace before the senate concerning *reverendus vir, Ricardus Bentley, Collegii Trinitatis Magister*, who had thus treated his court with contempt. The grace concluded:

Placeat vobis ut dictus Ricardus Bentley ab omni gradu, titulo et jure in hac Universitate dejiciatur et excludatur.

The grace was carried by majorities of more than two to one. The only head of a house who abstained from joining the majority was Dr John Davies, president of Queens'.

'So the great Dr Bentley was reduced to be a bare Harry-Soph,' one wrote in his diary; which means that on the night of October 17 and for many days and nights to come, the Master of Trinity resided at his lodge in the status of an undergraduate.

18

Flails and Fiddlesticks

There is something so singularly rude and barbarous in his
way of treating all mankind, that whoever has occasion to
relate it will, instead of aggravating, find himself obliged to
qualify and soften the harshness of his story, lest it should pass
for incredible.

CONYERS MIDDLETON, *A Full and Impartial Account, etc.*

What had happened to him can be stated thus briefly, but it was
the culmination of a whole series of actions which had held the
university spell-bound over several weeks, including the master's
defiance of the vice-chancellor's order for his arrest and the
locking up at Trinity Lodge of the officer sent to carry it out.
'He would not,' he told the vice-chancellor to his face, 'be judged
by him and his friends over a bottle.' As for the esquire-bedell,
Edward Clarke, incarcerated all through a long afternoon in the
master's dining-room, Bentley had treated him as a trespasser.
His 'decree' or warrant for arrest was a scrap of paper. Once he
had got hold of it, the master refused to give it back to him. Only
the king, he said, and certainly not the vice-chancellor, was the
judge of a master of Trinity and a Regius professor. When a
second esquire-bedell came to him a day or two later, the master
sent him off to get a warrant, for, he was pleased to say, he was
now ready to be arrested. He actually submitted to this second
decree, one of the fellows of Trinity going bail for him.

He was playing for time until, as he openly boasted, powerful
friends at court should come to his rescue. Meanwhile, he made
merry at the discomfiture of vice-chancellor, esquire-bedells
and heads of houses in court and senate assembled. Immediately
after his degradation he petitioned the king as supreme Visitor,
complaining that he had been suspended from his degrees without hearing or summons; though he made no reference to his
having failed to surrender to his bail. In consequence of this, the

vice-chancellor was called to the Council Board to give an account of his proceedings. The council first postponed the hearing and then sent the matter to a committee, thus causing a tremor of anxiety to run through both universities lest a royal commission should be set up to inquire into things in general. There can be little doubt that party feeling was involved in the quarrel from the beginning, the Whigs championing Bentley as the victim of Tory animosity as a ministerialist, the Tories rejoicing in his humiliation as a bully and despot. The twentieth is by no means the first century in which university issues have been head-line news, even if in the eighteenth century there were as yet no head-lines.

Personal, and even class, animosities went even deeper. At the head of Bentley's opponents at this time was Thomas Gooch, Master of Gonville and Caius and vice-chancellor, who was not only a Tory (and some suspected of Jacobite sympathies), but a man of breeding from a county family in Suffolk. Thomas Gooch was as certainly a gentleman as Richard Bentley was not. He had fine manners and what is called 'address'. His face looks down from his portrait where it hangs today in the University Combination Room, with the smooth self-satisfied expression of a thoroughbred. It is the expression of a man who knows that he is surveying a crowd of non-fellows eating their lunch from a snack-bar, a man who passes every day through the gate of honour of his college as to the manner born, and has long ago shut the gate of humility behind him. To such a one Richard Bentley, the man from the north with the deathless Yorkshire tang in his voice, his mocking lips, his utter disrespect for all establishments, high or low, except those of which he himself was the head, and his relish for a fight whether it concerned a corrupt text or a four-guinea fee, must have been extremely distasteful. For one thing Bentley used nicknames. Once at a discussion when the Master of Jesus had said that a certain point was not yet quite clear to him, the Master of Trinity had asked, very audibly, 'Are we then to wait here until your mud has subsided?' Among such pleasantries he was wont to refer to Dr Sherlock as Cardinal Alberoni, and to Dr Gooch as 'the empty gotch of Caius'. It is easy to understand that the Master of Caius had had more than enough of Dr Bentley some time before it became his duty to suspend him from his degrees in October 1718. Nor is there any reason for surprise that all but one out of the ten heads of houses present on that occasion voted against him. Whether or not Bentley, or one of his friends, tried to assassinate Dr Gooch by shooting with a gun into the Master's Lodge, a rumour to that effect was afoot at the time and was long preserved at Caius College, along with a hole in the wainscot of the master's study. Trinity College is next-door neighbour to Gonville and Caius, and Dr Monk thought that the habit of discovering sham plots in the course of party-warfare in the preceding century may still have been in vogue. 'Sham' plots seems something of an understatement here, for the dean of Peterborough went on to record that a bullet was found in the wall when it was stripped for certain repairs 'a few years ago'.

Pamphlets rather than bullets flew freely in the period that followed the master's fall. He continued to hope for relief at the hands of 'persons in high places'. Conyers Middleton wrote, 'we are threatened indeed every day with the expectation of a Royal mandate to re-establish him; and he himself, I hear, gives assurances of it to his friends'. The writer went on scornfully to repudiate the notion of royal or ministerial intervention on behalf of 'a person so justly odious, so void of all credit and interest amongst us. . . .' It was from Conyers Middleton's suit against the master for the debt of four guineas that his fortunes had been brought to their crisis, and he was one of the first to take up his pen in the subsequent war of words. The fact was, however, that all parties to the quarrel were alike repudiated by those in authority, ministers consistently advising the king not to interfere in any way with what Carteret called 'the frenzied struggles of cloistered bigots'. Academic warfare spent itself in print after the familiar pattern of disputation in the Age of Reason. It assumed such titles as *A Full and Impartial Account of the late Proceedings in the University of Cambridge, The Case of Dr Bentley Truly Stated, A Second Part of the Full and Impartial Account, The Case of Dr Bentley Further Stated, Some Remarks upon a Pamphlet, A Review of the Proceedings Against Dr Bentley . . . in Answer to a late pretended Full and Impartial Account. . . .* This envenomed literature is not quite dead today. Conyers

Middleton's *Full and Impartial Account*, in spite of – perhaps because of – its lying title, remains eminently readable. Bentley's own intervention in his *Review of the Proceedings*, however, is scarcely worthy of the mighty Aristarchus, the veteran of the flail and the chamber-pot of *The Battle of the Books*.

Dr Johnson once said that the attacks of Bentley's opponents were 'owing to envy, and to a desire of being known by being in competition with such a man'. The doctor, he said, never answered his opponents but 'let them die away'. By beating them, he would have given them a measure of immortality, and it is true that his most embittered enemy, Conyers Middleton, did on at least one occasion confess that a fight with Bentley afforded him 'some chance of being known likewise to posterity . . . dragged at least by his great name out of my present obscurity and of finding some place, though a humble one, in the future annals of his story'. Besides, Johnson added, 'in his hazardous method of writing, he could not but be often enough wrong; so it was better to leave things to their general appearance, than own himself to have erred in particulars'. It would be more accurate to say that he let his allies answer for him, rarely intervening *in nomine proprio*. His *Letter to the Bishop of Ely* in 1710 was printed under the name of 'A Gentleman of the Temple'. Now, in 1718, his case was put under the name of Arthur Anthony Sykes.

Sykes had no standing in the university, nor had he any intimate relationship with Bentley. His life has been called 'one long altercation', and he chose to regard the treatment of the master as an attack on the low church party, to whose cause Sykes was passionately devoted. He sprang to the defence of the master as the victim of tyranny and injustice, with two letters to the *St James's Post*, professing to give a full account of the overbearing conduct of Dr Gooch and the scandalous way in which the greatest scholar of the age had been treated by the university in the matter of his degrees. Perhaps only an observer on the side-lines could have hoped to win support for the doctor as the victim of academical oppression, but once a low-church spokesman had championed his cause an answer had to be produced by the high-church faction of the Establishment. It came from Dr Thomas Sherlock, Bentley's 'Cardinal Alberoni' in the typical eighteenth-century form of *A Letter to a Noble Peer*, or *The Proceedings of the Vice-Chancellor and University of Cambridge against Dr Bentley, Stated and Vindicated.* Sherlock was to become a best-seller in 1750 with his *Letter on the Occasion of the Late Earthquake,* which sold 105,000 copies, but this was nothing to do with Bentley, who died eight years before it appeared, when Sherlock was Bishop of London. In 1718 he was Dean of Chichester. He had been vice-chancellor in 1715, when he was Master of St Catharine's Hall, and a prime-mover in the anti-Bentley faction. Now, with his *Letter to a Noble Peer,* or *The Proceedings Vindicated* he lived up to, or down to, Bentley's soubriquet of the cunning cardinal by giving the impression that the cause of the master's degradation had been his insistence on a four-guinea fee for making doctors of Divinity and his rough treatment of the esquire-bedell. He also gave the impression that what had happened was likely to lead on to the ejection of the miscreant from the chair of Regius professor of Divinity.

Sherlock was followed almost immediately by the gentleman whose resistance to the four-guinea fee, and whose suit against the professor for debt in that sum at the vice-chancellor's court, had put in train the course of events which culminated in his degradation. Conyers Middleton, like Sykes, was at this time something of a bystander. Although he had been among the fellows of Trinity who signed the Articles of Complaint against the master in 1710, he had left his fellowship[1] and was now living a happy domestic life in the town. He was singular, too, in his possession of a distinct literary flair, an elegant and polished English style which can still be read with pleasure when the issues for which he contended are as dead as mutton. His *Life of Cicero,* long supplanted as a work of scholarship, remains as fresh and readable today as the essays of Macaulay remain readable on subjects on which few would any longer think to depend upon him for enlightenment. This made him the most redoubtable of Bentley's enemies in print, for it is a sad fact that a good writer in a bad cause may enjoy, at least for a time, all the advantages of an immediate, even if ultimately a

[1] Bentley was not alone in thinking that he acted meanly in concealing the fact of his marriage for some months in order to continue as long as possible to enjoy the benefits of his fellowship.

spurious, triumph. Not that Conyers Middleton's cause was entirely bad. Rather, his attractive style made it seem a great deal better than it was. There was generally a sufficiency of truth in what he wrote, but by the power and velocity of his prose he was able to carry his readers with immense rapidity to frequently unwarrantable conclusions. It is perhaps significant that this skilful writer was a devoted amateur musician. Bentley liked to refer to him as 'Fiddling Conyers', or 'Fiddleton'.[1] If Bentley wrote with a flail, certainly Conyers Middleton wrote with a fiddlestick, and sometimes what he wrote was a matter of fiddlesticks too.

For sheer elegant chicanery there is little to surpass his argument (following upon Sherlock's line) for depriving Bentley of his professorship.

> For besides, that its forfeiture might be fairly argued from his present want of degrees; that by its foundation it is made inconsistent and incompatible with the mastership of Trinity College; that he obtained it by bullying, and holds it by violence: besides all this, I say, as the statute has made it a necessary qualification of a Professor, that he have no blemish or infamy upon his character, I would desire no other foundation to prove the necessity of his being ejected. He has been publicly accused by his Fellows of many great crimes, which he never has nor can clear himself of. And his trial which never came to a sentence, has left the marks of such infamy upon him, as by all the notions which the civil or canon law has of it, would be sufficient not only to incapacitate him from being chosen Professor, but to deprive him when in possession.

We need only to recall that Bentley's 'want of degrees' was the effect of a sentence pronounced in his absence and without his being heard in his defence, a sentence that was to be quashed by the Court of King's Bench some five years later as defective in 'natural justice'; when we remember that he had never been

---

[1] Bentley's contempt for the man is to be found everywhere in his writings. 'That puppy Middleton . . . that silly fellow . . . ' are his commonest mode of reference. Bentley suspected that the puppy not only fancied himself as Regius professor of Divinity when the master had been ejected from it, but even as his successor at the Master's Lodge. Such pretensions on the part of 'an arrant Pagan'!

found guilty of the 'many great crimes' charged against him in the Bishop of Ely's court; that his conclusionless trial had only left 'the marks of such an infamy upon him' in the opinion of those whose minds were made up before the proceedings began; that the category of 'notorious offender' in the absence of a formal action at law had been defunct since the times of the Saxon and Anglo-Norman kings: then Conyers Middleton's case is seen to be the offspring of personal animosity and linguistic craft. Again, the writer of this so-called 'Full and Impartial Account' calls to his aid the 'plain marks of a judgment and infatuation', which he had detected in a man whom the gods had obviously made mad as a step on the way to destroying him.

Quem Juppiter vult perdere dementat prius.

For, after all, he could have saved himself all the calamities that had fallen upon him 'by restoring of four guineas which he has shamefully extorted'. What Middleton calls 'an easy, and perhaps private submission' would have served, but of course he had sacrificed everything to his pride, to 'the glory of never having been known to submit':

> We may strip him of his titles, but we never can, we see, of his insolence; he has ceased to be a Doctor, and may cease to be a Professor, but he can never cease to be Bentley. There he will triumph over the University to the last; all its learning being unable to polish, its manners to soften, or its discipline to tame the superior obstinacy of his genius.

19

Bentley's Bubble

It has been noted by his enemies, and lauded by his eulogists, that whenever the tide of accusation was strongest against him, he was sure to come out with some book which turned the public attention from his delinquencies to his abilities, and indisposed the world to believe that so much learning could lack honesty.

HARTLEY COLERIDGE.

But indeed most people are agreed in opinion that he has borrowed this scheme from Change Alley, and in this age of bubbles, took the hint to set up one of his own . . . and does not in the least question but that Bentley's Bubble will be as famous and profitable as the best of them.

CONYERS MIDDLETON.

The grand strategy of scholarship was never better evinced, in the general opinion, than in the year 1720 when the master came forth with the prospectus of his edition of the New Testament. He had been meditating the scheme for some time past, and had indeed broached the project to the Archbishop of Canterbury in the spring of 1716. At that time, lately returned from the proceedings at Ely House, he had reason to believe that another petition against his maladministration at Trinity was in preparation. In fact, almost exactly a month after his letter to the archbishop, nineteen of the fellows petitioned the king to clear up the question of the visitatorial power with regard to their college. It was undoubtedly important for the master to be able to rely upon the good offices of the Archbishop of Canterbury, who had already interested himself in the troubled state of affairs at Trinity College, and had promised the fellows his support at the council-board for the sending of a royal commission to visit the college for the composition of its quarrels. Archbishop Wake had himself been engaged in certain learned investigations in the field of biblical criticism at an earlier stage of his career. What-

ever the archbishop may have thought of Richard Bentley as
Master of Trinity, he could hardly, as a patron of learning and
religion, show indifference to a proposal on the part of the Regius
professor of Divinity and the most celebrated scholar of the age
to apply himself to the production of a corrected and perfected
edition of the Gospel of Peace.

He appears to have received Bentley's proposal with respect if
not with evident enthusiasm. For one thing, the master's letter
found him busy with Convocation, and when he wrote again
Bentley apologised for troubling him at such a time. 'I condemned myself that I should be so immersed here in books and
privacy,' said the archdeacon, 'as not to know a more proper
occasion of address to your Grace.' He had been in a desperate
hurry in approaching his Grace 'about those unfashionable
topics, religion and learning', in case 'a casual fire should take
either his Majesty's library or the King's of France', in the event
of which dreadful calamity, not all the world could do what he
was proposing to do. He would wish to know 'if the extrinsic
expense to do such a work completely (for my labour I reckon
nothing) may obtain any encouragement either from the Crown
or public?' His scholarly enthusiasm breathes in every sentence.
Nothing but sickness, he avows, shall prevent him from
prosecuting the task to the end, for the project has not only
engaged him but enslaved him. '*Vae mihi*, unless I do it,' he
exclaims. Woe there was certainly to be, but not quite in the
way he anticipated. His plans for a perfect edition of the Gospel
of Peace were to plunge him, with the irony which so often
accompanied his undertakings, into yet another chapter of the
Forty Years' War that constituted his reign as Master of
Trinity.

He was at this time engaged in war on two fronts. His war
with the university had left him worsted by the loss of his degrees, and still without evident prospect of recovering them,
though even the University of Cambridge might find it embar-
rassing to accept a perfected Greek Testament *edidit* RICH-
ARDUS BENTLEIUS, *tout court*. In his war with the fellows of
Trinity his prospects, though still darkened by the threat of
another petition, and a possible visitation, were brightening
under the prospective defeat of both Edmund Miller and Conyers

Middleton, the leaders of the first two phases of the resistance movement. Since the virtual ejection of Miller from his fellowship in 1714, that stricken hero had played into the master's hands by his own folly. He had written a critical book about Cambridge, always a tactless thing to do unless one is a fellow of King's. It was called *An Account of the University of Cambridge and the Colleges There*, and it was intended to assist Parliament in their (supposedly) forthcoming task of reformation. Statutes and ordinances were out of date and needed bringing into touch with the modern world. Like most academic reformers of the clever type, Miller betrayed his despotic temper and succeeded in arousing all sections of opinion against him. Even his old flock of dissident fellows of Trinity were cured of their infatuation, and dissociated themselves and their cause from him. The heads of houses asked the High Steward of the University, the Earl of Manchester, to dismiss him from his office as deputy, and the senate censured his book as a notorious libel on the honour and privileges of the university.

Bentley, of course, had come in for plenty of Miller's venom in the *Account*. He took his revenge by dressing down the sergeant in conjunction with Conyers Middleton in his *Review of the Proceedings*, effectively showing him to be 'the completest blockhead he ever met with'. At the same time, he proceeded to make common cause with the blockhead in his attempt to recover from the college the expenses he had incurred in serving the fellows over the petition to the Bishop of Ely in the years 1710–14. After all, Bentley was after his own expenses over that action too. The master and the sergeant had at least a common ground in financial matters, and Bentley was never a man to neglect a chance to benefit financially at the cost of a little diplomacy in the true eighteenth-century style. By a great deal of lobbying and brow-beating he got the fellows to agree to pay Miller £528 in prosecutor's costs, and the arrears on his vacated fellowship, together with a sum of £500 to the master for his own expenses in defending himself, not to mention a small item of £284 towards the purchase of certain choice furnishings for the Master's Lodge. Miller agreed to drop his petition against the master and to discharge the college and its members from all further claims. All this was carried in the name of future peace

179

and harmony. Each of the fellows, it was hoped, would agree to sign an undertaking which took the following form: 'I hereby declare that I sincerely wish that an end may be put to the contests which have so long disturbed the College; and in order thereto, I desire that the charges of each side may be defrayed out of the common stock of the College.' Bentley was not greatly concerned that Edmund Miller came off thus profitably, always providing that Richard Bentley did too. On the next occasion when the master appeared before the Bishop of Ely – some fourteen years later – the petition of the fellows of Trinity was to contain a full indictment of this transaction in Articles LIX, LX and LXI, and all three were to be confirmed by the court as legitimate items among his 'great and enormous crimes'. They constitute what Monk was to call 'the greatest malversation ever charged against Bentley in his disposal of College funds', and there is little doubt that they did more than anything else to deprive him of the mastership. But he had recovered his expenses and disposed of Edmund Miller, who from henceforth fades out of the master's story. He seems to have shunned both the Eastern Circuit and the university for the remaining dozen years of his life, becoming a Member of Parliament in the extreme Whig interest and one of the barons of the Exchequer for Scotland. Whether or not the master drank the blockhead's health during his late port-drinking days we are not told.

His successor in the leadership of the resistance movement was, for a time, Conyers Middleton, whose diatribes we have already seen. He, like Miller, let his facile pen lead him into trouble. The celebrated *Account of the Proceedings* of 1719 contained libel not only on the master but on the Court of the King's Bench. He had rather pertinently asked what had happened to the famous liberty of Englishmen, so much the envy of other nations and so rightly the boast of our own, when 'the meanest person knows where to find redress for the least grievance he has to complain of', while 'a body of learned and worthy men, oppressed and injured daily, in everything that is dear and valuable to them, should not be able to find any proper court of justice in the kingdom that will receive their complaints'. They had for several years past been labouring to procure a

180

public and decisive hearing. They had applied to every great man they could get access to. Their petition to the king in Council had been depending for above four years without any other effect than to find themselves trampled upon with spirit and insolence. This incautious observation was the beginning of an action in the King's Bench on the joint behalf of the king and Richard Bentley.

'Bellum', wrote Dr Arbuthnot, 'a tall, raw-boned man', the emperor's library-keeper, when he got into a quarrel immediately flung a great book at his adversary and, if his adversary flung one back, 'he complained to the Grand Justiciary that these affronts were designed to the Emperor. . . . By this trick he got that great officer on his side, which made his enemies cautious, and him insolent.' Dr Conyers Middleton was now to experience the wrath of both 'Bellum' and his master. He produced unavailing testimony to his peaceable character and to the truth of what he had written, but he had to dance attendance at Westminster Hall for weeks while awaiting sentence. The Chief Justice implored the two doctors of Divinity to come to terms out of court, and indeed Middleton in desperation did bring himself to ask Bentley's pardon. Bentley found this insufficient, and his lordship asked whether the plaintiff required the defendant to be paraded through Westminster Hall with his apology pinned to his hat? This brought the business to an end at last, and the university sought to compensate Middleton by creating a job for him as principal keeper of the University Library at £50 per annum. Bentley's costs were defrayed by Trinity College.

The year 1720 was to be long remembered as 'South Sea Year'. It marks the height of the mania for financial speculation which had been steadily increasing in intensity since Robert Harley had secured the incorporation of the South Sea Company by Act of Parliament in 1711. 'No peace without Spain!' had been the Whig war-cry in the later years of the War of the Spanish Succession. Which meant that Her Britannic Majesty did not intend to make peace until she was assured of an appropriate share of the trade of the Spanish empire in America. The South Sea Company was founded to exploit the riches of an empire which belonged to someone else, *videlicet* the king of Spain, who was kindly allowed a place on the Court of Directors, and it soon became fairly obvious to the critics of the company that there would be trouble when His Majesty woke up to the way he had been 'bubbled'. The company was bemused, as many Englishmen had been bemused ever since the days of Sir Walter Raleigh, by dreams of El Dorado, and the second decade of the eighteenth century saw the slow dawn of the light of common day. Not that the company's profits were negligible, but they were never so splendid as they had seemed to promise in prospect. More important, the activities of the company set off a 'whirlwind of speculation' which caught up innumerable projects, old and new, possible and visionary, sound and unsound. By the spring of 1720, 'the lunatic note of the nit-vendor – or selling of nothing – was already sounding clearly',[1] and for a time it seemed that everyone had a prospectus offering shares in some infallible form of gold-mine, from the manufacture of heat-resisting paint to a 'cleanly manner of emptying necessary houses throughout England' and making salt-petre from the 'soil'.

When, at the height of 'South Sea Year', Bentley published 'Proposals for Printing' his New Testament, it certainly bore some resemblance to the familiar type of prospectus then coming forth from the myriad stock-jobbers pullulating between South Sea House and 'Change Alley'. The project is described under four heads as concerned 'to do good service to common Christianity' by providing a text which can be fixed 'to the smallest nicety', dispensing with about four-fifths of the 'various readings' which at present cluttered up the margins. This was to be achieved by comparing the original Greek and St Jerome's Latin. The Greek and Latin manuscripts, by their mutual assistance will yield the standard version received by the fathers at the time of the Council of Nicea (AD 325). Use was to be made of the old versions, Syriac, Coptic, Gothic and Ethiopic, to confirm the lections, with notes on all the variants, so that 'the reader has under one view what the first ages of the Church knew of the text, and what has crept into any copies since is of no value or authority'. And, like a good projector, Bentley disclaims all 'divination' (a faculty for which he was by this time famous from

[1] John Carswell, *The South Sea Bubble*, pp. 141–2.

his editing of the profane authors), likewise all guesswork, all sleight-of-hand. 'The author is very sensible,' he says, 'that in the Sacred Writings there's no place for conjectures or emendations. Diligence and fidelity, with some judgment and experience, are the characters here requisite.' He declares therefore that 'he does not alter one letter in the text without the authorities subjoined in the notes'. If he wishes to suggest any changes in the text not supported by copies now extant, he will offer them separately in his *Prolegomena*. He is of no sect or party, and he will make no 'oblique glances'! His design is to serve the whole Christian name, and he offers the fruit of his labours as a 'Charter', a Magna Carta, to the whole Christian Church.

SUBSCRIPTION TERMS: Great Paper Edition, 2 volumes folio, produced with the best paper and type that Europe can afford, 5 guineas (2 in advance). Smaller paper edition, 3 guineas (1 in advance).

The work to be put to the press as soon as sufficient money is contributed to support the charge of the impression. No more copies to be printed than are subscribed for. Overseer and corrector of the press, the learned Dr John Walker of Trinity College. The 'issue' (whether profit or loss) to fall equally on him and the 'author'.

Again, like a good tradesman, Bentley provides a sample of his wares in the form of a specimen-sheet, consisting of the 22nd chapter of the Apocalypse – the last chapter of the New Testament – the choice of this particular sample serving to intimate that the whole work was already in an advanced state of preparation. For he was in a tearing hurry to get things moving. After all, there were good reasons to believe that his enemies were plotting to get him ejected from the chair of Divinity. And anyway, it was nearly ten years since his *Horace* had appeared. Nothing could better serve the regius professor of Divinity, let alone the whole Christian Church, than a handsome two-volume folio at five guineas headed:

'H ΚΑΙΝΗ ΔΙΑΘΗΚΗ. *Græce.* NOVUM TESTAMEN-TUM, *Versionis Vulgatæ, per S*^{tum} *Hieronymum ad vetusta Exemplaria Græca castigatæ et exactæ. Utrumque ex antiquis-*

simis Codd. MSS. *cum Græcis tum Latinis, edidit* RICHARDUS BENTLEIUS.

In drawing up his prospectus, Bentley worked at break-neck speed all through one summer evening. Candlelight shone from the windows of the Master's Lodge, the sweet chime of the college-clock told the hours and the voice of the fountain in the midst of Great Court murmured on to midnight and beyond. We have his own word for it that the 'Proposals for Printing' were drawn up 'in one evening by candlelight, and printed the next day from that first and sole draught'. Quoting St Jerome from memory he got one unimportant word wrong, and gave a handle to his enemies who were to accuse him of tinkering with his authorities. Not one of his critics could have done the work in a week.

When Dr John Colbatch, one of the Seniority, and professor of Casuistry, was shown a copy in hall, he was heard to say that the whole thing was a sham, and that the master's design could hardly be taken seriously, for everyone knew he had to interest the public while he was under threat of a visitation. As for the egregious Conyers Middleton, he rushed into print with more *Remarks*, this time *Remarks, Paragraph by Paragraph, on Dr Bentley's Proposals*. . . . He excelled himself in malicious innuendo and vulgar parallels. It was Conyers Middleton who started the jest about 'Bentley's Bubble', and the origin of the scheme in 'Change Alley'. To the master, whose financial enterprises (to put it mildly) were a byword, this must have been the most unkindest cut of all. He was accused of basely selling scholarship in the market-place, offering subscriptions in Holy Scripture, money-changing in the Temple. At a season when it seemed that the whole world was for sale at the hands of stock-jobbers, the Regius professor of Divinity had been branded as a stock-jobber.

And it was not true. Bentley's scheme was no 'bubble'. It had occupied his mind ever since John Wetstein, having obtained leave-of-absence from his duties in the Dutch army, had visited him at Trinity College and at the King's Library at St James's in 1716, offering him the collations he had been making of New Testament MSS in France, begging him to undertake an edition

as the fittest scholar in the world for the task. Bentley had himself collated the Epistles of St Paul with the Alexandrian MS,
'the oldest and best now in the world', which was under his
especial care at the king's library.[1] He had recruited the services
of 'the learned Dr John Walker', a product of the master's old
school at Wakefield, and newly elected to a fellowship at Trinity,
to collate important MSS in Paris. Walker was in Paris for
almost twelve months, at Bentley's expense, over this task, and
performed it with exemplary care and diligence. He received
hospitality and learned collaboration from the Benedictine
monks of St Maur, and especially from the learned Father
Montfaucon, who even offered to send MSS treasures of his
house to Cambridge for the use of the great scholar. The intellectual traffic between the Master's Lodge and the Convent of
St Germain des Prés at this time remains a lively witness to the
fraternity of the learned world, in ironic contrast to the insectual
back-biting which went on in the cloisters beside Cam's
slumbrous stream where Drs Colbatch and Middleton fleshed
their stings.

Conyers Middleton's *Remarks, Paragraph by Paragraph
. . .* was perhaps the most disgraceful specimen of the *odium
theologicum* that the master encountered in these, the darkest
years of his pilgrimage. . . . *Où sont les neiges d'antan?* Is it
worth while to parade at this time of day the whitening bones of
learned guttersnipes long gone to dust? Shall these dead bones
live? Perhaps, if only to set the academic feuds of the twentieth
century in a just perspective. Nothing we have seen of donnish
critics in recent years can rival for sheer impudence Middleton's
charge of 'low and paltry higgling to squeeze our money from
us' against Bentley's plan to publish by subscription, coming as
it did from a man who did not hesitate to indulge in the same
perfectly normal and reputable procedure when he published his
own best-remembered book.[2] The master's *Full Answer* to
Conyers Middleton was not merely impudent, it was virulent. It
might be said to carry off the prize for full-blooded abuse even in
the century of Swift, Junius and John Wilkes. Conyers Middleton is ignored, except for a passing reference to the pillory, a

[1] See above, p. 86.
[2] *The Life of Cicero.*

punishment which hung over 'Fiddling Conyers' anent his libel upon the Court of the King's Bench. The cannonade is directed upon Dr Colbatch as the man behind the fiddler's mask. Colbatch is not named. The master said that he declined to foul his letter with his name 'since he himself thought it too scandalous for his own pamphlet', but he makes it crystal-clear that he is addressing the professor of Casuistry by reference to 'a casuistic drudge', and by unmistakable reference to well-known facts about Colbatch's career. He also paints a disparaging but recognisable portrait of his physical appearance: his swarthy skin (he had lived in Portugal), and his unfortunate habit of screwing up his head and shoulders and glaring horribly when delivering himself of some sententious reference to his conscience. This, it was notorious, the professor did at the slightest provocation. 'He never broaches a piece of mere knavery without a preface about his conscience; nor ever offers to us downright nonsense, without eyes, muscles and shoulders wrought up into the most solemn posture of gravity.'

The Master was to be at war with John Colbatch for the rest of his life, and a brief reference to his *Full Answer* leaves one in no doubt that the wounds inflicted in 1721 infected the enmity between the two men with the most deadly poison that can afflict the academic mind: the poison of contempt. For the academic mind is particularly prone to self-contempt, because it is dimly conscious that academic activities are not proper to a whole man as a full-time occupation. Dr Colbatch was now addressed as a 'cabbage-head', a snarling dog, a gnawing rat, a maggot, a worm and an insect. He is made to appear silly, trivial and ridiculous. He is said to be a man for whom 'a College squabble is necessary to keep up his spirits'; a noisy little Cassandra who 'in the midst of College plenty, with five thousand pounds surplusage above all expenses . . . can bawl, with tragic tone, and lungs stronger than a smith's bellows, *Destruction, Dilapidation, Ruin*, upon the laying out of five pounds'; an absurd mannikin, a 'scribbler of the dark' with jaws as wide as a fish, and forever 'smiling horrible like Satan in Milton'. He was even accused of having for a brother the Rev George Colbatch, vicar of Abington, 'much the better of the

two', but scarcely less absurd, since he let his beard grow down
to his waist at the behest of some vow or vision. Evidently the
brothers Colbatch were under the influence of the moon, or,
quite literally, lunatic.

One sees the candle-flames in the master's study windows wink
and flicker a good deal through the long evening when he composed the *Full Answer*, and no doubt the world in general
wondered at the mighty scholar's versatility when he took time
off from his New Testament. For although the *Full Answer* was
described on its title-page as by 'A Member of Trinity College',
and refers to Dr Bentley throughout as 'our Master', no one was
deceived. Nor was it intended that anyone should be. The *Full
Answer* contains at least one proprietorial reference to *The Letters
of Phalaris*. Dr Colbatch secured a majority resolution from the
seniority that the work was 'false, scandalous and malicious',
and that proceedings should be brought against its author if he
were discovered to be a member of the college. The heads of
houses in the university declared it to be 'a most virulent and
scandalous libel, highly injurious to Dr Colbatch, contrary to
good manners and a notorious violation of the statutes and
discipline of the University. . . .' Again, if the author were
discovered, he should be censured as the statutes of the university
provided. Conyers Middleton, of course, promptly published
Some Further Remarks, Paragraph by Paragraph. . . . He ex-
plained that the author of the *Full Answer* had been mistaken in
attributing his previous 'Remarks' to Dr Colbatch. His new
production was four times as long as its predecessor. In it he
uttered his famous avowal that he would stick to Dr Bentley as
his best hope of immortality.

'I heartily congratulate you . . .' Dr Colbatch wrote to him
'. . . you have laid Bentley flat upon his back.' He also rejoices at
the master's failure to get from the Treasury permission to
import duty-free paper for his New Testament.

But the 'bubble' was floated. There was no question of its having
been pricked by Conyers Middleton. The great work was to go
on. Before long the subscription had topped 2,000 guineas, and a
story was going about that 200 guineas had been raised by a

whip-round at the Duke of Bolton's dinner table while Bentley was out of the room. On his return, the master is said to have shaken the guineas in his hand and exclaimed: *Quis, nisi mentis inops, oblatum respuit aurum?* or 'None but the poor in mind would refuse gold when offered.' Whatever else he may have been, Bentley was never poor in mind. Nor, after his youthful years, was he ever poor in pocket.

20

The Martyrdom of Dr Colbatch

The vicarious immortality hoped for by Conyers Middleton in 'sticking to the Master' was, in fact, to be enjoyed (if that is the right word) by Dr Colbatch. Colbatch infested the master for more than twenty years, outlived him by some five years, and finally died a haggard shadow of a man in his rectory at Orwell at the age of eighty-four. He had fought the master over Orwell rectory in the crucial years 1719–20, the years which saw the beginning of their deathless vendetta, inflicting upon him his first serious defeat, and boasting that he 'fairly threw Bentley on his back'. Thereafter, to say that he was a thorn in the master's flesh would be to associate Bentley with the more trivial pains and weaknesses of flesh and blood. Like most people who lived beside 'Cam's slumbrous stream' at that time – and at most times – he suffered from a cold in the head for much of the year and a bronchial catarrh in the winter months.[1] He never took exercise, although every day when the weather was fine he walked on the terrace he had built in his garden, on the river-side. Otherwise he enjoyed the occasional exercise incidental to travelling up and down to London and occasionally to Bath. People had little need to 'seek' exercise in the centuries when a summer journey meant jogging on horse-back over roads like

[1] When, in their final petition against him the fellows charged him with not attending chapel for more than twenty years, he replied that since 1718 or 1719, when he reached the age of sixty, he had been subjected to 'almost constant colds and dangerous coughs by changing his habit and putting on a Collegiate or academic one', although 'in order to stay in that spacious chapel, and to secure him from the cold and damp of the marble . . . he had a carpet carried by his servant to chapel for that purpose . . .' but even this was insufficient to prevent him from catching cold every time he went there, so that he was 'necessitated to decline going thither, or to any other place out of his own house, by advice of his physicians'.

corrugated iron or a winter excursion involved wading through swamps in coaches with wheels like drums. Nothing that Dr Colbatch could do to aggravate the discomforts of the master's life after 1720 can have been more than a slight headache. He did everything he could, but if we have sympathy to spare, it must be for the Professor of Casuistry rather than the Regius Professor of Divinity. The unfortunate man was to be finally celebrated in an essay by Lytton Strachey entitled *The Sad Story of Dr Colbatch*. It was a posthumous irony that this martyr to gravity and precision should be commemorated in a comical and somewhat inaccurate essay by the pen of a master-hand in the art of the flippant and the absurd.

The fact is that John Colbatch was a disappointed man when at the age of forty he returned to his old college from his sojourn as English chaplain to the factory at Lisbon and as bear-leader to the Earl of Hertford, eldest son of the Duke of Somerset, chancellor of the university. The duke, and Gilbert Burnet, Bishop of Salisbury, to whose eldest son Colbatch had also served as private tutor, not to mention Richard Bentley himself, all had fostered his hopes of preferment in the church and a liberal income. Burnet had given him a prebend at Salisbury worth £20 per annum. The duke had dismissed him abruptly with 'expressions of displeasure', and the exact proportion of his salary due to him at the date of his dismissal. Bentley gave him kind words and smoothed down the duke's roughest aspersions. But the result of it all was that John Colbatch found himself back at Trinity with an assured income of £20 per annum, a chip on his shoulder, and the sense of having been robbed of the best years of his life. The chip was not to diminish even after the university elected him Professor of Casuistry in 1707, which meant that he was to spend the remainder of his days discoursing to the young on the principles of moral philosophy. He was to need all the moral philosophy he could muster. Not that he appears ever to have had the least difficulty in maintaining the loftiest and most inflexible principles in all things. His friend Conyers Middleton spoke of his virtue as 'by some deemed too severe'. Another friend, William Whiston, thought that his virtue 'seemed to have somewhat of the disagreeable'. It is obvious that life, and perhaps nature, had made John Colbatch more than a little of a prig, and – a later age would say – a sour-puss.

What was needed to cope with the situation at Trinity in 1720 was not a Dr Colbatch but a Dr Strangelove, a man who had learned not to worry and to love the bomb that was Bentley. Bentley, the tall, raw-boned man with a conscience like leather and the fighting temper of a rhinoceros, the man for whom everything had always gone right, was confronted by a man of severest virtue, for whom everything (or almost everything) had always gone wrong. The son of Captain Bentley, the armed man with the rusty sword, stood face to face with a professor of Casuistry who believed his strength to be as the strength of ten because he believed – and too often said – his heart was pure. 'He never broaches a piece of mere knavery without a preface about his conscience,' said the master. 'Commend me to a man who with a thick hide and solid forehead can stand bluff against plain matter of fact.'

At first their relations had been amicable enough. After all Colbatch was by principle and temperament a pillar of properly constituted authority. He had also reason to be grateful to Bentley for assistance in the matter of his ungrateful patrons. He strongly approved of the master's early efforts to raise the standards of scholarship in the college by a stricter management of examinations and appointments, even if he remained critical of the high-handed methods by which the master was inclined to promote these desirable ends. He was reluctant to participate in the first great campaign which petered out at Ely House in 1714, and only signed the petition with reservations. He deeply deplored the fellows' accepting the leadership of Edmund Miller, a person of whom he strongly disapproved. When in 1714 the vice-mastership fell vacant, Bentley offered it to Colbatch and was plainly hurt when he declined it. Colbatch was not yet of the Seniority, and no doubt he suspected (doubtless correctly) a move to recruit him to the master's party at the cost of his liberty of conscience as a critic. At this point the relations of the two men took a decisive turn for the worse. If Colbatch had felt able to accept the vice-mastership he might have exercised a moderating influence on the master in the period of extremely high-handed behaviour that was now opening. As it was, becoming a member of the Seniority at this moment, the man of inflexible virtue was more than ever morbidly sensible of his duty to stick by both the letter of college statutes and the rules of propriety, with the utmost rigour.

Having come away from Ely House scot-free and utterly unrepentant, the master seemed determined to clinch his victory – such as it was – by giving a repeat performance of his former misdeeds, thereby justifying the ways of masters to men. For example, 1714 was the first year in which he frustrated any attempt by the fellows to raise effective objection on the college accounts by sitting on the books until it was too late for the audit. He was, at this time, once more intent upon adding to the amenities of his lodge – and, of course, of the college – by various forms of reconstruction, at college expense, to the tune of some £900. He tore down a ruinous summer-house and built a new one adjoining his study, adding a bath with water piped from the college conduit. Bentley's 'banqueting-hall' his critics called this enterprise. A double-vaulted wine-cellar was another item, and no expense was spared in the laying out of the grass-plots and walks in the master's garden. A terraced walk was constructed for his exercise along the bank of the river. But what raised most opposition was his conversion of a dove-cot and a lumber-room in the back premises of his lodge into a granary for the reception and storage of the master's wheat and malt brought by river-barge from his rectory-farm at Somersham, for in these years it seemed that the master was intent – as Conyers Middleton put it, with customary exaggeration – upon making himself 'the greatest farmer and maltster in the country'. He was accused of selling his wheat and malt to the college bakehouse and brewery at his own price, much to the detriment of the college ale by weevil-damaged malt, though this charge was never made out against him to the satisfaction of any but his most inveterate enemies. What is certain, however, is that he managed to overcome opposition to his levying of the cost of his granary upon the college by similar methods to those he had employed earlier in the matter of his staircase.[1] This time, however, instead of threatening to send the junior bursar into the

[1] See above, Ch. 14.

Sir Thomas Gooch, Bart., 1674–1754
Master of Gonville and Caius College,
1716–54. By an unknown artist,
c. 1716–37

John Moore, 1646–1714, Bishop of Ely.
By Isaac Whood, 1736, after Sir
Godfrey Kneller's portrait, 1705

Conyers Middleton, 1683–1750
By an unknown artist, *c*. 1730–5

The Avenue of Limes, and the Bowling Green, Trinity College.

The Avenue of Limes leads from New Court to the 'Backs'. Tennyson in *In Memoriam* speaks of passing along the Lime Walk on the way to his friend Hallam's rooms:

> Up that long walk of limes I past
> To see the rooms in which he dwelt. (*Stanza 87*)

country to feed his turkeys, he recruited a new junior bursar in the person of the Rev Richard Walker, curate of Upwell, in the fens, henceforth distinguished by the name of Frog Walker.[1] This gentleman managed to get the college expenses and those of the master so confused that no one was ever able to distinguish the one from the other. Walker was to become the master's most devoted henchman for the rest of his life, the perfect Mosca to his Volpone.

And, as ever, Bentley served Trinity, and Cambridge, as handsomely as himself. It was in the years 1717–18 that he transformed 'the back-green' into the 'Backs', the glory of Cambridge.[2] Some thirty acres of fenny pasture, the unkempt grazing-land of a few cows and sheep and ponies, became a true type of 'the Groves of Academe', with gravelled walks and avenues of elms and limes. Across the river, beyond Wren's library and the master's granary, and his terrace, a pattern of landscape-gardening in the happiest style of eighteenth-century domestic amenity was to commemorate forever not the least enlightened of the enlightened despots. This particular enterprise cost some £500, but for once no voice was raised neither in opposition nor dissent.

The despot's enlightenment was perhaps less evident in his handling of fellowships than in his handling of trees. Fellowship elections now tended to become magisterial nominations. By treating all college appointments like personal patronage, he not only showed himself unabashed by what had happened in 1710–14, but assured the security of his autocratic rule in future by strategically-placed friends and allies. After Colbatch's refusal of the vice-mastership, for instance, he kept that office vacant for some months, and then appointed George Modd, a feeble old man in failing health and destitute of the elementary qualification of a

---

[1] To distinguish him from Dr John Walker, the Master's learned assistant in the New Testament enterprise. See above, p. 185.

[2] A note in Rud's diary records that in February 1716, 'all the old elms behind the Library, and on each side of the walk leading to the bridge, were rooted up and felled, and a new walk of limes planted there' – part of 'that long walk of limes' of Stanza LXXXVII of Tennyson's *In Memoriam*. Rud also records details about the stubbing up of old hedges along the walks, the plashing of others, and the planting of new ones.

degree in divinity. He dealt out college preacherships in the same fashion, regardless of statute. Preacherships were particularly prized because they qualified a man for preferment, and especially for presentation to a college living, and a college living – especially one near Cambridge – was treasured as affording the incumbent the means to enjoy marital bliss and domestic amenities without retiring into the depths of rural solitude beyond reach of hall, senior combination room, library, and all the pleasant politics and gossip of university life. We hear of Mr Malled and Mr Craister waiting upon the master at his lodge in order to solicit such favours, and finding themselves taken by the shoulder and firmly propelled out of the front door. In fact, the master was like a man playing a game of living-chess, autocratically waving his hand with a 'come here' or a 'go there' as it pleased him. Mr Bradshaw was to have Flintham, a small and rather poor parish in Nottinghamshire, despite the fact that six of the seniors wanted it to go to Mr Fernihough, for the master had said that his vote was equal to the vote of six fellows. Barrington, which is near to Cambridge, and therefore most desirable, was to go to Mr Hacket, one of the master's party among the fellows, even though Mr Rud, another of his party, thought it should be his. And if the master found his faction among the fellows insufficient to carry a particular measure, he could always depend upon the vote of Mr Brabourn, 'an unfortunate personage of impaired intellects' and an unfailing supporter. It was in somewhat the same spirit that Over was given to a young bachelor of Arts whom the master confessed never to have set eyes on, but who was said to deserve reward for consenting to marry Mrs Bentley's maid. A nephew of Mrs Bentley was put into a fellowship, and so was a nephew of the master's friend, Mr Hacket. There were, someone said, three scholars and two nephews in the college scholarships.

Yet this sort of aspersion was less than just, for although Bentley did things in his own way, the things he did were very often good things. Young men of promise, men of what the century called 'parts', were more frequently among his nominees than were mere 'blanks' put in to make votes. As usual it was not so much what he did as how he did it that caused offence, and very often scandal. When Archbishop Wake began to take an interest in sorting out the troubled affairs of Trinity College, it was not because he thought that Bentley was packing the college with nephews and noodles but because his autocratic way of doing things, and his indifference to the letter of the law in statute ('it must be broken in order to be kept' he liked to say: presumably in the interest of some 'higher law' of which the master was sole judge), made life at Trinity unbearable for anyone who crossed him, and was making the college a byword for scandal. Wake confined himself to describing Bentley as 'the greatest instance of human frailty that he knew of'. How strange that with such 'good parts' and so much learning, the man could be so insupportable! It was hardly the age, and Wake was hardly the man, to talk about Original Sin. What was most strange was that an archbishop of Canterbury should profess such innocence of the complex character of academic persons.

Dr Colbatch, the righteous man, kept all these things in his heart, and when Dr Wolfran Stubbe died in 1719 he put up a stubborn fight for his prerogative, as senior doctor of Divinity, to succeed to the rectory of Orwell. With considerable courage and address, he outmanoeuvred the master and his following who strove either to exclude him or to compel him to vacate his fellowship if he were presented. When, after some six months of rather vicious in-fighting, the professor was victorious, he was unwise enough to say, in understandable jubilation, that he 'fairly threw Bentley on his back'. The master hated to be worsted, but he rarely bore malice once he had beaten his adversary into the ground, which he now proceeded to do in his notorious *Full Answer* to Middleton's *Remarks* on his proposals to print the New Testament. A few years later, when completing the decoration of the chapel and the installing of a new college clock, he presented the old clock to the rector of Orwell for his parish church. *Timeo Danaos et dona ferentes*[1] may well have been the rector's comment. As for the fulminations of Bentley's *Full Answer*, with their unseemly references to snarling dogs, gnawing rats, maggots, worms, insects, cabbage-heads, and such personal features as swarthy skin and the long beards of brothers, the professor took advice before he ventured upon a retort, and particularly on the question 'how far it may be lawful to publish

[1] I fear the Greeks even when they come bearing gifts.

the notorious crimes of any Wicked Man'. For the master had shown that he knew the law of libel well enough to cost Dr Middleton heavily in time, money and painful experience of the Court of King's Bench.[1] Dr Colbatch, however, as usual thought himself armed with the strength of ten because his heart was pure and his quarrel just. He also thought he knew more law than the gentleman of the profession. Was he not, as professor of Casuistry, deeply learned in both civil and canon law, and more especially in *Jus Academicum*? That was the title he gave to a pamphlet, copies of which he caused to be presented to judges and barristers, to instruct them in (as his sub-title put it) 'the peculiar jurisdiction which belongs of common right to UNIVERSITIES in general . . . to those of ENGLAND in particular'. The doctor was intent on 'shewing that no Prohibition can lie against their Courts of Judicature, nor appeal from them, in any Cause like that which is now depending before the Vice Chancellor of Cambridge. . . .' This cause was, of course, Dr Colbatch's action against the Master of Trinity, author of the *Full Answer*.

If there is anything more silly and presumptuous than the nonsense of a 'barrackroom-lawyer' it is the nonsense of a senior combination room lawyer. As soon as the great luminaries of the Common Law tumbled to the fact that the professor of Casuistry was questioning the jurisdiction of the king's Courts over the jurisdiction of the vice-chancellor, and indeed libelling the judicature, Colbatch's publisher was clapped into prison on a charge of libel, and when Mr Wilkin declared that Colbatch was the author, the Chief Justice told him that the court would serve the author in the same way if brought before them. The professor, learned in the law, went into hiding and sought to move heaven and earth to save him from a spell in prison, which would probably detain him all through the long vacation. Lord Carteret mocked gently at 'University men who sucked in notions which

---

[1] In November 1721, Middleton was writing to Colbatch: 'the losses which all my friends have had in South Sea make it necessary for me to put an end to my trouble and expence as soon and as cheaply as I can'. He was therefore moving for judgment as early as possible, regardless of the issue. Bentley was content to wait upon the court's good time, if only because it might result in Middleton's financial ruin.

they called principles and were resolved strictly to adhere to and die martyrs to them', but Dr Colbatch's martyrdom was alleviated by release on bail in the sum of £200 for himself and £100 for his sureties. When his case came on in the following winter term, he was sentenced to a fine of £50, to remain in prison until it was paid, and to be bound over for good behaviour for a year. His actual stay in prison was one week. If he had been able to refrain from correcting his Lordship's Latin, setting him right in a quotation from Horace, it seems he would have got away with a fine of one mark.[1]

It was on the backwash of Dr Colbatch's brush with the Court of King's Bench, that Bentley secured a *mandamus* for the restoration of his degrees. King's Bench was not feeling particularly tender towards the jurisdiction of university courts after the affair of Colbatch's *Jus Academicum*, and when Bentley's case against the university came up in the Hilary Term, 1723–4, Chief Justice Pratt gave judgment for the plaintiff. After all, Bentley's offence had been contempt of the vice-chancellor's court, not of the senate, and yet it was the senate which had degraded him, and that without either summons or hearing, which was contrary to natural justice. King's Bench therefore caused a writ *mandamus* to be served on the university requiring it 'to restore Richard Bentley to all his degrees, and to every other right and privilege of which they had deprived him'. The university submitted reluctantly, perpetrating a final meanness in postponing the grace of restitution until one day after March 27, 1724, so that the Master of Trinity should be precluded from taking his place at the ceremonies fixed for that day in connection with the laying of the foundation-stone of the new building at King's College, now known as the 'Gibbs building',

---

[1] i.e. 13s 4d.

The quotation from Horace (declared by the judge to be his most virulent verse) was the motto of Colbatch's book: *Jura negat sibi nata, nihil non arrogat.* . . .

The judge misread 'arrogat' as 'abrogat', and took it that the accusation of 'abrogating' the law of the land was intended for the judges of King's Bench, whereas Colbatch had intended it to apply to Bentley. Colbatch's persistence in correcting his Lordship's misreading no less than three times was, to say the least, foolhardy. Lytton Strachey in his sketch of Dr Colbatch makes more than the most of this episode, even imputing the cry of 'Arrogat, my Lord!' to the wretched man on his death-bed.

or more colloquially – because of its deep and roomy central archway – 'the Jumbo-house'. The master had been without his degrees for some five-and-a-half years, and this slight additional delay is unlikely to have caused him much pain and grief. After all, he had had a good run for his (mainly other people's) money. He held the university record for suits in the Court of King's Bench. He had been a party to six of them in three years, and had won them all. He now wiped the slate clean by paying Conyers Middleton his four guineas, plus a few shillings in costs. He was not a man to bear malice after victory, and he had kept the fiddler waiting for nearly eight years.

21

Richard's Himself Again

With the recovery of his degrees, Bentley had found himself (as Dr Monk puts it) 'the first citizen of the academical Commonwealth'. It might have been expected that after so complete a victory, and advancing into his sixties, he would settle down into the serenity of a scholarly old age. There was for one moment the possibility of his translation to a bishopric. The see of Bristol was offered by the Duke of Newcastle, recently appointed Secretary of State for the Southern Department, and setting out upon more than forty years of office, chiefly in the loaves-and-fishes department. Newcastle was always gratified to present his somewhat horse-faced image to the minds of bishops as a pattern of their maker. He was not to enjoy such gratification from Richard Bentley, however, for when his Grace asked the Master of Trinity what kind of preferment he desired, or expected, he is said to have received the reply 'such preferment as would not induce me to desire an exchange'. Since this might have been taken to imply either the archbishopric of Canterbury or the Kingdom of Heaven, neither of which was at that time in the duke of Newcastle's power to bestow, Bentley remained Master of Trinity. Perhaps his Grace thought he saw in his translation a convenient way of settling the affairs of Trinity College for the future. Certainly it would have been hard to persuade Bentley to retire from the field of his triumphs in the hour of victory. Why, to put it in terms that the Duke of Newcastle would have understood, should he consent to be kicked upstairs? Bentley would have said downstairs. To change the metaphor once more, he had other fish to fry, of whom Dr Colbatch was one. And there was his old rival, Dr Francis Hare, who had just brought out an edition of *Terence*, which required at the very least that Aristarchus should bring out a better one. There was, too, the Greek

New Testament. That 'bubble', as fiddlers and cabbage-heads had dared to call it, was still in laborious process of inflation. There was an edition of the Fables of Phaedrus to be got out in order to forestall Hare, who had promised one, and there was Manilius who had been waiting since Oxford days, and he meant to produce his 'digammated' Homer if it was the last thing he ever did.

Working at top speed, as usual, he had his *Terence* out early in 1726, together with the *Phaedrus*. Not only did he suggest about a thousand corrections in the text of the plays, with a running commentary on the notes of Doctor Hare's edition (firm, but polite, and without once mentioning the dean by name) but he added a dissertation on Terentian metres, showing with his celebrated 'divination' just how (in his view) the ancient comedians spoke their lines. Bentley's *Terence* is one of his finest works, and his dissertation on the metres still entitles him to be remembered as a pioneer of such studies in the Latin drama. When Westerhof, the Dutch scholar, produced his fine edition of *Terence* at The Hague, he scoffed at the idea that anyone could possibly recapture the ancient modes of dramatic delivery. To the delight of everyone but Westerhof, lo and behold Bentley had done it! And when his edition brought a rapid demand for a second edition, he had it printed in Amsterdam, and the publisher entrusted the work on the index to no less a person than Westerhof himself. It was typical of Bentley's genius that he never forgot that the first purpose of a play is to be acted, and like many another arrogant character, he excelled as a mimic, and would have made a great comic actor. There is a story that Lady Granville reproached Lord Carteret for keeping a country parson up late and making him so drunk that he sang in a ridiculous manner. Her son was actually entertaining the Master of Trinity on one of his visits to town, and was being treated to a rendering of Terence 'according to the true *cantilena* of the ancients'. Bentley supplied his *Terence* with accentuation in every line, an enormous labour, especially at the proof-reading stage.

If the doctor left the plays of Terence fit for the production of prompt-copies, he left the *Fables of Phaedrus*[1] scandalously ill-

---

[1] Phaedrus, c. 15 BC – AD 50. His *Fables* in iambic verse are based on Greek collections, generally attributed to Aesop. *The Fables* of La Fontaine have been called 'mainly Phaedrus transmuted from silver to gold'.

served in both notes and emendations, thereby exposing himself to a withering review by the affronted dean of Worcester. Hare's *Epistola Critica* also contained some animadversions upon Bentley's *Terence* couched in much less mild and polite language than the master's comments on the notes to his own edition. Bentley's old friend and admirer, Sir Isaac Newton, deplored the spectacle of two distinguished divines 'fighting with one another about a play-book'. To the law-giver of the Newtonian universe it must have appeared like the scuffling of mice in a cupboard. The great man of science died in the spring of that year, and Bentley composed his epitaph in Westminster Abbey.

More important than the resentment felt by Dr Hare over the *Phaedrus* was the breach with an old friend, Peter Burman, with whom Bentley had corresponded for years. Burman had brought out his own fine edition of *Phaedrus* in 1727 and now came down on the side of Dr Hare, much to Bentley's chagrin. The breach was widened by a foolish misunderstanding over the edition of Lucan's *Pharsalia*.[1] Bentley's request for the loan of Burman's notes and collations for the purpose of an edition provoked Burman to undertake an edition himself. When, by way of excuse for declining this request, Burman told him of his project, Bentley postponed further work on Lucan until his old friend's edition should appear. Then Burman in turn postponed further work waiting for Bentley. Thus the two great men watched and waited for each other until two young scholars published editions of Lucan at Leipsig and Leyden, spoiling the market for their elders and betters. Burman did not produce his Lucan until 1740, and Bentley's notes were not seen in print until after his death. It is said that Bentley was so angry about this contretemps that he thought of publishing *Ovid* to get in the way of Burman's great edition then appearing after a twelve-year period of gestation. In the summer of 1727, he was 'mighty warm about an edition of *Ovid*, for no other reason but out of spite to Peter Burman, a foreigner, who had lately published *Ovid*'. Thus, wrote crabby old Thomas Hearne, one of the doctor's bitterest

[1] Lucan's *Pharsalia*, or *Bellum Civile*, recording the struggle between Caesar and Pompey. The epic, which owes much to Virgil, belongs to the first century AD. Bentley had a low opinion of Nicholas Rowe's translation, but Dr Johnson took the contrary view. One can see why Bentley was attracted to this imaginative, declamatory and often violent poet.

political opponents, 'thus does this poor old spiteful man turn all his thoughts upon revenge, and spends all his time in mere trifles'.

One 'mere trifle' now engaging the poor old spiteful man was the New Testament, the unpricked bubble of 1720, for which he was engaged to his subscribers, and upon which he placed some reliance for the restoration of his reputation as a good Christian occupant of the chair of Divinity. He now proceeded with arrangements for the completion of the collations at home and abroad, and particularly for the collation of the vital Vatican MS which had not been used by the Complutensian editors. His assistants in this ranged from Mico, an Italian amanuensis, and a learned German, Baron de Stosch, who served as a spy at the court of the Pretender at Rome, to young Tom Bentley, the master's nephew, at this time a rising master of Arts at Trinity College. Thomas Bentley was the son of James Bentley, the master's elder brother, who had inherited the old home at Oulton from their father. The great Richard by no means monopolized the brains and abilities of the Bentley family. Young Tom seems also to have inherited his uncle's share of the family amiability, for while he always remained a most reverential devotee of the master, he seems never to have sacrificed amicable relations with the opposition in college. As a young bachelor of Arts he had produced what was always known as his *Little Horace* – a smaller and cheaper edition of his uncle's great work of 1711, and while Uncle Richard's *Horace* was dedicated to the Earl of Oxford, nephew Tom's was dedicated to his lordship's son, Lord Harley. Alexander Pope sneered at him after his death as 'one Thomas Bentley, a small critic who aped his uncle in a *little Horace*'. It is unlikely that the doctor set eyes on the *little Horace* until it was printed, and it is quite absurd to say, as some did, that the master published it under his nephew's name. Thomas Bentley was a scrupulous scholar, and quite capable of producing the eighteenth-century equivalent of a paperback unaided.

This amiable young man went on a learned tour of Europe in 1725, spending more than twelve months in Paris, Rome, Naples and Florence. It is not true that he went at his famous uncle's behest and expense, though the master seems to have supplied some financial assistance when he was in difficulties in Rome. Young Bentley was about his own business, and only incidentally about the master's, having projected an edition of Plutarch. Neither in collations for his own purposes, nor in those for his uncle, did he prove the equal of Bentley's former assistant, John Walker. This was not for lack of application or ability but for lack of the robust health required for such rigorous pursuits. He was to die suddenly at Clifton, whither he had gone for his health, at the age of fifty in the same year that his uncle died at eighty. He is said to have indulged in the habit of reading in bed, a perilous practice in the days of tallow candles, tent-beds and timber houses. One night in 1733, Tom Bentley's lodging in the Strand caught fire and he narrowly escaped with his life; he did lose important manuscripts.[1] Uncle Richard's premises in Little Dean's Yard, close to Westminster School, where as keeper of the king's libraries he housed the bulk of the Cottonian collection and much other treasure from the king's collection at St James's, had caught fire one October night about two years earlier. On that occasion much damage was done to the Cottonian collection, but the doctor braved the flames and was seen emerging in his bedgown and his chevelure, bearing the priceless Alexandrian *codex* in his arms, a majestic spectacle, a true exemplar of the centurion, faithful unto death. This was just the eventuality he had prognosticated with such foreboding to Archbishop Wake when he broached his great design of the Greek Testament to him in 1716: 'My Lord, if a casual fire should take either His Majesty's library or the King's of France, all the world could not do this. . . .'[2] Here was another reason for his urgency to complete his labours on the great edition.

But he was to lose out on his prolonged endeavours. The year 1729 saw his great final effort to secure the long-awaited collations of the vital Vatican MS, the last remaining and indis-

---

[1] Including the uncompleted work of Dr John Davies on Cicero, entrusted to him to finish and publish, and some *scholia* he was copying for his uncle's edition of Homer. It was shortly after this calamity that he disposed of the old home at Oulton, which he had inherited from his father – Richard Bentley's birthplace.

[2] See above, p. 178.

pensable stones of the edifice.[1] His old ally at Rome, the Baron de Stosch, sent him a good deal of transcript material from the Vatican MS during the long vacation of that year, but he was fighting a losing battle with time. Perhaps had he gone in person to Rome that year . . .? But the doctor was never out of England in his life. He had never dared to turn his back on his enemies. Now he was approaching his seventies. In the early summer of the previous year he had fallen dangerously ill with a fever that had almost killed him. He had just entertained King George II at a banquet in the college hall during a royal visit from Newmarket which resembled that of his father in 1717, except that pre-cautions were taken to fix in advance the amount of the fees to be paid to the Regius professor of Divinity for the creation of doctors, of whom the professor created no less than fifty-eight on this occasion.[2] It was probably the strain of this mass-produc-tion of doctors of Divinity, and of standing for many hours beside the king's chair in hall during the banquet, that brought on the master's illness. He went to Bath to take the waters that summer, and returned in good trim for the wedding of 'Jug', his beloved daughter Joanna, to Denison Cumberland.[3] Twelve months almost to a day after the royal visit, Dr Greene, Bishop of Ely summoned him to appear at his court at Ely House, to answer sixty-four articles of accusation regarding 'sundry great

[1] For a valuable discussion of the nature and value of Bentley's labours on the New Testament project, see R. C. Jebb, *Bentley*, C.10. How late in life he remained optimistic, even exuberant, about completing the work is illustrated by a note preserved in his *Table Talk* in the library of Trinity College. He reiterates his intention to publish his Greek Testament according to the project as stated in the *Proposals* of 1720. (See above, p. 182.) He has collated all the Greek and Latin MSS then to be found in the world, 'none of which are of so low a date as the last eighteen-hundred years. I shall rely upon my own conjectures in twenty or more instances [not quite in accordance with the *Proposals*, this!] for which I shall give my reasons, some of which may probably raise a hubbub among the systematical Divines, which I shall laugh at.' Plainly, he was game to the end.

[2] The fee was fixed at 2 gns, together with the customary broad-piece: a compromise between the conflicting views of 1717.

[3] A son of Archdeacon Cumberland. Of this marriage was born Richard Cumberland, who spent much of his infancy at the Lodge and has left us a loving child's-eye view of his grandfather in his *Memoirs*. Inaccurate Cumberland may be in some particulars, as Dr Monk complains, but his portrait breathes with a sense of life.

and enormous crimes', drawn up by Dr Colbatch, of which Article VI accused him of having, for more than twenty years past, 'lived a very irreligious life . . . more particularly by constantly and habitually absenting yourself from divine service in the chapel of the Said College at the usual hours of morning and evening prayers. . . .' No wonder that in the long vacation of this year the master showed peculiar avidity to complete his edition of the New Testament. After all what better reply could a doctor of Divinity make? Of course he would explain also that his propensity to colds kept him away from the chapel, with its marble floor, cold despite his portable carpet. Anyway, he had made a great effort to attend more regularly since the restoration of his degrees. There had been an awkward moment when attending chapel for a concert, and finding himself shut out of his stall because the lock on the door had rusted with disuse, he was obliged to send for a locksmith to let him in. . . .[1] He took the trouble to make sure that the chapel-clerks lighted the candles of his stall in future, suspecting that the rascals had been making away with the unlighted candles as perks.

The sixty-four articles of accusation presented to Bishop Greene in 1729 contain a much more comprehensive indictment than the fifty-four presented to Bishop Moore twenty years earlier, and afford a tolerably accurate history of the master's régime at Trinity College since his first appearance at Ely House in the last year of Queen Anne's reign. It is not that they were much more numerous, but rather that they contained certain charges of greater import and gravity, concerning so many affronts to those twin deities of the eighteenth-century mind, from Locke to Burke, property and contract. Much was made of the master's alienation of college land, more especially the leasing of Massam House and other tenements in York 'by your fraud and contrivance . . . to your brother, James Bentley', and thereafter at much less than the market-value to Priscilla Bentley. The use of the college seal for his nefarious devices without the requisite compliance of the Seniority had become, it seems, a habit. So too had his practice of evading the quarterly college audits, when the

[1] Another version has it that the doctor 'went over his seat', meaning presumably that he jumped in. *The Gentleman's Magazine*, 1732, p. 920.

bursars and steward were by statute required to present their respective accounts to the senior fellows. Not once during the time of his mastership, ran Article LXIII, had the accounts been brought in and examined according to the statutory requirement. Moreover, it was charged, when one of the seniors demanded to see the accounts quarterly, pursuant to statute, 'you, the said Dr Bentley, replied, with great disdain, "Don't tell me of statutes" '. Considering the master's profligate ways with the college stock, his shyness – or boldness – on such occasions is hardly to be wondered at.

Once it had been a staircase, sash-windows, marble fireplaces, and wainscoting, which by the year 1715 had run the college into an expenditure of £2,000 for the beautifying and improving of the Master's Lodge. Since that time he had expended many other large sums, over and above the £2,000, exorbitantly and unnecessarily upon double-vaulted wine-cellar, water-side terrace, summer house with a bath for bathing, granary, cow-house, three new coach-houses, and a garden laid out and formed 'after a new model'. There had been a new coach for his wife and daughters and refurnishing of the lodge far beyond the original profusion of nine marble chimney-pieces, to wit: a scarlet cloth bed, and chairs and stools, a damask bed and quilt, two large looking-glasses, a silk squab, japan and walnut tables, to the amount of at least £400 sterling, all paid for out of college stock. Another £800 of college money had already been spent in building himself a country house on part of the college estate at Over, in the county of Cambridge, 'fit for the reception of a person of rank and quality'. For the master liked fishing-parties, and had spent much thought upon planning a summer residence, erected with London bricks and by London workmen, with sash-windows and wainscot, and a chimney with a window behind it so that one could read by the fireside: a feature which revealed for whose use it was intended, although he made much of the convenience of the place for members of the society serving the curacy at Over, and actually got the seniority to agree to the project instead of going ahead on his own initiative, as was his usual mode of proceeding. One way and another the Bentley family was well looked after throughout.

Along with detailed complaints about college appointments

and the master's dubious activities as a dealer in malt and wheat, there were grievous charges about the relaxation of college discipline. According to Article XX, the master had ruled that term in the college should begin much later and end sooner than term began and ended in the university at large, and by neglecting to keep the porter up to his duties in the matter of bringing him the keys when the gates were closed each night, and by allowing the porter to act by a deputy, paid by persons going out or coming in, all manner of persons – as well as members of the college – were at liberty to come and go at all hours of the night. Another liberty, particularly favourable to the master's family, had been the election of the master's son, Richard Bentley junior, to a fellowship before he had completed his degree of bachelor of Arts. Not all of these articles were allowed, and some few were withdrawn, but one's general impression of what had been happening in recent years must be that since the restoration of his degrees, Richard had been very much himself again.

He ignored Bishop Greene's citation until the last minute, and then applied to the Court of King's Bench for a writ of prohibition, requiring the bishop to show cause why he should not be prohibited from acting. The bishop showed cause, and the judges gave him leave to proceed. On June 10, therefore, the master appeared before the bishop at Ely House[1] – and entered objection to him as the Visitor of Trinity College. The bishop modified the Articles of Accusation in a few particulars, and appointed a day when he would receive them once more in their amended form. This gave the master time to apply again to the Court of King's Bench, and the judges again required the bishop to show cause why he should not be prohibited from taking action. His counsel argued that it was evident the master was merely playing for time. They did not suggest that he was anxious to have the long vacation free for his work on the New Testament, but when the judges continued the prohibition for a further spell it was upon the New Testament project that he expended the time. He was much concerned about the Codex Montfortianus

---

[1] It was on his appearance at Ely House in June 1729 that the master appeared in a purple cloak, which caused a whisper to go round: 'Cardinal Bentivoglio'.

in the library of the University of Dublin and the textural warrant of the 'Heavenly Witnesses' (I John, v. 7, 8).[1] These were not the witnesses that Dr Bentley's opponents expected him to be interested in. When the case came up again in the Michaelmas Term, the judges extended the prohibition indefinitely, pending intricate procedures concerned with writs of consultation, replication and demurrer. It was quite true, as a barrister had told Dr Colbatch in 1721, that it was wisest not to get into legal proceedings with the Master of Trinity 'who now knew the way into Westminster Hall', and (he might have added) knew the way out again. The present proceedings cost Dr Colbatch and the prosecution very nearly £1,000. They cost Bentley slightly more, but his expenses, as usual, were paid from the college-chest.

By 1731, however, the judges had arrived at the decision that the Bishop of Ely was the General Visitor of Trinity College. There was only one further action that the master could resort to: a petition to the king to secure a *fiat* from the law officers of the crown against the bishop as a would-be invader of the jurisdiction of the crown – the lawful Visitor, according to Bentley's argument from start to finish. The prosecution decided to carry the case to the House of Lords by writ of error. When Parliament met in the early months of 1732, it was more than possible that the peers would overturn the decision of King's Bench, and the run of the old fox would be over. The old fox while awaiting the new session set about producing another big book.

[1] See above, p. 161, fn. 1.

Trinity College Chapel.
Bentley is buried in the corner to the left of the altar.

Richard Bentley. Roubiliac's bust in the Wren Library.

Richard Bentley, junr. Only son of the Master, 1708–82. From a portrait, once at Strawberry Hill, by W. Greatbatch.

Dr Thomas Bentley. Nephew of the Master, 1693(?)–1742. From a drawing made in Italy by Ghezzi.

22

Paradise Improved

In the year 1732 Bentley reached the age of seventy. He celebrated by publishing the English work which was to secure him the interest and attention of the twentieth century. 'Milton's *Paradise Lost*, A New Edition, by Richard Bentley, DD,' was delivered to the world as a handsome quarto volume by Jacob Tonson and his associates. Bentley received one hundred guineas, the most he ever received for a book in his life, and exactly twenty times the sum paid to John Milton on publication of the first impression in 1667.[1] Unlike Milton's edition, however, Bentley's earned no more. 'First sales', in his case, were the only sales, and the book has never been reprinted. It was met with a roar of fury, not at all to his surprise, and still less to his dismay. He might have minded forty years earlier, he said. At that time it would have been prudent to suppress such a work 'for fear of injuring one's rising reputation'. At seventy he was 'without any Apprehension of growing leaner by Censures or plumper by Commendations'.

Was it that the author of *Epistola ad Millium* and the *Letters of Phalaris* had lost all sense of proportion or propriety? Was it that he had now entered into his dotage? It was neither. It was simply that Bentley was continuing to be Bentley, and thinking in terms of strategy. His edition of *Paradise Lost* was timed to appear with a new session of Parliament in January 1732, a session likely to be concerned – among other things – with the last round in his thirty years' war with the fellows of Trinity College. If this round went against him, he was likely to be deprived of his mastership. If paradise were to be lost, better

---

[1] When, after two years, 1,300 copies had been sold, Milton received the second payment of £5 provided for in the contract. In 1680 the publisher compounded with Milton's widow for £8 in return for sole and entire property in the poem.

that it should be the one in the poem. If anyone were to be dis-
lodged, better that it should be John Milton than Richard
Bentley. Who shall cast the first stone at Aristarchus in an age
when the dislodgment of Milton has become almost a critic's
pastime?

Besides, Queen Caroline was understood to have said that she
would like to see Dr Bentley exercise his fabulous critical
powers upon the great English epic. It was all very well for such
powers to be exercised upon fragmentary and uncertain texts
surviving in the ancient tongues. How revealing to see them
applied to the familiar and accessible text of an English poet of
not much more than half a century ago! Let the great conjuror
perform for once in daylight. Then perhaps one might have some
sense of what a Grecian or Roman of taste, restored to life,
would have thought of Bentley's emendations in the text of the
ancient classics, a sense which is blunted or extinguished to us
by our unfamiliar command over the two languages. The queen
did not put it like that. It was Coleridge who threw out the idea
a century later, much to the indignation of Thomas de Quincey.
De Quincey would simply liken Queen Caroline's 'womanish
folly' to that of Queen Elizabeth I in 'imposing upon Shakespeare
the grotesque labour of exhibiting Falstaff in love', laying her
commands upon Bentley 'for a kind of service which obliged him
too frequently to adjure all his characteristic powers and
accomplishments'. De Quincey thought that Bentley had a
suspicion that Her Majesty was making him play the fool for her
amusement, making him into 'a comic performer'. Bentley in his
Preface says nothing of this. Only when he comes to the final and
most outrageous emendation in Milton's text does he offer the
excuse for his presumption that the song he has been singing is
not his own composition but 'imposed by authority'. . . . *Non
injussa cecini*.

Bentley was never a man to take evasive action once he had
settled to a cherished task of emendation, correction, or
'divination', let alone to hide behind the skirts of a woman,
though she were a queen. No doubt he was concerned to please
Queen Caroline; but he maintained his forthright Yorkshire
manner to the end, more especially where value for money was

concerned. The first words of his Preface are: "'Tis but common Justice to let the Purchaser know what he is to expect in this new edition of *Paradise Lost.*' Having told him in no uncertain terms, he expresses a certain wonder at his own temerity in having dared to oppose 'the Universal Vogue' by removing so much 'miserable Deformity . . . and not seldom flat Nonsense' which have been passed over for more than sixty years in imposing this poem upon the whole nation for 'a perfect, absolute, faultless composition . . . rivalling if not excelling both Homer and Virgil'. The trouble is that readers have been possessed by too much 'Awe and Veneration from its Universal Esteem' to trust their own judgment. They have been prepared to suspect their own capacity rather than to admit that anything in the book could possibly be amiss. Aristarchus alone has dared to 'risque his own Character while he labour'd to exalt Milton's'. Although he had no reason to suspect it, Bentley had enlisted himself in the critical ranks of the twentieth century. At one stride he had aligned himself, 200 years in advance, with the school of literary critics that has come to bear the name of the 'Anti-Miltonists', and has been at work for several decades of the present century 'dislodging' Milton from his pedestal. The old man has been able to do nothing about it. Instead of stamping on their fingers as they scrabbled around his feet on his plinth, he has simply continued to look down his nose at them, scarcely interested enough to be angry with them, sublimely confident that God takes care of His own. Probably he agrees with Bentley that no man was ever written out of reputation but by himself.

The apostles of modern criticism ('new' it is wrongly called) have a 'case' against Milton. They generally talk about 'cases', assuming the intellectual postures of the barrister, while the accused is assumed to cower in the dock, except that nine times out of ten he is already dead. Or else the critic assumes the appalling mien of the embattled theologian, the Grand Inquisitor, a Calvinist of the Consistory, or a bearded ruffian of the Council of Trent, filled to the teeth with the *odium theologicum*. The 'case' against Milton is, briefly (though the prosecutor is never brief), that he is not Shakespeare, or John Donne, or even D. H. Lawrence, and principally that he doesn't use English in the English way, nor even (mercifully) the jargon used by his critics, but a kind of Anglo-Italian, Anglo-Latin, or 'poetic' language (than which, in a poet, nothing could be less forgivable). Worse still, since the anti-Miltonists are dons, or near-dons, a race who have a peculiar hatred for each other, Milton has been turned into a solemn bore by the orthodox professors, those pious worshippers chanting solemn rituals in praise of Milton . . . 'august, solemn, proud, and (on the whole) unintelligent and uninteresting Milton'. You see, Milton used words for their musical value, not for their 'significance' (precious word). He did not follow *actual* speech and thought when he wrote poetry, but donned the bardic robes, loosed the strings of the lyre, stroked instead of striking them, pulled out all the stops of the organ and 'let the pealing organ blow, to the full-voiced quire below. . . .' The result is not 'serious poetry' but rather 'a solemn game', not a sharp challenge to a critical awareness, but a laxative, weakening our sense of relevance and our grasp of sense. Too often, Milton's verse is not grand but grandiose. He manipulates language, not from an inner necessity but from the literary habits of a master of rhetoric. He does not use simile to sharpen definition or to focus our perception of the relevant, but imprecisely, insensitively, too often ready to sacrifice sense to sound, setting a shocking bad example to younger or lesser poets of striking a 'poetic' attitude instead of getting on with the job. In short, as his housemaster might say, John Milton has been a bad influence.

Bentley too had a case against Milton, and it was near enough to this case to make him interesting to the twentieth-century critics. Professor William Empson greeted him in 1935, almost exactly 200 years after the publication of the edition of 1732, with the salutation of a brother, though Professor Empson could not but regard his work as eccentric, and as unfortunate in its influence upon the critical tradition. For Bentley's 'famous failure' scared later critics into anxiety to show that they were sympathetic to the maltreated poet, and scandalized, and resolved that such a disrespectful thing should never happen again. They tended to fall over each other in respectful prostration before the old idol. Instead of grappling with the questions which concern the essence of the poetry they were considering, they tended to talk with 'the mild and tactful hints, the air of a waiter anxious not to interrupt the conversation'. In fact, for long enough Bentley's performance had an inhibitive influence, just as some twentieth-century criticism has had, tending to close the ranks of orthodoxy in a defensive attitude which would have us believe, as the editor says, that 'this correspondence is now closed'.

Of course, Bentley was not in the least interested in a critical tradition, or in softening up Milton for the offensives of the future. He was simply concerned to show his own celebrated powers in action for once on familiar ground, or to give 'a performance', like the great virtuoso he was. His preface does not lack suitable obeisance in the direction of the master. 'What a wonderful performance . . . was this *Paradise Lost*, that under all these disadvantages could gradually arise and soar to a national applause and admiration. . . . What native, unextinguishable Beauty must be impress'd and instincted through the Whole, which the Defoedation of so many Parts by a bad Printer and a worse Editor could not hinder from shining forth?' In fact, he proposed as he put it 'to risque his own Character while he labour'd to exalt Milton's'. His task was 'a restoration of the genuine Milton'. The great man had been ill-served by a slack and stupid amanuensis; and who might be expected to know more about this kind of disservice than the man who had had to deal with Thomas Bennett, of the sign of the Half Moon in St Paul's Churchyard?[1] Who knew more about such fellows than the scholar whose life had been spent in scraping the faces of palimpsests, the Hound of Heaven on the trail of the authors of the New Testament?

> Our celebrated Author, when he compos'd this Poem, being obnoxious to the Government, poor, friendless, and what is worst of all, blind with a *Gutta Serena*, could only dictate his Verses to be writ by another. Whence it necessarily follows that any Errors in Spelling, Pointing, nay even in whole Words of a like or near Sound in Pronunciation, are not to be charg'd upon the Poet, but on the Amanuensis. . . .
>   If any one fancy this *Persona* of an Editor to be a mere

[1] See above, p. 93.

Fantour, a Fiction, and Artifice to skreen Milton himself; let him consider these four and sole Changes made in the second Edition. . . .

Bentley gives these four changes and shows them to be for the worse, challenging the reader to contend that they are the poet's own. He continues:

But now, if the Editor durst insert his Forgeries, even in the second Edition, when the Poem and its Author had slowly grown to a vast Reputation, what durst he not do in the First, under the Poet's Poverty, Infamy, and an Universal Odium from the Royal and triumphant Party?

Dr Johnson, referring to the fact that Bentley imputed verbal inaccuracies 'to the obtrusions of a reviser whom the author's blindness obliged him to employ', called it 'a supposition rash and groundless, if he thought it true; and vile and pernicious, if, as is said, he in private allowed it to be false'. However this may be – and it is doubtful whether in his arrogance he either knew or cared whether such an editor had ever existed or not – the device fails to serve him, for the changes made in the second edition actually amounted not to four but to thirty-three, and any villainy that he imputes to the 'phantom editor' is insignificant when compared to what Masson called 'the utter monstrousness' of the proceedings of Richard Bentley. ' 'Slife, Sir, are you mad?' as one critic cried when the edition came out. 'Did ever such a piece of prophane drollery come from a doctor of Divinity?' The author of *A Friendly Letter to Dr Bentley*, calling himself a Gentleman of Christ Church,[1] went on to suggest that Dr Bentley understood his 'classicks' no better than he did his Bible. *Monstrum horrendum, informe, ingens, cui Lumen ademptum* was the epigraph of this onslaught upon the doctor's work. *The Grub-Street Journal* charged him bluntly with having invented his phantom editor in order to avoid a head-on attack on Milton. 'What a prodigious Man is Dr Bentley,' cried the author of another of the numerous derisive parodies called forth by his 'sacriligious intrusion' under the title *Milton Restor'd and*

---

[1] The second edition was signed 'Semicolon'.

Bentley Depos'd. 'He corrects the Numbers of Horace and raises the sense of Milton.' This time the epigraph was 'Sing Heavenly Muse, from pedantry be free'.[1]

The fact is that Bentley's edition of *Paradise Lost* was evidence neither of madness nor of failing powers, save in the sense *quem Juppiter vult perdere, prius dementat*, or 'whom the gods would destroy they first make mad'. Long success as a textual critic of classical texts had led him to limitless confidence in his powers. All that he saw before him when he set to work on *Paradise Lost* was simply another text, like those of *Callimachus* or *Terence*, to whose work he had restored a shape in spite of all the difficulties of time's corruption. He knew far less about English literature than he knew about the literatures of Greece and Rome, and thereby exposed himself far more to attack because his author's text was so generally accessible. He was unable to give up the attitude of victorious superiority to which he had become accustomed. He conjectured as freely in editing Milton as he had done in editing *Callimachus*. The way to retrieve the poet's own words, he affirms with his customary confidence, is by 'Sagacity and happy Conjecture'. Of course, a manuscript were better still. But – where no manuscript existed? Or where the textual sources were corrupt, contradictory, or obscure? Here was his favourite field of battle, the field in which he had won the brilliant victories which had made his name. 'His real genius and perhaps unequalled power of divination in the field of conjectural criticism', was the way in which Jacob Mähly put it, when he gave the Germans a Bentley biography in 1868.[2] 'Happy divination' Mähly called it, *geniale Divinationsgabe. . . . Conjectural kritik.* In his preface, he undertook to 'cast into the Margin and explain in the Notes all the conjectures that attempt a Restoration of the Genuine Milton . . . So that every Reader has his free Choice whether he will accept or reject what is here

---

[1] For some of the best of these attacks, reference may be made to *Studies in the Milton Tradition* by J. W. Good (Illinois 1925), pp. 177–9. The best counter-attack to Bentley's edition however is not a parody but a perfectly scholarly *Review* by Zachary Pearce, a fellow of the master's college (1732), which refutes many of Bentley's attacks, using his own brand of textual criticism against him, and informed by a properly historical grasp of Milton's work.

[2] *Richard Bentley, eine Biographie* (Leipzig, 1868).

offer'd him'. As he warms to his task, however, his footnotes
leave this prefatory modesty behind. Of course, he was in a
tearing hurry, as usual, working on a large quarto copy of the
first volume of Tickell's edition (Tonson 1720) with his
nephew, Richard Bentley, serving as amanuensis – and trying
to put the brake on, quite unavailingly.[1] 'I made the Notes
extempore, and put them to the Press as soon as made', he tells
us, and we may believe him without difficulty. The job was done,
with its more than 800 emendations, in a few hectic weeks of the
winter of 1731–2.

Nonetheless, as Professor Mackail has said, we are compelled to
acknowledge the justice of many of Bentley's strictures, and
Dr Monk thought that Milton himself would have accepted not
a few of them. The first and the last have often been singled out
for especially severe comment, but they are not wholly typical.
When he argues that 'the secret top of Horeb' in Book I, l. 6,
should read 'sacred' top, it is easy enough to reply – as de
Quincey, among others, was to do – that 'secret' is justified by
the mere physical fact that the top of a mountain is not visible
from below. As for the concluding lines:

> They hand in hand with wandering steps and slow,
> Through Eden took their solitary way.

It was little but an Augustan perversity to propose instead:

> Then hand in hand with social steps their way
> Through Eden took, with Heav'ly Comfort cheer'd.

Very improper, Bentley objects, to talk about *wandering* steps
and *slow*, if they were guided by Providence and after Eve at
least 'had professed her Readiness and Alacrity for the Journey'.
As for *solitary* way, there were only the two of them in Eden, and
they were not more solitary now than they had been before.
Why dismiss our first parents in anguish and melancholy after
they had accepted their fate with peace of mind, full of consola-

---

[1] The late Professor J. W. Mackail tracked down the actual copy, and
established once and for all the speed at which the work was done. See his
Warton Lecture for 1924 in the *Proceedings of the British Academy*, vol.
XI.

tion, or at least in two minds whether to be sad or joyful? Some
reference to heavenly comfort would seem called for. . . . Such
literalness reminds us of the famous quarrel Bentley had with
leviathan stretching out his huge length on the burning lake.
This, too, was improper, Bentley would have us know, 'for the
whale cannot stretch out or contract any of his Joints; he is
always the same length'. It was, said the man of Natural Science,
simply a matter of natural history. So, too, was Milton's error
about the whale's skin in the same passage,[1] and the possibility
of a seaman anchoring on a whale in mistake for an island. 'The
whale has no scales', and if he had them they would be far too
thick and solid for a seaman to fix his anchor in them. Though
Bentley will allow that it might be possible to fix an anchor in a
whale's *skin* without his noticing it. . . . Not that Bentley's
cavillings are often either so comic or so insensitive as these
instances would suggest. Often, by changing a single letter, or a
word sometimes, where a misprint is likely, he shows the value
of genius in textual criticism. Some of these changes have been
accepted into the received text by later editors, and some others
are highly plausible even if they have not been generally
accepted. His note of Book VII, 451, where he corrected 'Let the
earth bring forth Fowl living in her kind', to '. . . soul living in
her kind', was but using his commonsense and his knowledge of
Genesis. His note on 'the smelling gourd' at line 321 of the same
book is perhaps the best instance of how judicious emendation
should be conducted. He was sure that Milton gave it 'the
swelling gourd', and that 'smelling' was 'a mere mistake of the
Printer'. He cites Propertius: *caeruleus cucumis, tumidoque
cucurbita ventre.*

'Those that stiffly maintain that smelling was Milton's word,
and interpret it the *M*elon, seem not to attend, that he had the
word *smelling* two lines before, and would not have doubled it so
soon again, and that he does not name here any particular plant,
but whole tribes and species; the *V*ine, the *G*ourd, the *R*eed, the
*S*hrub. . . . Gourds are as numerous a family as most of the
others; and include the *M*elon within the general *N*ame; which
though it smells, it swells likewise.'

[1] Book I, lines 200–14.

217

What are not acceptable are emendations arising from Bentley's misunderstanding of the text, generally from failure to follow out sympathetically Milton's long-breathed prosody, or from his inability to resist pouncing on a sentence as apparently lacking a verb. 'Here's a sentence without a verb!' he cries, at Book III, line 345. Sometimes, as Professor Empson says, he will let a couple of verbs into a sentence like a couple of ferrets. Often he reminds us of a schoolmaster correcting a schoolboy's exercise, crossing out repetitions under some rule about not using the same word twice in a sentence. Most monstrous of all are the cases where 'slashing Bentley' gets to work with the famous 'hook', excising whole passages that offend his notions of sense and decorum. He cuts out 147 lines in the first three books, demolishing some of Milton's most typical passages, as for instance The Paradise of Fools in Book III, lines 443–97, as 'a silly Interruption of the Story' and an 'insertion by his Editor'. As for Book I, lines 579–87, the jewelled passage adorned by Trebizond and the Afric Shore and Charlemain with all his Peerage . . . Bentley dismisses it as 'a heap of barbarous words . . . a silly boast of useless reading', best attributed to the editor. Only that egregious man would have suffered the epic work to be clogged and sullied with such 'romantic trash'. The list of lovely places, from the fair field of Enna, the sweet grove of Daphnae, and the inspired Castalian spring, down to Mount Amara and Nilus' head (Book IV, lines 268–85), goes out with a slash and a curt command to the editor: 'Pray you, Sir, no more of your patches in a poem quite elevated above your reach and imitation.' As for Book II 650–86 with its procession of horrors, from

> Vexed Scylla, bathing in the sea that parts
> Calabria from the hoarse Trinacrian shore,

with its night-hags, lapland witches, fiends and monsters: here again the editor has chosen to 'contaminate this most majestic poem with trash', not to mention the impropriety of retailing such 'idle and dangerous stories to his young and credulous Female Readers'. At least one of John Milton's female readers of the present century seems prepared to forgive Dr Bentley for this, and much else, on account of his 'tenderness for women',

especially his considerate treatment in his notes of 'our grandmother Eve'.[1]

In his anti-romantic animadversions Bentley entirely missed
Milton's point and purpose in piling up the imaginative treatment of historic and fabulous allusion. There is, he insists, a
certain decorum of language to be observed in an epic, especially
an epic in English, 'an impolite Gothic tongue, inferior to Greek
and Latin'. Not only is he rigorous in ruling out 'romantic
trash'. He is ruthless towards those simple, idiomatic expressions
which often preserve Milton's style from excessive solemnity.
We find it a relief to have Adam ('the Patriarch of Mankind')
and Eve ('our general mother') holding converse

> Under a tuft of shade that on a green
> Stood whispering soft . . .[2]

but Bentley at once launches into a reproof against the poet for
fancying himself in some country village, forgetting that the
scene is supposed to be Paradise. 'Poor stuff indeed. . . .' As if
any old green would do. As for the Apostate Angel speaking
'though in pain', the expression is 'low and vulgar'. (*Book I*,
125).

Insensitivity to the romantic temperament was the weakest
side of the classical period of our literature. Where it shows itself
in Bentley's criticism of *Paradise Lost* it was more than that. It
was the weakest element in Bentley's equipment as a critic, and
often the product of sheer ignorance as well as of defective
sensibility. To rescue English poetry from 'provincial Chaos'
and waywardness in order to establish it in the mainstream of
European order and discipline may have been a natural and
laudable aim in his day and age. Unfortunately he knew hardly
anything of the post-Elizabethan poetry with which Milton grew
up, and precious little of the Italian poetry to which Milton owed
so much. This last is hardly surprising, for very little Italian was
then known, let alone taught, in English universities, and there
was no real guide to Milton's prosody until the work of Robert
Bridges in the twentieth century. But quite apart from his

---

[1] See Helen Darbyshire's 'Milton's Paradise Lost', in her *Addresses and
Other Papers*, London, 1962.
[2] Book IV, p. 325–6.

slender knowledge of pre-Milton poetry, if we except some Spenser and some Chaucer, Bentley lacked temperamental sympathy with the romantic reaction that was beginning to affect English literature in his life-time. His mind at seventy remained what it had been at twenty-five. Milton, to him, required to be purged of those elements of imperfect civility which he derived from the literary anarchy of the early seventeenth century, elements which detracted from his claim to truly classical stature even after Dryden and Addison had done their best for him.

Bentley's notion of style was that of the literary majority of his age. He deemed his task to be the reconciliation of 'high Language with Philosophy and true Sense',[1] and true sense must exclude any deviation from the simplest and most direct mode of expression. 'The simplest and nearest word is the best.'[2] He accused Milton of 'deserting Propriety while he's hunting after Sound and Tumor', like a twentieth-century critic making 'the case against Milton' as a manipulator of language who sacrifices sense to sound, setting a bad example to the young by striking 'poetic' attitudes and assuming postures of orotund bardic solemnity. His grossest errors sprang from incapacity to understand metaphorical language and hidden associations, especially of an emotional (or, to use the fashionably pejorative term of today, 'emotive') character. He often destroys Milton's subtler distinctions of syntax in his search after simplicity and regularity, missing the poet's finer shades of meaning. For he takes English as a *spoken* language, as he more justly took Latin and Greek, misprising or failing to grasp its *literary* qualities.[3] It is odd that he so often fails to grasp the spirit of Latinity in Milton, as if he found it difficult to recognise classical peculiarities when detached from classical texts. It is not simply that his mind was essentially prosaic, that his approach to poetry lacked the

[1] See his note to line 219, Book VI.
[2] See his note to line 741, Book V.
[3] If only because they preceded the invention of printing, and much of their literature was composed for delivery in song, chant, or stage-performance. Indeed, all literature until fairly modern times gave priority to verbal delivery, as 'silent reading' is a modern practice. One imagines the master's study at Trinity Lodge humming like Lord Carteret's drawing-room when the master was at work on his edition of *Paradise Lost*.

imaginative touch, though both charges (if we are to talk in terms of 'charges' and 'cases') are abundantly true. Nor is it enough to dismiss the problem with Mackail's verdict that he was 'out of his depth', as the undergraduate essay once complained of Plato. The fact is that he was suffering from the occupational disease of the 'emendator' – the final inability to leave well alone. And, as was to be expected, his strictures on Milton's rhythms, metrical habits, word-order, cumulative imagery, and so on, only serve to draw attention to his almost magical rightness, and, even more often, to his critic's impertinence. He said himself that an emendator should be 'a tenacious textuary', and that in these matters his maxim was *Nobis et ratio et res ipsa centum codicibus potiores sunt*.[1] But what if *res ipsa* be deficient, or (according to Bentley's own statement) no manuscript exists? Then surely *ratio*, in the form of sagacity and 'happy conjecture', must come to the rescue. And, again, what if conjecture turn out not to have been so happy after all? Not even Bentley's knowledge that the Gods of Greece bled *ichor* instead of blood will satisfy every reader that he was right to emend 'nectarous humor' to 'ichorus humor' when he comes to the substance that flowed from Satan's wound at lines 332–3 of Book VI.

The late Dr Helen Darbyshire, in a lecture on *Paradise Lost* in 1951, bracketed Bentley with Dr Johnson as a critic of Milton. He provides us, she affirms, with 'an excellent way-in to what matters in Milton's text, and further to what may be called the texture of the poem', just as Johnson provides us with the best way-in to what matters in estimating its *content* along with its form. The astringency of both men as critics acted as 'a good tonic to our tired taste', and both have the virtues of the best critics because 'they ask the right questions, even if they often give the wrong answers'. This judgment would put Bentley's *Milton* on a level with his *Horace* in its penetration into 'those places . . . which need looking into, whether for their weakness or their characteristic strength'. It was the first time an *English* text had been subjected to critical treatment by a great classical scholar, and Dr Darbyshire concluded that for astute examination of text and verbal texture she knew no commentary 'so

[1] Meaning, 'For me, reason and the subject matter are worth a hundred manuscripts.'

animating, enjoyable and instructive. He gave Milton what he deserved. . . .' And Dr Darbyshire gave Dr Bentley what he deserved. She called him a rogue. For she claimed to have caught him out over his pretence that 'there was no manuscript'. She had seen the copy in which he wrote his notes for his edition, as Mackail had, and she had formed the opinion that he not only saw the manuscript of Book I but collated it carefully, marking certain readings in the margin MS. He had to maintain the pretence that there was no manuscript, she would say, or give up 'his whole ingenious theory about the meddling editor, on which his scheme of emendation is founded'. This is what Dr Johnson suspected when he said that Bentley's obtrusion of a reviser was 'a supposition rash and groundless, if he thought it true; and vile and pernicious, if, as is said, he in private allowed it to be false'. Such Nemesis upon conjectural criticism Bentley would have found unthinkable. Perhaps he preferred to be a rogue, even if it brought upon him the fate of a fallen angel.

It has often been said that the key to any man's response to *Paradise Lost* must be found in his attitude to Milton's *Satan*, and it is only in his treatment of Milton's portrait of Satan that Bentley departs from his one-sided logical consistency. He will admit that Milton 'generally rather aims at Strong Expression than smooth and flowing Numbers'. He had learnt from Homer and Virgil that the nature of the subject may sometimes make a *rough* verse preferable; and where Satan was concerned Milton was almost prepared to forget his devotion to faultlessly regular versification out of sympathy with intense and energetic expression. In any case, one might have expected the strong and austere passion of Milton to call forth the sympathy of Bentley's own energetic character in all its *superbia*, its invincible pride. In one place, indeed, he even finds Milton's *Satan* somewhat deficient in defiance. It is where he refuses to accept *Infernal World* at line 251 of Book I. He persuaded himself that Milton had given it: *Hail*, ETERNAL WOE! The meddling editor had doubtless thought it 'a saying too desperate, even for the Devil himself, and therefore changed it into *Infernal World*'. Bentley thinks that 'Satan's character is the better kept up by his saluting and congratulating *Eternal Woe*', thereby showing 'a temper and disposition truly Satanical'. After all, Satan can take it. 'He was

not scared with the mere word.' His welcoming Eternal Woe
'paints him to the life, his obdurate mind, his unconquerable will,
his courage never to submit or yield'. These are almost precisely
the words of fiddling Conyers when he deplored the master's
obduracy over a four-guinea fee for making him a doctor of
Divinity – holding out 'for the glory of never having been
known to submit'.[1] One is also reminded of the occasion when
Coleridge lectured for an hour on the character of Hamlet, and
someone in the audience was heard to observe: 'This is a satire
on himself.' Henry Crabb Robinson reflected: 'No, it is an
elegy.'

Although it has never been reprinted, and may never be,
Bentley's *Paradise Lost* deserves remembrance not simply as a
literary curiosity but as a landmark in literary criticism. Even
if his classicism was pedantic and his sensibility severely limited,
his rigour and his logical consistency help us to assess both the
achievement and the limitations of literary criticism in the Age
of Reason. To fix the standards of scientific scholarship, and to
transmit them to posterity, was a necessary work in the vindication of English studies as a branch of the higher learning. In
addition to his claim to be remembered among the founders of
the Natural Sciences at Cambridge, Bentley could claim to be not
wholly without honour in the Cambridge school of literary
criticism.

[1] See above, p. 176.

23

Gone to Earth

And it would almost seem to me peculiar to Him: had not
Experience by others taught me, that there is that Power in
the Human Mind, supported with Innocence and *Conscia
virtus*; that can make it quite shake off all outward uneasinesses,
and involve itself secure and pleas'd in its own Integrity and
Entertainment.

Bentley's Preface to *Paradise Lost*.

Was Bentley's prefatory portrait of Milton in his grandeur and
his misery at the time of composing *Paradise Lost* intended also
as a self-portrait? He wondered, he said, not so much at the poem
itself (though worthy of all wonder) 'as that the Author could so
abstract his Thoughts from his own Troubles as to be able to
make it', that he could find solace in 'spatiating' at large
through the whole universe and all time. What must have been
the strength of spirit that made him capable of such solace!
Certainly, if this were intended as a self-portrait, it was not
intended as an elegy. There was still his *Manilius* to come, after
forty-five years of gestation, with what Housman was to call 'the
firm strength and piercing edge and arrowy swiftness of his
intellect, his matchless facility and adroitness and resources. . . .'
There was still his project of a Homer and the restoration of the
Æolic Digamma after two thousand years. Nor was the master
in the least disposed to submit to the impertinence of Bishop
Thomas Greene, backed by the Court of King's Bench, or the
House of Lords, or Satan's legions led by Dr Colbatch.

Can Bentley have ever supposed that his *Paradise Lost* would
serve to disarm his enemies, to charm the queen, to win the court or
the ministry, for a policy of intervention on his behalf, or even to
raise a 'disposition' in his favour? Surely things had gone much
too far for that. Even had he been so besotted as his critics made
out, he was hardly capable of deluding himself with the notion
that his latest display of learned ingenuity afforded a belated

testimonial to his purity of heart or the rectitude of his conduct as Master of Trinity. The process which had been for so long under way for bringing him to book was only at a stand until the re-assembling of Parliament at the New Year. Then the House of Lords would entertain Bishop Greene's appeal against his prohibition by the Court of King's Bench.[1] In effect, the Lords would decide whether there was a 'true bill' against the Master of Trinity, whether the bishop might proceed to try him in his court as visitor, and on what charges. They would have to examine the articles of accusation, and determine which ones were *prima facie* allowable, and which (if any) were to be prohibited. The House of Lords, indeed, would serve as 'the Grand Jury of the Nation'. The Master's affairs would occupy the central stage, would 'chime', as he had always liked, with the national business, even from time to time to delay it. No doubt in Bentley's mind it was highly appropriate that they should. Were not the affairs of the master of the royal college as important as the bills then awaiting their lordships' consideration, among which stood prominently (and perhaps ironically) certain measures concerned with frauds on Charitable Corporations?

When the appeal came on in the spring of 1732 the country (or as much of the country as took any notice of such things) was to be regaled by the spectacle of the highest court in the king's dominions attending to the question of whether or not the Master of Trinity had, or had not, been remiss in his attendance at chapel. By the time that Parliament was prorogued on June 1, their lordships had proceeded only so far as to nibble at this, the first (and to the bishops among them, the paramount) article of the indictment, and it was decided to postpone further business until the next session – which meant the next year, which suited Bentley very well, since his main tactic throughout was a delaying action. When, in January 1733, the article-by-article inquest was resumed, it was before a crowded House, for many of their lordships were either old Trinity men, or sons of Alma Mater in some sort, who were intent upon enjoying themselves at the spectacle of what soon became a public inquiry into the whole mode of life and discipline at the university. They even resorted, on at least one occasion, to the unheard-of practice

[1] See above, p. 208.

of sitting on a Saturday rather than miss the next instalment of the enthralling story.

Their lordships whittled down the sixty-four articles of accusation to twenty, a reduction that was facilitated by the withdrawal of a certain number by the prosecution in the course of the hearing. They showed an extraordinary lack of consistency. The most glaring example was their decision in the master's favour with regard to his unstatutable mode of conducting college business in the matter of the presence of the Seniority, and (on the same day) their decision against him in the matter of his unstatutable use of the college seal. They decided in his favour about his alienation of certain college property (notably the lease of Massam House), and against him in the matter of the bargain with Edmund Miller. While the articles concerning his conduct with regard to elections to fellowships and scholarships were withdrawn, their lordships insisted on maintaining the charges concerning his extravagance in rebuilding and adorning his lodge and other premises, and the cost of his granary and the country-house at Over, indeed even his household consumption of coals. In many of these items the voting was nearly equal on both sides of the question, and the impression is often to be gained that, while their lordships enjoyed the details, they would have been willing to toss up for a verdict. After the parade through the senate of the empire of coal-scuttles and bricklayers' wages and Mrs Bentley's snuff-box (which she used to send to tradesmen and the college buttery to authenticate her orders for supplying the Master's Lodge at college expense), there still remained a substantial list of articles for the master to face when he came to the Bishop of Ely's Court. They included absence from chapel, non-appointment of Catechetical lecturers, unstatutable use of the college seal, alienation of one piece of land, extravagance in building on the master's premises, the building of the country-house at Over, wasteful household expenditure, and the bargain with Miller.

The master's champion among the peers was that great lover of classical literature and port-wine, Lord Carteret. His lordship was principally concerned to set the master free in body and mind so that he might carry through his great edition of Homer, the project with which Bentley was (after his wont) already busily occupying himself during the intervals of legal proceedings. Carteret exerted all his considerable influence to secure for him books and manuscripts to this end. If ever Bentley's 'learned strategy' bore fruit, it was with the influence and eloquence of Lord Carteret, who left the House of Lords in no doubt that in entertaining the charges against Bentley they were playing the game of a bunch of pygmies worrying a giant. It was at this time that he delivered his celebrated contemptuous reference to 'the distempered frenzies of cloistered zealots'. By referring to 'a late Bishop of Ely'[1] who would have scorned to countenance such charges against such a man, he removed all ambiguity as to his opinion of Bishop Greene. 'No man of tolerable sense of learning,' his Lordship declared, 'could with a grave face expel a Master upon this charge; nor even admonish him, without the censure of dullness and incapacity, and the amazement of mankind.' Carteret was particularly warm on Articles XIX and XX which charged the master with having neglected to insist on keeping up 'disputations', a form of intellectual exercise which, in so far as they were based on the Physics of Aristotle, at least, served only to maintain reverence for loads of 'medieval lumber'. He was not alone in this, although the bishops scouted his criticism. At least one of the lay peers must have reddened the swarthy cheeks of Dr Colbatch, by denouncing disputation as perpetuating the horrid jargon of the Schoolmen as employed by the Jesuits. It is evident that not everyone in an assembly like the House of Lords in the eighteenth century took it for granted that every departure of the master from the ancient ways was culpable. Articles XIX and XX, charging him with neglect of disputations were both prohibited. Apart from his personal absence from chapel, and the neglect of Catechetical lectures, no complaints against the master of a properly academical nature were allowed. Those that were allowed might be said to have been ineluctable for a house containing the bishops. It was appropriate that he should have been left to face charges concerned with little else than property.

Judgment was pronounced by the House of Lords on February

---

[1] Bishop Fleetwood, who always avoided attempts to get him to intervene. The father of the 'cloistered zealots' no doubt was Dr Colbatch.

15, 1733, and Bishop Greene was given permission to try the Master of Trinity on twenty out of the sixty-four articles of accusation. As regards costs, Bentley as usual came out very well, Bishop Greene being required – as plaintiff in error – to pay him £100, while the expenses of the parliamentary proceedings (nearly £1,000) were met out of the college chest. Otherwise he had gained nothing but time, and at the age of seventy-two he probably regarded time as of more value than money. He would fight for time to the end of time, if needs be. And there was a point, between the conclusion of the proceedings in the House of Lords and the opening of the proceedings in the bishop's court at Ely House, when for one moment it seemed that Bishop Greene might die like Bishop Moore twenty years earlier. Even Dr Colbatch was in a parlous state of health towards the end of that long winter of 1732–3. If either of the elderly gentlemen had died, proceedings would have had to begin again at the beginning, and would probably have been quashed. The master, however, seems to have enjoyed rude health throughout, and went on with his Homer in between fits of happy laughter.

However, when the bishop did hold the first session of his court on June 13, it soon became apparent that he intended to take a strong line and to bring the interminable contest to a definitive close. It took him another nine months, largely because he decided, for reasons best known to himself, that all the evidence should be submitted in writing. Both depositions and cross-examinations were taken down at great length, while Bentley himself simply put in a 'Defensive Plea' which probably suited him a great deal better than long and wearisome personal attendance. For the most part he took the line that the charges were simply untrue, or exaggerated, or based on misunderstanding of his motives. For instance, the country house at Over had been intended to lodge the incumbent of the college living, and anyway had been the repair and rebuilding of the house, not a splendid construction *de novo* 'fit for the reception of a person of rank and quality', and neither the master nor his family had ever resided there. Similarly with the Master's Lodge. Considering that it was 'the residence of the Royal Family when they honour the University with their presence, as also of the Lords the Judges in their circuits', it was not disproportionately splendid compared with the Master's Lodge at other colleges. Much that had been done on the master's premises had been done for the whole society, not simply for the personal use of the master. As for all the stuff about Catechists, preachers and lecturers, he had appointed as many as, or more than, his predecessor had done. The pipe conducting water to the bath in the Master's garden was 'only lengthened by an addition of two feet of lead to supply the cistern of the said bath', and had been there for a century or two. Similarly, the 'large spacious granary' was intended for housing college stores of grain, and not in order to allow the master to carry on trade as a farmer or maltster in his private capacity.

The master's tone scarcely suggests that he took such matters with great seriousness. In one thing, however, he showed real gravity and feeling. He strenuously denied that 'he had lived a very irreligious life, and notoriously neglected the public worship of God', and he professed himself to be, and always to have been, 'a devout, pious and religious man'. His non-attendance at chapel in recent years had been wholly the consequence of his physical infirmities, 'a tenderness contracted by his sedentary and studious life'.[1] He knew very well the paramount importance of this, the pious reputation of a master of Trinity, whose statutes required him to be 'a person no less eminent above all other members of the said College in his piety and integrity of life than he is superior to them in the dignity of his place. . . .' The charge of laxity and irregularity in this respect had loomed large in the discussions in the House of Lords, and the master made his reply to it the pre-eminent head of his defensive plea. Nothing that he could say, however, was likely to impress Bishop Greene, who had quite obviously prejudged the case. When on April 27, 1734, the bishop appeared in his court to pronounce judgment, it was ominous that his two Assessors were not present. These two gentlemen, Dr Audley and Dr Cotteril, were known to the master's friends to be in favour of an acquittal. When Dr Andrews, counsel for the master, asked whether his lordship would defer judgment until these two gentlemen could be present, he replied shortly: 'No, I shan't', and when Dr Andrews begged to know whether the two gentlemen were consenting,

[1] See Appendix III.

the bishop replied: 'They are consenting and desirous of it', which might well be taken to mean that they consented to his pronouncing judgment, but not necessarily that they consented to his sentence. The bishop's sentence was that Richard Bentley, having been proved guilty of dilapidating the goods of the college and of violating the statutes, was deprived of the mastership.

Thus the great chase came to an end, a chase that had lasted five-and-twenty years, and the old fox had been run to earth at last. Like the reign of Queen Victoria, it must have seemed when it ended that one of the normal conditions of life had been taken away, that some feature in the landscape of physical nature had been removed by a seismic disturbance or a change in the earth's atmosphere. It had outlasted the academic lifetime of many men, and many others who had ridden to the first *view-halloo!* were now old. Many could not remember a time when peace subsisted between the master and the fellows of Trinity. Some there may have been living beyond the gates of Trinity College, and even some within them who regretted the change, for at least they could be certain that university life would never be so eventful again. Those who, like Dr Colbatch, rejoiced that the old fox was no longer running, however, still did not know their master. He had been run to earth. But who was going to dig him out?

As he lay there, snug in the earth where he was to live for another eight years, and where he was to die, did he wish like Caligula that all his enemies shared one neck, that he might cut it through at a single stroke of his 'rusty sword'? Perhaps, as Thomas de Quincey surmised, he wished for them 'one common set of posteriors, that in planting a single kick he might have expressed his collective disdain of them, their acts, and their motives'.

24

Port after Stormie Seas

Sleep after toyle, port after stormie seas,
Ease after warre, death after life, does greatly please.

EDMUND SPENSER.

Bishop Greene sent out three copies of his sentence of deprivation,
one to Dr Bentley, one to be posted on the college gates, and one
to the Vice-Master of Trinity whose duty it was – according to
statute – to carry it out.[1] The vice-master was Dr John Hacket,
no lover of the master, but at the same time no hero to 'bell the
cat'. Bentley sat tight in the Master's Lodge, waiting for something to happen. He amused himself by setting as a theme for the
candidates in the scholarship examinations that summer, a line
from Terence[2] which might be roughly translated: 'they are
kicking me out; but, then, life is full of ups and downs'. He was
reported to be in the best of spirits. He had lately taken to
smoking, and he was improving his taste for port, thus affording
a basis for Pope's line in the *Dunciad*:

Where Bentley late tempestuous wont to sport
In troubled waters, but now sleeps in port. . . .

The college, to its everlasting credit, rallied round the old man
in what anyone but Bentley would have supposed his darkest
hour. Dr Colbatch and his faction, however, pestered the vice-
master to carry out the sentence, and Colbatch as senior fellow
even petitioned the House of Lords, without success. Fellows of

[1] Dr Monk held the view that the framers of the statute, instead of *'per
eundem VICE-MAGISTRUM . . .'* had probably intended to enact *'per
eundem VISITATOREM officio Magistri privetur'*, and that the shoulder-
ing off of the duty of deprivation upon the vice-master was the result of a
clerical error. Professor Jebb, however, assures us that Monk was not
arguing on the original copy of the statutes, and that *'Vice-Magrm'* is the
original and correct term. (Monk's *Life*, c. XIX; Jebb's *Bentley*, c. VII).
[2] *hoc nunc dicis,*
Ejectos hinc nos; omnium rerum heus vicissitudo est.

colleges (apart from the Colbatches of this world) ultimately find it hard to abide interference by outside authority, and now that the Bishop of Ely had actually condemned their master and ordered the vice-master to turn him out the fellows of Trinity were reluctant to proceed further. The long process had cost their college large sums of money, and it was time for retrenchment and the end of the scandal. By 1735 the fellows had come to a compromise with the ancient squatter at the Master's Lodge. They would abstain from further action for his removal, while he would no longer interfere in the elections and government of the college.

As for the bishop, Bentley still knew his way into Westminster Hall, and he held him at bay for four years. Three times Dr Greene secured a *mandamus* from King's Bench requiring the vice-master to do his duty. Each time, the *mandamus* was defeated on a legal technicality or a defect of wording, until it began to look as if the judges were seeking suitable hairs to split in order to reprieve the old hero. After all, even Bentley could not live for ever. Only after King's Bench had quashed the third successive *mandamus* on April 22, 1738, did the Bishop of Ely come to the conclusion that the world belonged to Caesar. A few days later, he took to his bed and died. The invincible archdeacon was always fatal to the Bishops of Ely. John Moore had lost his life in trying him. Bishop Fleetwood saved his life by letting him alone. Bishop Greene died promptly on discovering that he could never succeed in executing his sentence. Some began to believe that the master was in league with mysterious agencies beyond the scope of mere bishops or fellows of colleges to trace or to influence. Was he, after all, in treaty with the Prince of Darkness? Certainly he had devilish eyebrows that went off at the outer corners, and he always had Mephistophelian lips, the very impress of Pride, which is the sin of the fallen angels. Did he not admire Milton's Satan? Was he not passionately devoted to cats?

The fact is that the master was safe from his enemies from the day and the hour in the merry month of May 1734 when the seniors accepted the resignation of Dr John Hacket and appointed Dr Richard Walker in his place. Thenceforth Bentley may be said to have been his own vice-master, for 'Frog' Walker, the

man from Upwell in the Fens, whom he had put in as junior
bursar at the time of the quarrel over the master's granary in
1717, was devoted to the master with the complex devotion of a
cross between Mosca and Sancho Panza. Yet Walker was neither
a knave nor a fool. He had the intelligence and the insight to
recognize genius when he saw it, to love it, and to serve it, and
thereby – as Carlyle would say – to share in it. Nor was Walker
the master's knave as Mosca was Volpone's. He was trusted,
indeed liked, by the fellows: witness their ready acceptance of
him as vice-master of their college, and his decisive part in
bringing about the compromise with the master in 1735. From
henceforth Frog Walker was the master's willing slave, his
smoking companion, his hat-bearer, even – one suspects – his
male-nurse after the master's partial stroke in his seventy-
seventh year. He became, like his hero's shadow, almost as
famous as the master himself. In Pope's description of the 'awful
Aristarchus' we straightway hear of Walker:

> His hat, which never vail'd to human pride,
> Walker with rev'rance took and laid aside. . . .

The Frog appears to have harboured rather pride than resentment at such servitude, for he kept the master's hat – which might
be said to have resembled the hat of the Quangle-Wangle-Quee[1]
– hanging in his rooms for reverent admiration long after
Bentley's death.

This, then, was the last scene of Richard Bentley's forty years'
sojourn at Trinity, an old man, partially paralysed, seated by the
fire smoking with his faithful Frog, his hat on his head against
the draughts, his glass of port at his elbow, and his Homer on his
knees. The everloving Joanna, the wife of nearly forty years of
idyllic domesticity, died in 1740, when he had but two years to
live. The younger Joanna, his beloved 'Jug', took up residence
at the lodge with her children, and revived for him that domestic
warmth and serenity which he had always loved so well. Ever
and anon the laughter of children at play, and other more

---

[1] The Quangle-Wangle's Hat, in Edward Lear's *Nonsense Song* of that
title, was of enormous size, and used as a dancing floor by a diversity of
strange creatures.

riotous sounds, penetrated to the old man's ears from regions overhead. He supported such interludes with a rare patience. Once, when young Richard was making a vast racket upstairs, his grandfather called him down and wished to know why. When the boy replied that he had been playing battledore and shuttlecock with Master Gooch, son of the Bishop of Norwich,[1] the master forgave him with the remark, 'And I have been at this sport with his father.' He added 'thine has been the more amusing game; so there's no harm done'. Richard Cumberland also tells us of his sending away a man who had been caught stealing his plate, with the advice to take a more honest occupation. 'Harkee, fellow, thou see'st the trade which thou hast taken up is an unprofitable trade, therefore get thee gone, lay aside an occupation by which thou canst gain nothing but a halter.' To those who urged him to prosecute the thief he said: 'Why tell the man he is a thief? He knows that well enough without thy information.' The man was penitent, and the master bade him go his ways and never steal again. It is not every day that a great scholar bears out his scholarly critics with such a practical example of his sanity and good sense. It was in these years – to be precise, in 1739, when he was seventy-seven – that he at length brought out his edition of *Manilius* (after forty-five years of gestation),[2] and it was of his *Manilius* that A. E. Housman was to write as an example of 'his sanity, his great and simple and straightforward fashion of thought'. How glorious to turn from 'the smoky fire' of other scholars' genius, to 'the sky and air of Bentley's....'

One last scene remains with us, redolent of his irrepressible humour. In the year of *Manilius*, the master took part in the proceedings of the vice-chancellor's court against a young man who bore the charming name of Tinkler Ducket, a fellow of Caius who had been converted to atheistical principles by Samuel Strutt's *Philosophical Enquiry into the Physical Springs of Human Actions*.[3]

[1] Thomas Gooch, Master of Caius, who had taken away Bentley's degrees in 1718. Later Bishop of Ely.

[2] See above, p. 84.

[3] Published in 1732. Strutt seems to have been known to Ducket as 'the adorable Father Strutt'. He had been a writer in *The Craftsman*, organ of the opposition to Walpole.

The Reverend Tinkler had given what the orthodox were pleased to regard as 'a remarkable specimen of the practical results of atheism' by attempting to seduce a young woman under the persuasion that God would not have given us passions unless he meant us to gratify them. To clinch the argument, he told her that he had an infallible preventive against pregnancy. Bentley was unable to attend the court at the schools, so the court met at the Master's Lodge at Trinity. After all, it was a high privilege to meet in the drawing-room of the first Boyle lecturer of the year 1692; the Christian advocate who had harrassed the atheists of the wicked old days of Hobbes; the celebrated author of *The Confutation of Atheism*, not to mention the *Remarks on Anthony Collins' Discourse of Freethinking*. A very big gun to bring up against poor little Tinkler of Caius, one would have thought. The Christian advocate himself appears to have thought that atheists had shrunk since the days when he had tackled the Hobbists. Looking round the court for the atheist, he was astonished to have little Tinkler pointed out to him. The master let out a roar. 'What! Is that the atheist? I expected to have seen a man as big as Burrough the Beadle!'[1]

Aristarchus never published his Homer, although he worked at his edition until his paralytic seizure in his seventy-eighth year,[2] when he was mid-way through the sixth Book of the *Iliad*. His ambition had been to furnish the world with an edition restoring

---

[1] Mr Burrowes and Mr Burrough, the esquire-bedells of that day, were both portly gentlemen; for then, as now, the stately bearers of the university insignia accompanied a long line of vice-chancellors to all feasts and festivities for years on end.

[2] In *A Short memorandum of some learned discoveries made in a late Conversation*, preserved in the library of Trinity College under the title of *Bentley's Table-Talk*, there is a typical example of his persistence with his design late into his life, although precisely how late it is impossible to say, since the record is without either date or signature. 'I shall bestow on the world (though it does not deserve it of me), a new edition of Homer, e'er it be long, in which that Poet will make another sort of figure than he has hitherto done. I shall then show how ill he has been used by dull Commentators and pretended critics who never understood him. . . . In short, by the happy discovery I have made that Homer frequently made use of the Aeolick MM Digamma everywhere in his poem I shall render multitudes of places intelligible which the stupid scholiasts could never account for but by Licentia Poetica.'

the lost *digamma*, that mysterious letter which had disappeared from the Greek alphabet for some two-thousand years and (he held) was necessary for the correct prosody of Homer's epic. 'The lost digamma' might have become the doctor's King Charles's head in his last years but for two things. In the first place, his intellect remained unimpaired to the end, and in the second place he was right. The lost consonant disappeared when the Ionian Greeks made Greek a literary language, probably because they disliked its harsh sound – the same reason that Dr Monk suggested for Bentley the north-countryman's liking for it. He had decided for its recovery as early as 1713, when he was in his early fifties, and it became the last ambition of his life as the genius of 'conjectural Criticism' to bring it back into use. He wrote it as a capital F and he pronounced it as a W. Homer was punctuated with sounds reminiscent of the Red Indian 'wah' or 'waugh', as he declaimed the *Iliad* in recitative sessions in his last years. He certainly made the lines scan by the way he used it, although he was attempting something impossible in contemplating a printed 'digammatized' edition of the Homeric epic. A printer can only cope with the digamma by setting it on the line, where it 'towers' above the other letters, as Pope said, 'like Saul', which was not in the least what Bentley intended when he wrote it. Thus Pope's last mockery of the *Dunciad*:

While tow'ring o'er your alphabet like Saul
Stands our digamma, and o'er tops them all.

His other favourite recreation in these years was to pursue Dr Colbatch with a final lawsuit in the Consistorial Court of the Bishop of Ely for the sum of 3s 6d which he claimed was due to him as archdeacon for 'proxies payable to the ecclesiastical visitor' – actually travelling expenses for the archdeacon of Ely who, as Colbatch complained, never visited. Bentley had not once visited the churches and parsonages of the diocese in person in thirty-seven years, and Dr Colbatch was not going to pay. But, finding it dull after so long to have no lawsuit pending, the archdeacon, like the old gentleman in the comedy, decided to get up an action against his dog. Dr Colbatch would serve excellently for the prosecuted dog, for the master had always accused him of snarling. The rector of Orwell, at length had to pay the 3s 6d together with 2s 6d in arrears, and £20 in costs. Like John Hampden, John Colbatch was less concerned with the money than with the principle. In future, however, he confined his arguments to a very learned and totally unreadable book with a very long title: *The Case of Proxies Payable to Ecclesiastical Visitors Fully Stated: and the Question Discussed, whether those Payments can on any Account become due from Parochial Clergy to an Archdeacon who doth not Visit them and their Churches in Person? With some remarks on* . . . etc, etc. . . . The book appeared in 1741. In the following year, Dr Colbatch's old persecutor died, preceding him by seven years to a place where, it may be hoped, dons no longer dispute.

25

Envoi

' "Walker, our hat!" – no more he deigned to say.
But stern as Ajax' spectre strode away.'

Bentley's conduct throughout his learned life has led to much
speculation whether he would not have been better fitted for the
career of a lord chancellor or a field-marshal than for that of a
divine or a don. The answer must be that as a lawyer he would
have been promptly disbarred, while as a soldier he would either
have been quickly court-martialled or (more likely) have run a
catastrophic course as a Bonaparte or a Tamerlane. As a divine,
or a don, in the age of the unreformed universities, he could
rejoice in a career virtually untrammelled by effective discipline.
In the life of letters, as he himself observed, no man was ever
written out of a reputation save by himself; and in matters of
academic propriety a bold man was a cat among pigeons or a
wolf among sheep. Besides, Bentley was never 'a mere moloch of
human nature' seeking whom he might devour. Rather, he was
Voltaire's *'animal méchant . . . quand on le bat, il se défend'*. He
simply went on his way rejoicing, and when he trod on other
people's corns he was genuinely astonished at their attempts to
trip him up. The final tripping-up was generally done by
Bentley, and he was perfectly justified in his boast: 'It is no
practice of mine to trample upon the prostrate.' He really could
not understand the malignity of an Alexander Pope. And he
could be merciful to Joshua Barnes, whose edition of Homer of
1710 was directed at Bentley as *homo inimicus* with a great deal
of scurrility, because he knew that Barnes had spent most of his
small fortune on his edition. 'I would not, without the utmost
provocation, hurt the sale of his book,' he said in a letter of
criticism addressed to a friend of Barnes with instructions not to
publish it. He would put up with a great deal of provocation

before he aimed a blow in retaliation. His only inveterate enmity
was for the impostor, for the pretentious, for the second-rate
posturing as genius. In a world of dons and *petits-maîtres*, whet-
ting their beaks on each other's books and patting each other on
the back in hope of the same attentions in return, Bentley was
simply the white bird in the rookery, the one who was different
and therefore due to be set upon and pecked to death. Only his
beak was sharper, and his eye brighter, and his plumage had the
infuriating habit of looking the more resplendent for the dust of
battle.

He was often rude, rough, dictatorial. He could be arrogant,
vituperative, overbearing. When once the feathers began to fly
he loved a fight with a true Yorkshire gusto. He was grasping,
tenacious of financial advantages, always with an eye to the main
chance. He came from a part of England, and from a social background, where 'brass' was respected, the more because it was
hard to come by. His home was a home where every penny
counted, and he had made his way against heavy odds. He came
from a grammar school, and when he went to Cambridge he
lived among the sizars. It would be easy to misread the situation
by translating it into present-day terms. The notion of colleges
full of gentlemen in gold-laced gowns and silver-tasselled caps
holding at bay a horde of obscure Judes is nonsense at any time.
The fantasy of a university dominated by gentlemen with what
came to be called 'Public School accents', took on a semblance of
reality in the nineteenth century, and had a life of about 100
years. In Bentley's day, fellows of colleges were not young
aristocrats. For the most part they were promoted sizars, men
of lowly or middling birth, and often of coarse and common
fibre. College life, with its official celibacy and its peculiarly
secular type of monasticism, was unlikely to transform them into
gentlemen. They had too little to do, and tended to turn rather
readily to the bottle and the bawdy-house. Throughout the
eighteenth century, the aristocracy were inclined to shun the
universities as schools for their sons and to rely upon private
tutors and the Grand Tour. 'Dens of dunces', and 'schools of
vice', were the soubriquets in common use when Oxford and
Cambridge were mentioned. Every age gets the kind of universities it deserves. Drinking and drabbing and idleness were the

common occupations of young men at the university because they were the common occupations of the extra-mural world in a coarse, masculine, and brutal society. The exceptions were the 'heads of houses', who were often men of birth and breeding put in by aristocratic patrons. Bentley's predecessor as Master of Trinity was Dr John Montagu, fourth son of the first Earl of Sandwich. Montagu's predecessor, Dr North, was the fifth son of Lord North, and younger brother of the first Baron Guilford. The sizar who jumped over the wall from St John's in 1700 (he was not even a fellow) at any rate made a change.

Bentley seems to have had few of the vices of the young men of his time, or indeed of any other time, but there can be no doubt that he was, if not plebeian in any obvious sense, homely enough in everything but his princely gifts of scholarship. He retained certain home-spun characteristics derived from his good Yorkshire origins all his life, including a fondness for thee-ing and thou-ing his familiars, and a perfect contentment with a simple, indeed often an abstemious, diet. In the great age of port and prejudice, he certainly went easy on the port, though he admired it and gave a certain attention to its niceties in his old age. After all, it was the great Whig drink, and he liked to say of the Tory claret that 'it would be port if it could'. Becoming head of a house, and such a house as that of the Holy and Undivided Trinity, at the age of 37, he must have appeared if not an upstart, at any rate a man from the north come among the softer southerners. We know that Joanna Bernard's family looked somewhat askance at the ambitious and brilliant young northerner, and we also know that his relations with Dr Gooch of Caius were like those of vinegar with oil. It would be absurd to read Bentley's troubled career in terms of class-warfare, but it is as well to remember that although he learnt to wear the purple as one to the manner born, he never lost the common touch, using that term in the pejorative as well as the laudatory sense.

In any weighing of the evidence he must be adjudged guilty of most of the misdeeds charged against him by the fellows of his college. There is neither justice nor candour in de Quincey's argument that he should be pardoned because he was so eminently superior in force and scholarship to his enemies; that 'the little dogs should be sacrificed to the great one'; that 'the current of our sympathies with an illustrious man should be cleared of ugly obstructions, enabled to flow unbroken, which otherwise might be unpleasantly distracted between his talents on the one hand and his knavery on the other'. It is still true, however, that for all his railing and invective, he seems to have been one of those rare men who knew how to *use* anger, and this was probably because he was always conscious of a paramount concern, an over-riding destiny, beyond the brawls which filled the fore-front of his life. There is something splendid about his ability to turn his back on the dancing dervishes at his door, and, after shutting the door in their faces, to retreat to his study and get on with his work. He had an infinite capacity for what might be called, without contradiction, 'good-natured contempt'. It is to be discerned in the man's eyes, in the cut of his big, strongly-featured face as Roubiliac left it in his marble where it looks down from its place in the Wren Library at Trinity. To read the voluminous letters of Dr Colbatch under that slightly supercilious but finely human gaze makes one wonder what all these little men thought they were doing in their comings and goings between Cambridge and King's Bench and Ely House, their backstairs sneakings to make 'interest' with great men and to make Archbishop Wake lift up his hands and turn up his eyes at their tales of the goings-on of the Master of Trinity? Their business is, one feels, but a busy-ness. The man who looks down from over yonder seems not to abide our question. He seems not to hear it. He is probably thinking of Homer and the great digamma.

Bentley's last days were a true Indian summer. In the closing passage of his essay, de Quincey calls it 'a sweet mimicry of summer . . . less gaudy than the mighty summer of the solstice . . . sweet, golden, silent, happy though sad . . . a spiritual echo of the music that had departed . . . frail and transitory as it was solemn, quiet, and lovely'. And death, when it came upon him, came with a proper stealth, as if even the greatest of his adversaries knew the need for circumspection in his dealings with Dr Bentley. He had never really recovered from the stroke of 1739. Now came a pleurisy, laying hold of him in his weakest spot, where the damps and draughts of chapel and the schools had for so long besieged him. His last public act, within a month of his death, was to examine for the Craven scholarships. One of the two successful candidates was Christopher Smart.

The day of his death was July 14, 1742. It would certainly have pleased Dr Colbatch that the death of a tyrant should in later years be recalled on the day that commemorates the fall of the Bastille. Nevertheless Bentley had celebrated his eightieth birthday in the previous January. He had said that he would die at eighty, and what Bentley said he would do he generally brought to pass. In eighty years, he liked to say, a man could read everything that was worth reading. *Et tunc magna mei sub terris ibit imago.* It was the last example, perhaps, of the great critic's celebrated faculty of divination.

APPENDICES

Appendix I

Articles of accusation against Dr Bentley relative to his trial before Bishop Greene

Article
confirmed by
the House of
Lords.
Imprimis, We article and object to you the said Dr Richard Bentley, that you the said Dr Richard Bentley do know, believe, and have heard, that Queen Elizabeth of blessed memory, formerly Queen of this realm, did by Letters Patent, bearing date the 4th of the Calends of April, in the second year of her reign, make, constitute, appoint, and ordain certain rules, constitutions, or statutes, for the good government, order, and discipline, and for the better preservation of the estates, and administration of the revenues of the Royal College of the Holy and Undivided Trinity in the University of Cambridge, of the foundation of King Henry the Eighth, her father: and the said statutes were by her confirmed under the broad Seal, and received and accepted by the Master, Fellows, and Scholars of the said College. *Et hoc fuit et est verum, et objicimus et articulamur conjunctim et divisim et de quolibet.*

Confirmed. II. *Item,* We article and object to you the said Dr Bentley, that in and by the fortieth chapter of the said statutes, the Bishop of Ely, for the time being, is appointed, authorized, and empowered, at any time, to examine the Master of the said College, upon and concerning sundry great and enormous crimes in the latter member of such statutes particularly enumerated and expressed, as in and by the said statutes now remaining among the archives of the College, to which the party proponent referreth himself, doth and may appear. *Et hoc fuit et est verum, et objicimus et articulamur ut supra.*

Confirmed. III. *Item,* We article and object to you the said Dr Richard Bentley, that you the said Dr Richard Bentley was, in and about the year 1699, by a grant or letters patent from his late Majesty King William the Third, constituted and appointed Master of the aforesaid College of the Holy and Undivided Trinity in Cambridge, and was afterwards duly admitted Master thereof, and have ever since possessed and enjoyed, and do now possess and enjoy the said Mastership. *Et hoc fuit et est verum, et objicimus et articulamur ut supra.*

Confirmed.　　IV. *Item*, We article and object to you the said Dr Richard Bentley, that you the said Dr Richard Bentley did, at the time of your admission into the Mastership of the said College, take the oath, enjoined and prescribed by the second of the said statutes of Queen Elizabeth, to be taken by every Master at and before his admission into such Mastership, and that you then swore (*inter alia*) in the words following, viz. *Ego*, Richardus Bentley, *a Regia Majestate Magister hujus Collegii Sanctæ et Individuæ Trinitati dedicati designatus, juro et Deo teste promitto ac spondeo, Primo me veram Christi religionem omni animo amplexurum, &c. Deinde, me omnia dicti Collegii sacerdotia, fundos, prædia, possessiones, dominia, reditus, proventus, jura, libertates, privilegia, omnia denique bona sine imminutione aut vastatione (quantum in me situm erit) conservaturum, statuta Collegii in omnibus servaturum, et eadem vere sincere et omnino secundum sensum grammaticalem interpretaturum, omnes et singulos socios et discipulos, pensionarios, sisatores et subsisatores et cetera Collegii membra ex iisdem statutis ac legibus sine ullius generis aut conditionis aut personarum respectu, gratia odiove recturum et defensurum, atque ut omnes, officiarii socii ac discipuli, ceteraque Collegii membra diligenter suum faciant officium, curaturum; postremò, si munere Magistri vel sponte abiero, vel jure ac legitime abdicatus fuero, me omnia Collegii bona quæ in mea potestate custodiave sunt, aut esse debent, Vice-Magistro Decanis et Thesaurariis Collegii, vel statim, si id commode fieri poterit, vel intra quindecim dies, sine controversia tergiversatione aut aliqua eorundem diminutione redditurum; et si quam pecuniæ summam id temporis Collegio debuero, obsides sufficientes daturum Vice-Magistro et ceteris Collegii sociis et scholaribus de eadem pecunia penitus ante finem trium mensium proxime sequentium dissolvenda; nullam litem, actionemve Collegio aut his qui me legitime abdicaverunt ea de causa unquam in posterum intentaturum. Hæc omnia in me recipio,*

Deoque teste me pro virili facturum polliceor: sicut me Deus adjuvet et haec sacrosancta Dei Evangelia. Et hoc fuit et est verum, &c. et objicimus et articulamur ut supra.

Prohibited by the House of Lords.

V. *Item*, We article and object to you the said Dr Richard Bentley, that you have, ever since such your admission to the Mastership, lived and acted in open violation of many of the said rules and constitutions, or statutes, so made and provided for the good government of the said College, and in breach of the oath so as aforesaid by you taken. *Et objicimus et articulamur ut supra.*

Confirmed, except the words within brackets.

VI. *Item*, We article and object to you the said Dr Richard Bentley, that by the second chapter of the said statutes it is (*inter alia*) ordained and provided, that the Master of the said College for the time being, shall be a person no less eminent above other members of the said College for his piety and integrity of life, than he is superior to them by the dignity of his place: notwithstanding which you, the said Dr Bentley, have, for more than twenty years past, in violation of the said statute, and in breach of your said oath, lived a very irreligious life, and notoriously neglected the public worship of God; and more particularly by constantly and habitually absenting yourself from divine service in the chapel of the said College at the usual hours of morning and evening prayers, [and suffered or permitted the officers of the said College in the like manner to neglect the same.] *Et objicimus et articulamur de quolibet alio temporis spatio, &c. et ut supra.*

Prohibited.

VII. *Item*, We article and object to you, the said Dr Richard Bentley, that you have for several years successively elected, and by arbitrary methods procured several persons to be elected Vice-masters of the said College, notwithstanding that such Vice-masters did not at any time in the first year of their being Vice-master, nor in any of the following years, attend the public worship of God in the chapel of the said College at the usual hours of prayers in the morning, as by the statute they ought to have done; and that you, the said Dr Bentley have, from time to time, and at all times, suffered such open neglect of duty in the said Vice-masters to pass without censure, and unpunished, in violation of the said statutes of the said College, and of the oath so as aforesaid by you taken. *Et hoc fuit et est verum, &c. Et objicimus et articulamur, &c. Et ut supra.*

Prohibited.   VIII. *Item,* We article and object to you, the said Dr Richard Bentley, that by the first of the said statutes it is provided, that there shall be four persons in orders of priesthood, to serve as chaplains daily in the chapel of the said College, as by the said statute, reference being thereunto had, will more fully appear. *Et objicimus et articulamur ut supra.*

Prohibited.   IX. *Item,* We article and object to you, the said Dr Richard Bentley, that ever since you have been Master of the said College, the persons appointed to be chaplains thereof have been allowed by you to be non-resident and absent from the said College, and to enjoy and reside upon livings and other benefices in places very distant and remote from the said College; and that not any of the said chaplains have at any time been called upon by you, the said Dr Bentley, to reside there, or censured by you for such their non-residence. *Et hoc fuit et est verum, &c. Et ut supra.*

Confirmed.   X. *Item,* We article and object to you, the said Dr Richard Bentley, that by the 11th of the said statutes, it is ordained and provided, that there shall be a lecture read on some part of the Catechism, on every Sunday and Holiday, in the chapel of the said College, after the public sermon in the afternoon; and by such statutes five or six of the Fellows ought to be appointed to perform that religious and important duty; and from the time of making the said statutes, the names of the several Fellows appointed to read such lectures have been entered in the book called the Conclusion Book, or some other book belonging to the College: and that out of the number of those who had been so appointed, and gone through a course of such lectures, the College preachers ought to be chosen by the Master and eight Senior Fellows, when and so often as any vacancy shall happen among them; as by the said statutes, reference being thereunto had, will more fully appear. *Et ut supra.*

Confirmed.   XI. *Item*, We article and object to you, the said
            Dr Richard Bentley, that for twenty years past and
upwards, you have not only neglected, but absolutely refused,
though often called upon and required so to do, to appoint or fill
up the prescribed number of Fellows to read the said lectures; so
that the same have been frequently interrupted, neglected, and
discontinued for many months, and sometimes for whole years
together. *Et objicimus et articulamur de quolibet alio temporis
spatio, &c. Et ut supra.*

Confirmed.   XII. *Item*, We article and object to you, the said
            Dr Richard Bentley, that more particularly on or
about the 22d day of April, 1719, there being then several
vacancies in the prescribed number of Fellows to read the said
lectures, it was at a public meeting of members of the said
College, that day held, proposed to you the said Dr Bentley, by
one of the senior Fellows then present, and the rest of the senior
Fellows of the said College, did then earnestly desire of you,
that such vacancies might be supplied and filled up; and a list of
several learned and worthy Fellows of the said College, well fit
and qualified to read those lectures, particularly Mr Malled,
Mr Craister, and others, were then offered to you, the said
Dr Bentley, for that purpose; but that you, the said Dr Bentley,
absolutely refused to name or allow of, nor did you name or
allow of any other person to perform that laudable and necessary
exercise; but with great contempt and disdain told them, 'it was
nonsense to talk of putting up five persons to catechise at the
same time,' or to that effect. *Hocque, &c. Et objicimus et articulamur de quolibet alio tempore, &c. Et ut supra.*

Confirmed.   XIII. *Item*, We article and object to you, the said
            Dr Richard Bentley, that soon after the premisses
in the next precedent article mentioned, the aforesaid Mr Malled
and Mr Craister several times waited upon you, and earnestly
desired and entreated you, that they might have leave to read
the lectures upon the Catechism, according to and in pursuance
of the said statutes, in order to their being statutably capable of
being elected College preachers; but you absolutely refused
them, and turned them away from you with great rudeness and

ill manners. And the said Mr Craister waiting upon you at another time with the like request, you, the said Dr Bentley, refused him, and took him by the shoulders, and thrust him out of the doors. *Hocque, &c. Et ut supra.*

Prohibited. XIV. *Item,* We article and object to you, the said Dr Richard Bentley, that when any vacancy hath happened among the College preachers, you, the said Dr Bentley, have refused, though often called upon and required so to do, to call the eight Senior Fellows together, within the time prescribed by the said 11th statute of Queen Elizabeth; so that there have been very frequently several vacancies of College preachers at one time; and some years there were seven, and in other years there were nine places of College preachers vacant together; to the great prejudice and discouragement of such of the Fellows of the said College as were capable of being, and ought to have been elected into such vacancies. *Hocque, &c. Et objicimus et articulamur de quibuslibet aliis annis, &c. Et ut supra.*

Prohibited. XV. *Item,* We article and object to you, the said Dr Richard Bentley, that by the 30th of the said statute, it is ordained and provided, that when any livings, in the gift and presentation of the College, shall become vacant, the same shall, within one month after notice of such vacancy, without further delay, be conferred upon such Fellow of the College as shall be the then senior by degree, as by the statute, to which the party proponent refers, will appear. *Et ut supra.*

Prohibited. XVI. *Item,* We article and object to you, the said Dr Richard Bentley, that you, the said Dr Bentley, in violation of the said statute, and in breach of your said oath, have frequently, when livings, in the gift of the College, have become vacant, for private purposes of your own, and in order to carry on your evil practices, mentioned in these articles, unstatutably delayed and denied to join in presenting such senior as hath been then statutably qualified to take and hold such living, or any other person whatever, thereto, till more than five months have passed from the notice of such vacancy.

250

Hocque, &c. Et objicimus et articulamur de quolibet alio temporis spatio, &c. Et ut supra.

Withdrawn.   XVII. *Item,* We article and object to you, the said Dr Richard Bentley, that by the said 11th statute of Queen Elizabeth, it is further appointed, that every Fellow of the said College, before he can be chosen a College preacher, shall preach a sermon before the Master for the time being, and the Fellows and Scholars of the said College; and such sermon ought to be approved by the Master and four Senior Fellows of the said College. *Et ut supra.*

Withdrawn.   XVIII. *Item,* We article and object to you, the said Dr Richard Bentley, that you have not, for twenty years last past, been present to hear any one of the said probation sermons, save and except on the 23d day of August, 1719, being on a Sunday, when Mr Barnwell preached; and on that day you did not come into the chapel till the Communion Service was begun; but you, the said Dr Bentley, have frequently, and with great scorn, declared, that you approved and disapproved of such sermons as you were not present at, by report only; and that you did so by Mr Whitfield's and Mr Bouquet's sermons in particular. *Hocque, &c. Et objicimus et articulamur de quolibet alio numero annorum, &c. et de quolibet alio tempore, &c. Et ut supra.*

Prohibited.   XIX. *Item,* We article and object to you, the said Dr Richard Bentley, that by the 18th chapter of the said statutes, it is ordered and provided, that in every week of each term appointed by the statutes of the University, there shall be three disputations in the College chapel, viz. one on Monday in philosophy, at which the head lecturer is to preside; another on Wednesday in philosophy or divinity, at which the junior Dean is to preside; and another on Friday in divinity only, at which the senior Dean is to preside and moderate; and that each of such disputations is to continue for the space of two hours, between one respondent and three opponents, on which every Fellow and Scholar is to perform his part in turn in person, as appointed, unless excused on some weighty cause, to be allowed of by the Master and Dean of the said College; and in such case the person so excused may appoint a substitute to dispute in his stead, but is obliged in person to perform the like duty, as soon as the cause on which he was excused is removed or ceases. *Et ut supra.*

Prohibited.   XX. *Item,* We article and object to you, the said Dr Richard Bentley, that you have for these twenty years past totally eluded the force and effect of, and have violated the said statute as is hereafter mentioned, viz. first, by directing and appointing that the term in the College shall begin much later and end sooner than the term in the public University begins and ends; and by such your appointment, the term in the College has very frequently not lasted more than half the public term. Secondly, by suffering the disputations on Mondays and Wednesdays to be totally discontinued, and on those days the respondent reads a thesis only, and no opponents ever appear to dispute; and this through your wilful neglect. Thirdly, by allowing the disputations in divinity on Fridays to be performed by a respondent and one opponent only; and this exercise is seldom or never performed more than once in each term, and sometimes not at all; and this through your wilful neglect. Fourthly, by allowing the Fellows and Scholars of the said College, without any weighty cause, or good and sufficient reason, to appoint substitutes to perform their exercises, and not requiring them, when such pretended cause is removed or ceases, to perform the same in person; and by reason of this last-mentioned neglect in you, there are not now, nor for many years have been, above five of the Fellows of the said College at one time, who have regularly and statutably borne any part in the public disputations, either as respondents or opponents. *Hocque, &c. Et objicimus et articulamur de quolibet alio temporis spatio, &c. Et ut supra.*

Withdrawn.   XXI. *Item,* We further article and object to you, the said Dr Richard Bentley, that by the last mentioned statute it is further appointed and provided, that on every Tuesday, Thursday, and Friday, there shall be disputations held in the hall of the said College, in rhetoric and logic, by the senior sophists and others; and that the head-lecturer and the other lecturers shall preside thereat in their turns. And by the ninth statute of the said Queen, it is likewise ordained and provided, that the head-lecturer shall take care that the sub-lecturers under him perform their respective duties diligently and faithfully; and by the same statute it is further appointed, that the said lecturer shall go, at least once in every week to each class, and examine each of the scholars of the said College, to know what proficiency they have respectively made from time to time, as by the said several statutes, to which the party proponent refers, will appear. *Et ut supra.*

Withdrawn.   XXII. *Item,* We article and object to you the said Dr Bentley, that at the time appointed for the election of lecturers and other officers of the said College, in the year 1727, you the said Dr Bentley, proposed one of the Fellows to be head-lecturer, and one other of the Fellows to be Latin lecturer for the succeeding year: and although one of the Senior Fellows of the said College then objected thereto, on account that both the said Fellows so proposed by you, had totally neglected the duty of their respective offices in the preceding year, you replied as you had frequently done, that 'such objection concerned the time past only:' and then you asked if they, meaning the aforesaid Fellows so proposed by you to those offices, were not to take the oath, meaning the oath required by the statutes for the due discharge of their respective offices; and thereupon you, the said Dr Bentley, immediately with your own hand, wrote down the names of the said two Fellows, whom you had so proposed, as appointed to such offices. And that neither of the said Fellows, so as afore-said appointed to those offices, did during that whole year per-form any part of the duty incumbent upon them, nor have they at any time been censured or punished by you for such their neglect. *Hocque, &c. Et objicimus et articulamur de quolibet alio tempore, &c. Et ut supra.*

Withdrawn.   XXIII. *Item,* We article and object to you the said Dr Richard Bentley, that by the 31st of the said statutes, it is ordered and appointed, that the several gates of the College shall be opened and shut by the porter, at certain hours therein mentioned; and that at night, when all the gates are shut, the keys shall be carried to the Master, and in his absence to the Vice-Master, and deposited with him; and the porter is obliged personally to perform that duty, as by the said statute to which the party proponent refers will appear. *Et ut supra.*

Withdrawn. XXIV. *Item,* We article and object to you the said Dr Richard Bentley, that in violation of the said statute, and contrary to the true intent and meaning thereof, the keys of the College have not, at any time during these twenty years past, been brought by the porter, and deposited with you the Master, as by the said statute they ought to be, by which means all manner of persons, as well members of the said College as others, are at liberty to, and frequently do go in and out of the College gates at all hours of the night: and the college porter doth not officiate in that duty himself, but is with your privity and consent allowed to act by a deputy, who hath no salary, or other consideration for doing that duty, but only the money given by such persons as make a practice of going in and out of the College gates, at such unstatutable and unseasonable hours; of all which you have been informed, and have had notice, *Hocque, &c. Et objicimus et articulamur de quolibet alio numero annorum, &c. Et ut supra.*

Prohibited. XXV. *Item,* We article and object to you, the said Dr Richard Bentley, that by the third of the statutes, it is ordained and provided, that when any one of the eight Senior Fellows goes out of the said College, he shall substitute the Fellow who is next in seniority to the eight, and not before deputed by another, to act for him in his absence; and shall enter such deputed Fellows' names in the registry of the said College. *Et ut supra.*

Prohibited. XXVI. *Item,* We article and object to you, the said Dr Richard Bentley, that you the said Dr Bentley, in breach of your said oath, and in violation of the said

254

last mentioned statute, have all along suffered such of the eight Seniors as had occasion to be absent from the said College, to depart from thence without appointing any substitute, or entering the name of any substitute upon the Register Book; and you have very often called Junior Fellows of the said College, who to your knowledge were not deputed by any of the Seniors, and who by their standing and distance from the Seniority, to your knowledge were not capable of being deputed, or of transacting any of the affairs of the said College, to make conclusions, and to do other business, which by the said statute ought to be transacted by the Master and eight Senior Fellows, or by their statutable deputies only, and by no other Fellow whatsoever; and such their conclusions, acts, and doings, have been constantly entered by you or by your order, in a book kept for that purpose, as the acts of the Master and eight Senior Fellows of the said College. *Et hoc fuit et est verum, &c. Et ut supra.*

Confirmed. **XXVII.** *Item,* We article and object to you, the said Dr Richard Bentley, that by the 34th of Queen Elizabeth's said statutes, it is ordered and provided, that the public seal of the said College shall not at any time be affixed to any instrument or writing whatsoever, but in the Chapel, and in the presence of the Senior Fellows of the said College, and of the eight other Fellows, next immediately in seniority to them; and that unless eight of that number should agree with the Master, to the affixing the said seal to any writing or instrument, it shall not be affixed thereto, as by the said statutes to which the party proponent refers will appear. *Et ut supra.*

Confirmed. **XXVIII.** *Item,* We article and object to you, the said Dr Richard Bentley, that you the said Dr Bentley, in breach of your said oath and in violation of the said statute, have frequently caused the public seal of the said College to be affixed to writings and instruments of great moment and concern, when there have not been sixteen Fellows met together for that purpose; more particularly as in the following articles is mentioned. *Et ut supra.*

Confirmed.   **XXIX.** *Item*, We article and object to you, the
said Dr Richard Bentley, that some time in the
year 1726, you the said Dr Bentley, caused or suffered the said
College seal to be affixed or put to a certain writing or instrument, enabling one John Kent, or some other person, in behalf
of the said College, to make seizure of a certain quantity of hay
in the parish of Over, in the county of Cambridge, in order to
commence a law-suit with the said parish, when no more than
thirteen of the Fellows of the said College had been assembled
together in the Chapel, and part of that number, viz. Dr Ayloffe,
Mr Parne, and others, withdrew from the Chapel, before the
seal was so affixed, and put to such writing or instrument, and
refused to give their consent thereto; *hocque, &c. Et objicimus et
articulamur de quolibet alio tempore, &c. Et ut supra.*

Confirmed.   **XXX.** *Item*, We article and object to you, the
said Dr Richard Bentley, that on the tenth day of
August last past, you the said Dr Bentley, in further breach of
your said oath, and violation of the said statute, did cause and
procure the public seal of the said College to be affixed and put
to a writing, purporting to be a petition of the Master, Fellows,
and Scholars of the said College to the King's most excellent
Majesty, at the sealing whereof five of the eight Senior Fellows
were absent from the said College, and had not deputed any
other of the Fellows to act in their stead; and two only of the
three Seniors who were then present, were consenting thereto,
and most of the rest of the Fellows then present were Junior
Fellows, not deputed, nor by their seniority capable of being
deputed, to transact any of the affairs of the said College, but
were purposely sent for by you to be present thereat, although
there were several Fellows at that time in the College, who were
of much longer standing than many of those present; and the
whole number of Fellows present were fifteen only. *Et hoc fuit
et est verum, &c. Et objicimus et articulamur de quolibet alio
tempore, &c. Et ut supra.*

Withdrawn.   **XXXI.** *Item*, We article and object to you, the
said Dr Richard Bentley, that by the 13th of the
said statutes, it is appointed that no student whatsoever, who is

in possession of, or heir-apparent to, any land after the death of his father, exceeding the sum or rent of ten pounds a year, shall be allowed to appear as a candidate at the usual time of election of scholars into vacant scholarships of the said College, for any such vacant scholarship; as by the said statute, to which the party proponent refers, will appear. *Et objicimus et articulamur ut supra.*

Withdrawn.   XXXII. *Item,* We article and object to you, the said Dr Richard Bentley, that in the year 1721, there being many scholarships of the said College then vacant, you, the said Dr Bentley, at the usual time of election of scholars into such vacant scholarships in the said year, in breach of your said oath, and violation of the said statute, did permit and suffer one Andrew Hacket, who was then heir-apparent to an estate in lands of more than the yearly rent of 600*l.* sterling, to appear as a candidate at the said election, for one of the said vacant scholarships; and although it was then objected to you, that the said Mr Hacket was, by reason of his being heir apparent to such an estate, incapacitated from being a candidate, yet you did not only over-rule such objection, but did give your vote, and procure him, the said Andrew Hacket, to be chosen a scholar into one of the said vacant scholarships, and did afterwards admit, or procure, or suffer him to be admitted into such vacant scholarship, by virtue of such election. *Et objicimus et articulamur de quolibet alio tempore, &c. Et ut supra.*

Withdrawn.   XXXIII. *Item,* We article and object to you, the said Dr Richard Bentley, that by the twelfth chapter of the said statutes, it is ordered and provided, that all such Scholars of the said College as have completed the degree of Bachelor of Arts, and such only, shall have the right to become candidates at every election of Fellows of the said College; notwithstanding which you, the said Dr Bentley, in breach of your said oath, and violation of the said statute, did, at the election of Fellows of the College, in the year 1723, allow your own son, Richard Bentley, although he had not, to your knowledge at that time, completed his degree of Bachelor in Arts, to stand

R   257

a candidate for a vacant fellowship of the said College; and the said Richard Bentley was then elected into one of the fellowships of the said College then vacant: *Hocque, &c. Et objicimus et articulamur de quolibet alio tempore, &c. Et ut supra.*

Withdrawn.　XXXIV. *Item*, We article and object to you, the said Dr Richard Bentley, that both before and ever since the said year 1723, you, the said Dr Bentley, in further violation of the statutes, have not suffered, nor would suffer, any person whatsoever to stand as candidate for vacant fellowships of the said College, save Bachelors of Arts of the third year only, whereby great numbers of other Bachelors, who had completed their degrees, were every year hindered or prevented, from standing or offering themselves to stand as candidates for such fellowships: *Hocques, &c. Et ut supra.*

Prohibited.　XXXV. *Item*, We article and object to you, the said Dr Richard Bentley, that by the oath taken by you, at your admission to be Master of the said College, you are obliged to preserve the whole estate of the said College, and every part thereof, from all waste and diminution, and for the better preservation of the estate and possessions of the said College, it is by the 28th chapter of the said statutes, specially ordained and provided, that the Master and Vice-master, the Senior Bursar, and one other of the Fellows, who is a preacher for the time being, shall every year diligently visit and survey the College estates, in such manner, that all the several estates may be visited and surveyed once in three years; but no such progress as required by the said statutes hath at any time been made, either by you, the said Dr Bentley yourself, or by the Vice-master, Senior Bursar, and one of the Fellows of the said College for the time being, since you, the said Dr Bentley, have been admitted into the Mastership thereof; neither have you at any time, since your being Master of the said College, called upon, or required the Vice-master, Senior Bursar, or any of the Fellows for the time being, to proceed on such progress or circuit; but you have been wilfully negligent in the premisses: *Hocque, &c. Et ut supra.*

Prohibited.   XXXVI. *Item,* We article and object to you, the
said Dr Richard Bentley, that for want of such
progresses as are required by the last mentioned statute, the
improved values of the estates belonging to the said College
are not certainly known: and several leases have been let by
your evil contrivances, for much lesser fines than might have
been reasonably demanded for the same: and more particularly
in the year 1717, a lease of a large house, called Massam-house,
in the city of York, together with several tenements thereto
belonging, being all part of the estate of the said College, and in
very good condition and repair, and of the yearly value of more
than 50*l.* sterling, was by your fraud and contrivance, made and
granted to your brother, James Bentley, for twenty years then
to come, for the fine or sum of 40*l.* only, and no more: and he
the said James Bentley, was by a covenant in the said lease
allowed to receive and take to his own use the arrears of the
improved rent of the said house and tenements, which had
accrued to the said College, from the expiration of the former
lease; and which then amounted to the sum of 30*l.* and upwards:
*Hocque, &c. Et objicimus et articulamur de quolibet alio tempore, et
de quibuslibet aliis valore vel summa, &c. Et ut supra.*

Prohibited.   XXXVII. *Item,* We article and object to you, the
said Dr Richard Bentley, that in the year 1727,
upon the surrender of the said lease, so as aforesaid granted to
the said James Bentley, a new lease of the same house and
tenements was, by your privity and contrivance made and
granted to Priscilla Bentley, for the like term of twenty years,
for a fine of twenty pounds; although the said house and
tenements had been actually surveyed by the said James
Bentley, and the real value thereof certainly known to you the
said Dr Bentley, before and at the granting each of the said
leases: *Hocque, &c. objicimus et articulamur de quibuslibet aliis
tempore et summa, &c. Et ut supra.*

Confirmed.   XXXVIII. *Item,* We article and object to you, the
said Dr Richard Bentley, that notwithstanding the
statutes of the said College severely do forbid the alienation of
any part of the estates of the said College, yet you, the said Dr

Bentley, in violation thereof, and in breach of your said oath, did, in the year 1712, by your own sole authority, and without the consent of the eight Senior Fellows of the said College, bargain, and agree to alienate a piece of inclosed ground belonging to the said College, situate in the parish of Kirby-Kendall, in the county of Westmoreland, and an indenture bearing date the 23d of December, 1712, was by your privity, procurement, and direction, sometime in the month of June, 1715, prepared and brought into the chapel of the said College, ready to be sealed, whereby the said piece of inclosed ground was absolutely sold and granted to one Josiah Lambert, and to his heirs for ever, reserving only four shillings *per annum* rent to the use of the said College: *Hocque, &c. Et objicimus et articulamur de quolibet alio tempore, &c. Et ut supra.*

Confirmed.   XXXIX. *Item,* We article and object to you, the said Dr Richard Bentley, that upon reading of such indenture in the chapel of the said College, the time aforementioned, in the presence of the sixteen Senior Fellows of the said College, they all unanimously refused to affix the seal of the said College thereto, as being contrary to the 35th of the statutes of the said College, so made and provided by the said Queen Elizabeth: *Hocque, &c. Et ut supra.*

Confirmed.   XL. *Item,* We article and object to you, the said Dr Richard Bentley, that some time after the premisses in the next precedent article mentioned, you, the said Dr Bentley, caused the before mentioned indenture, with several erazures, interlineations, and obliterations, made therein, to be again brought into the chapel, in order to have the public seal affixed thereto, but the same was again unanimously rejected by all the sixteen Senior Fellows, who were then assembled together, and at such time, you the said Dr Bentley, sent a threatening message to the said sixteen Seniors so assembled, that in case they persisted in refusing to affix the College seal to such indenture, you would not suffer several leases of other estates belonging to the said College, and for which the fines had been actually paid, or agreed to be paid, to be sealed; but notwithstanding such your threats, the said sixteen Seniors did again refuse to comply with such your illegal and unjust desire: *Hocque, &c. Et ut supra.*

Confirmed. XLI. *Item,* We article and object to you, the said Dr Richard Bentley, that, notwithstanding the premisses, you did on or about the 28th day of November, 1713, in breach of your said oath, and in violation of the said statutes, procure the public seal of the said College to be affixed and put to the afore mentioned indenture of bargain and sale, and alienation of the said piece of ground; and the said estate is thereby wholly alienated from the said College for ever. *Et hoc fuit et est verum et objicimus et articulamur de quolibet alio tempore, &c. Et ut supra.*

Prohibited. XLII. *Item,* We article and object to you, the said Dr Richard Bentley, that you have at several times, since your being Master of the said College, made, and caused several leases to be made, of tithes, arable lands, meadow and pasture, belonging to the said College, without reserving one entire third part, or any part of the rent, to be paid in corn or in money, according to the market price of corn; and more particularly, in the year 1715, a lease of the parsonage of Swines-head, together with the rectory, or free chapel of Barthop, in the county of Lincoln, part of the estate of the said College, was, by your means and procurement, made and granted to one William Whiting, for and at the certain yearly rent of 100*l.* without any reserve of rent to be paid in wheat, or malt, or money, according to the market price thereof, and the sum of 100*l.* was then taken as a fine for the granting thereof. *Hocque, &c. Et objicimus et articulamur de quolibet alio tempore, valore, vel summa, &c. Et ut supra.*

XLIII. *Item,* We article and object to you, the said Dr Richard Bentley, that you have frequently, since your being Master of the said College, made, and caused several leases of estates belonging to the said College to be made and granted to several persons, wherein the price of corn hath been fixed at one certain set rent, for and during the whole term of such lease granted, and a covenant made with such persons, that they should pay their corn rent at one and the same rate and price during the whole term of such leases, as hereafter is mentioned, whereby the whole rent payable for such estates hath been reduced to one certain annual sum of money, notwithstanding that it was at all such times objected to by several of the Fellows then present, that such covenants, and reservations of abatements, were contrary to the true intent and meaning of the statute, and a great diminution of the proper income of the College. *Hocque, &c. Et ut supra.*

Prohibited.   XLIV. *Item,* We article and object to you, the said Dr Richard Bentley, that you did, on or about the 28th day of October, 1701, make and grant a lease of a tenement, close, pasture, and right of common in Shallow, in the county of Lincoln, part of the estate of the said College, for the term of twenty years, to Charles Firebrass, Esq. in which lease a third part of the rent payable for the same is reserved to be paid in wheat; and did cause or procure a clause or covenant to be inserted in such lease, whereby it was agreed, that it shall and may be lawful for the said Charles Firebrass to defalk and abate, during the whole term of such lease, so much out of the proportion of rent to be paid in money, according to the market price of wheat, as the price of wheat should on the market days next before such rent should become due and payable, exceed 4s. 8½d. per bushel; and that several leases of the same estate, with the same clauses and covenants therein inserted, have since the surrender or expiration of the said former lease, been made and granted by your means and procurement to the said Charles Firebrass, Esq. and others. *Hocque, &c. Et objicimus et articulamur de quolibet alio tempore vel summa, &c. Et ut supra.*

Prohibited.   XLV. *Item,* We article and object to you, the said Dr Richard Bentley, that you did, on or about the 15th day of November, 1715, cause or procure a lease of the tithes of corn, belonging to the rectory of Kirby Kendall, in Westmoreland, part of the estate of the said College, but bearing date at or about Christmas 1711, to be made and granted to Josiah Lambert, for a term of twenty years, in which lease a third part of the rent payable for the said tithes is reserved to be paid in corn, viz. in fifteen quarters of wheat, and 107 quarters of malt; and that you, the said Dr Bentley, did cause or procure a covenant to be inserted in such lease, whereby it was and is agreed that the said Josiah Lambert shall and may, during the whole term of such lease, defalk and abate out of the proportion of rent, to be paid in money according to the market price of corn on the market days next before such rent shall become due and payable, so much money as the price of wheat should exceed 1*l.* 13*s.* and half a farthing per quarter, and so much out of the price of malt as should exceed 12*s.* 4*d.* per quarter, whereby you reduced and set the price of wheat to 2*s.* 10½*d.* per bushel, and the price of malt to 1*s.* 6½*d.* per bushel, and not more. *Hocque, &c. Et objicimus et articulamur de quibuslibet aliis tempore, valore, et summa. Et ut supra.*

Prohibited.   XLVI. *Item,* We article and object to you, the said Dr Richard Bentley, that you did, some time in the year 1724, cause, procure, or suffer the said last mentioned lease to be renewed and granted to the said Josiah Lambert, with the same covenants and conditions, and with the same powers of defalcation and abatement, as were granted by the said former lease, and a fine of 250*l.* was then had and taken as a consideration for the renewal thereof. *Hocque, &c. Et objicimus et articulamur de quolibet alio tempore vel summa, &c. Et ut supra.*

Prohibited.   XLVII. *Item,* We article and object to you, the said Dr Richard Bentley, that on or about the second day of November, 1714, you did for and in consideration of a fine of 380*l.* likewise cause or procure a lease to be made and granted to the said Josiah Lambert, and others, of the Rectory of Aisgarth, in the county of York, also part of the estate of the said College, for the term of twenty years, and the third part of the rent payable by such lease for the same, is therein reserved to be paid in corn, viz. one quarter of wheat, and 212 quarters of malt; notwithstanding which, you, the said Dr Bentley, did cause or procure a clause or covenant to be inserted in such lease, whereby it was and is agreed, that the said lessees shall and may, during the whole term of such lease, defalcate and abate out of the proportion of rent to be paid in money, according to the market price of corn on the market days next before such rent should become due and payable, so much money as the price of wheat should exceed 13s. 4d. the quarter, which is after the rate of 20d. per bushel, and not more, and as the price of malt should exceed ten shillings per quarter, which is after the rate of fifteen pence the bushel, and not more. *Hocque, &c. Et objicimus et articulamur de quibuslibet aliis tempore, pretio, valore vel summa, &c. Et ut supra.*

Prohibited. XLVIII. *Item,* We further article and object to you, the said Dr Richard Bentley, that by settling and ascertaining the price of corn at certain and fixed rates in manner as in the preceding articles is mentioned, you have greatly wasted, impaired, and diminished the yearly revenues of the said College, and alienated so much of those revenues as the common and ordinary market price of corn shall exceed the rates by you so set as aforesaid, and particularly by fixing the price of the corn rent for the leases of Kirby Kendall and Aisgarth, at the rates in the two next precedent articles mentioned, you have thereby lessened the yearly revenues of the said College to the amount or value of 160l. per annum, or thereabouts, and thereby violated the 35th of the said statutes of Queen Elizabeth, and incurred the horrid guilt of wilful perjury. *Et hoc fuit et est verum, &c. Et objicimus et articulamur de qualibet alia summa, &c. Et ut supra.*

Prohibited. XLIX. *Item,* We article and object to you, the said Dr Richard Bentley, that on the 28th day of September, 1717, being the market-day in Cambridge, on which the price of corn to be paid to the Colleges for rent for the preceding half year was to be settled, you, the said Dr Bentley, did order and cause your bailiff, John Kent, to bring from St Ives a quarter, or some other quantity of wheat, into the market of Cambridge that day, and did likewise fraudulently invite and procure one —— Rule, a farmer, then living at Rampton, in the county of Cambridge, to bring the same day into the said market a like parcel of wheat, and promised the said —— Rule, that the said wheat should be bought of him at the rate of 5s. the bushel; and you, the said Dr Bentley did oblige and compel one William Porter, the College butler, to buy, and the said William Porter did accordingly on that day buy of them the said Kent and Rule, for the use of the said College, all the wheat so by them brought into Cambridge market that day, at the aforesaid price of 5s. the bushel, although the current and common price of the best wheat in the said market on that day was but 4s. 4d. and the best and highest price thereof was but 4s. 7d. and not more: *Hocque, &c. Et objicimus et articulamur de quolibet alio tempore, pretio, valore vel summa, &c. Et ut supra.*

Prohibited.   L. *Item,* We likewise article and object to you, the said Dr Richard Bentley, that you did on the said 28th day of September, 1717, cause the said John Kent, your bailiff, to bring a load of malt into Cambridge, and carry it to the College brewhouse, without going into the market, and did oblige one —— Barant, the then College brewer, to take the same off his hands, and to take it at the rate or price of 1l. 6s. per quarter, although the highest price of malt sold in the said market that day, was but 1l. 2s. per quarter, and not more: *Hocque, &c. Et objicimus et articulamur de quolibet alio pretio, &c. Et ut supra.*

Prohibited.   LI. *Item,* We article and object to you, the said Dr Richard Bentley, that you having, by the articles aforesaid, raised the price of wheat and malt so much above the real value as in the next preceding article is mentioned, did soon after Michaelmas, 1717, and before the Lady-day following, cause great quantities of your own tythe wheat and barley malted to be sold at the College bake-house and brew-house, at the extravagant price of forty shillings a quarter for wheat, and six and twenty shillings a quarter for malt, and did oblige all the College tenants to pay their wheat rent due for the preceding half year, according to such prices of forty shillings a quarter; and did in the succeeding years 1718 and 1719, oblige the College officers to take off about one hundred quarters of your own damaged malt, and great quantities of your own tythe wheat, at prices far exceeding the market price, upon the respective market days; *Hocque, &c. Et ut supra.*

Confirmed.   LII. *Item*, We article and object to you, the said
Dr Richard Bentley, that you have frequently since
your being admitted Master of the said College, in breach of
your said oath, and in violation of several of the statutes of the
said College, unnecessarily and profusely wasted and expended
several great and excessive sums of money, part of the common
stock of the said College; and particularly in some few years
after your being made Master of the said College, you did
expend or lay out near upon the sum of 2,000*l.* of the College
stock, in altering, fitting up, beautifying and improving the
Lodge belonging to you as Master, which was then in very
good condition and repair, and in no need of any such repara-
tions and improvements; and since that time, and particularly
since the year 1715 or 1716, you have over and above the said
sum of 2,000*l.* exorbitantly and unnecessarily laid out and
expended many other large sums of money out of the College
stock, in making many other unnecessary and superfluous
additional buildings thereto, and in other extravagances;
particularly by causing a double-vaulted cellar to be made or
sunk in your back yard, for keeping your wine cool; by ordering
and causing your garden to be laid out and formed after a new
model, and a terrace to be erected therein by the water-side; by
building a summer-house, or room of entertainment, in the
garden belonging to you as Master, and in that a bath, which
you have caused to be supplied with water and other conveniences for bathing; by converting two edifices belonging to
the College, into a very large and spacious granary, at the
expense of 400*l.* or at least 300*l.* for your own private use, to
carry on the trade or business of a farmer, or maltster, which
you followed for some time; by seizing upon two pieces of
ground belonging to the College, to keep a couple of cows in,
for the use of yourself and family; and by hedging, ditching,
and trenching the same for that purpose; by causing a new
brick house to be built at the back side of the College, for
wintering the said cows, and building three new coach-houses
for the use of particular persons; all which were paid for out of
the College stock, and amounted in the whole to the sum of
2,000*l.* or some other such large sum of money, as by the
accounts of the bursars of the said College, reference being

thereto had, will more fully appear. *Hocque, &c. Et objicimus et articulamur de qualibet alia summa, &c. Et ut supra.*

Confirmed.   LIII. *Item,* We article and object to you, the said Dr Richard Bentley, that you have further unnecessarily and profusely wasted and consumed great part of the common-stock of the said College, by building or causing a fine new country-house or seat to be built upon part of the College estate, at Over, in the county of Cambridge, for the use of yourself and family, fit for the reception of a person of rank and quality, and have already expended therein, though not yet finished, or furnished, more than 800*l.* of the College money; *Hocque, &c. Et objicimus et articulamur de qualibet alia summa, &c. Et ut supra.*

Withdrawn.   LIV. *Item,* We article and object to you, the said Dr Richard Bentley, that Dr John Christopherson, formerly Master of the said College, in the reign of Queen Mary, did by his last will and testament, give and bequeath all his hangings, bedsteads, tables, forms, chairs, wainscot, ceiling, and all the furniture belonging to his kitchen, to the said College, for the use of his successors, Masters of the said College for the time being, upon condition that every successive Master should oblige himself in the sum of two hundred marks to leave the same in as good condition as he found them, as by the said will now remaining among the muniments of the said College, reference being thereunto had, will appear. *Et ut supra.*

Prohibited.   LV. *Item,* We article and object to you, the said Dr Richard Bentley, that you upon your becoming Master of the said College, found the lodge belonging to you as Master, well and sufficiently supplied with all necessary and useful furniture, fit and sufficient for a Master of the said College, all which came to the hands or possession of you, the said Dr Bentley: *Et hoc fuit et est verum, &c. Et ut supra.*

Prohibited.   LVI. *Item,* We article and object to you, the said Dr Richard Bentley, that, notwithstanding the premisses, and notwithstanding there is not any allowance made by the statutes to the Master of the College, for the furniture of his lodge, yet you, the said Dr Bentley, have squandered away great and excessive sums of money out of the College stock, over and above those before-mentioned, for finishing and furnishing the said lodge; and particularly in setting up nine marble chimney-pieces, and furnishing the same with a scarlet cloth bed, and chairs, and stools, a damask bed and quilt, two large looking-glasses, a silk squabb, japan and walnut tables; and in buying a coach for the use of your wife and daughters, and several other goods and furniture, for the use of yourself and family, to the amount or value of 600*l*. 500*l*. or at least 400*l*. sterling; all which charge was by you paid for out of the common stock of the said College. *Hocque, &c. Et objicimus et articulamur de qualibet alia summa, &c. Et ut supra.*

Confirmed.   LVII. *Item,* We article and object to you, the said Dr Richard Bentley, that notwithstanding there is not by any of the statutes of the said College any allowance made to the Master of the said College, for the time being, for bread, beer, fuel, or any other provisions for himself and family at home, yet you the said Dr Bentley, have for these twenty-three years last past, yearly consumed and wasted great and excessive quantities of the common provisions and stores belonging to the College, and applied the same to the use of yourself and private family at home, to the amount of several hundred pounds per annum, viz. in bread, meal and beer to the amount of 150*l*. per annum, or upwards; and at the last audit the expense on that account amounted to 174*l*. in coals and other fuel to the amount some years of more than 100*l*. per annum, as by the College books of account, reference being thereunto had, will appear. *Hocque, &c. Et objicimus, et articulamur de qualibet alia summa, &c. Et ut supra.*

Confirmed.   LVIII. *Item,* We article and object to you, the said Dr Richard Bentley, that you have likewise for these many years past yearly spent and consumed several great sums of money out of the common stock of the said College, for linen and pewter, pretended to be used in your family at home, to the amount or value of 70*l*. 60*l*. or at least 50*l*. per annum; and particularly in the last year, to the amount of 90*l.* as by the College books of accounts, reference being thereunto had, will more fully appear. *Et objicimus et articulamur de qualibet alia summa, &c. Et ut supra.*

Confirmed. LIX. *Item*, We article and object to you, the said Dr Richard Bentley, that you did, sometime in or about the year 1719, fraudulently, unjustly, collusively, and unknown to the respective members of the said College, contract and agree with Mr Serjeant Miller, late one of the Fellows of the said College, to procure and obtain an allowance of 453*l.* to be made to him the said Serjeant out of the College stock, over and above the sum of 100*l.* before to him in hand paid, under pretence of reimbursing him the said Serjeant, the charge it was pretended he had been at, in carrying on a prosecution against you, the said Dr Bentley, before the Right Reverend Father in God, John Moore, late Lord Bishop of Ely, since deceased, as Visitor of the said College, for several great and enormous crimes by you committed, in the execution of your place or office of Master of the said College; but in reality and truth, such contract or agreement relating to the payment or allowance of the said sum of 453*l.* was by you made with no other design, view, or invention, than to avoid the pursuit of justice, and to engage and oblige the said Serjeant to withdraw a certain petition, that had been presented to his late Majesty King George I. on behalf of several of the Fellows of the said College, in order to ascertain the visitatorial power, and which the said Serjeant had by the said Fellows been entrusted to prosecute. *Hocque, &c. Et objicimus et articulamur de quolibet alio tempore et de qualibet alia summa, &c. Et ut supra.*

Confirmed. LX. *Item*, We article and object to you, the said Dr Richard Bentley, that in pursuance of such agreement you did, on the 19th day of June, 1719, at a meeting of the Senior Fellows of the said College, propose and insist to have the said sum of 453*l.* allowed and paid to the said Serjeant Miller out of the common stock of the said College, upon the pretence in the next precedent article mentioned, and at the same time insisted and peremptorily demanded to have the sum of 500*l*. paid or allowed to yourself out of the same stock, to reimburse you the charges which you pretended you had been at in defending yourself against such prosecution, but that such proposal and demands were all rejected by a majority of the Seniors then present; notwithstanding which, you the said Dr Richard Bentley did, on or about the 5th of December following, by vile and indirect practices, in the absence of three of the eight Senior Fellows of the College, and against the consent of three of those present, procure an order or conclusion to be made or passed by other Fellows of the College, not of the Seniority, nor deputed by any of the three absent Seniors, to allow and pay out of the College stock to the said Serjeant the said sum of 453*l*. and to yourself the aforesaid sum of 500*l*. upon the several pretences before mentioned; and that the said sums of 453*l*. and 500*l*. were afterwards paid to the said Serjeant Miller, and to you the said Dr Bentley, by virtue of such pretended order or conclusion, out of the common stock of the said College, to the great waste and diminution thereof, and to the great prejudice of the respective members of the said College. *Hocque, &c. et objicimus et articulamur de quibuslibet aliis tempore et summa, &c. Et ut supra.*

Confirmed.   LXI. *Item*, We article and object to you, the said Dr Richard Bentley, that the said Serjeant Miller, in consideration of the said sum of 453*l*. so paid to him out of the College stock or treasury, as before set forth, did, by a writing or instrument under his hand and seal, bearing date the 19th day of December, 1719, covenant and agree, that he would not at any time after prosecute or proceed upon the before-mentioned petition to his said late Majesty, but would withdraw, or cause the same to be withdrawn, and do all other acts in his power towards the preventing or hindering any further prosecution thereupon, as by the said writing or instrument now in the College registry, reference being thereto had, will appear. And the said Serjeant Miller did never afterwards follow or prosecute the said petition, or do or cause any act to be done thereupon, and hath ever since refused, and doth still refuse to deliver up all such papers, writings, and instruments as were entrusted in his hands, in order to carry on such prosecution.

Hocque, &c. Et objicimus et articulamur de quolibet alio tempore,
&c. Et ut supra.

Withdrawn.   LXII. *Item,* We article and object to you, the said
Dr Richard Bentley, that notwithstanding you are
by your oath, and by the 29th of the said statutes, obliged to
preserve all the moveables of the College, and to take care that
the Senior Dean and Junior Bursar do every year within one
month after their admission into their respective offices, make
or cause to be made two perfect inventories of all the goods,
moveables, plate, and other things belonging to the said College, one of such inventories to be deposited in the public
treasury, and the other with the Vice-master for the time being,
and at the same time to take an exact account of such goods,
moveables, plate, &c. as shall be at that time missing, by comparing such inventories with those made in the preceding year:
but for these ten years last past, and upwards, no such inventories
have at any time been made, neither have you at any time called
upon or required the Senior Dean and Junior Bursar, or either
of them, to perform their duty according to the said statute; nor
have you ever censured or punished them for their neglect therein, as by the statutes of the said College you are obliged and
ought to have done; by reason whereof a considerable part of the
College plate hath been for several years last past and is now
missing out of the College treasury, and no examination or
inquiry hath been made after it by you, the said Dr Bentley.
Hocque, &c. Et objicimus et articulamur de qualibet alia quantitate,
&c. Et ut supra.

Withdrawn.   LXIII. *Item,* We article and object to you, the
said Dr Richard Bentley, that by the 33d of the
said statutes it is (*inter alia*) ordained and provided, that the
Bursars and Steward of the said College, for the time being,
shall bring their respective accounts to be examined by the
Master, or in his absence by the Vice-master, and the eight Senior
Fellows of the said College, at the end of every quarter; but that
such accounts have not once, during the whole time that you have
been Master of the said College, been brought in and examined
according to the directions and intent of the said statute. And

when one of the Seniors demanded and insisted to have the accounts examined quarterly, pursuant to the said statute, you, the said Dr Bentley, replied, with great disdain, 'Don't tell me of statutes.' *Hocque, &c. Et ut supra.*

Withdrawn. LXIV. *Item,* We article and object to you, the said Dr Richard Bentley, that at the general audit of the accounts of the whole College, which is by the said last mentioned statute appointed to be on the 4th of December yearly, these accounts have for many years past, been passed in gross only, without entering into any particulars, or examining vouchers for any of the sums said to be expended therein; and at several times, and more particularly in the year 1715, when one of the Seniors at such meeting demanded that the orders by which great sums of the College money had been paid and laid out should be produced, and particulars of general sums specified, and the vouchers thereupon examined, you, the said Dr Bentley, with great insolence and foul language, hindered and prevented such examination, and by reason of your ill-treatment and behaviour, no objection hath of late been made to the accounts concerning the extravagant sums laid out upon the lodge, garden, and additional buildings, upon the aforesaid house at Over; nor to an article of 400*l.* demanded for velvet, and other materials said to be used in the Chapel; nor no inquiry made after the College plate so as aforesaid embezzled, lost, or missing; nor after the great sums of money laid out and expended in bread, beer, coals, and other fuel, linen, pewter, and other things for the use of you, the said Dr Bentley and your family, as in the precedent articles is mentioned.

LXV. *Item, Quod præmissa, &c.*

Appendix II

Dr Bentley's Defensive Plea
June 23, 1733

Article VI.   1. Whereas it is alleged in the sixth article of the pretended articles, exhibited and objected to the said Dr Bentley, to the effect following, to wit, 'That by the second chapter of the statutes of Trinity College, it is amongst other things ordained and provided, that the Master of the said College for the time being, shall be a person no less eminent above other members of the said College in his piety and integrity of life, than he is superior to them in the dignity of his place, notwithstanding which, he, the said Richard Bentley, hath for more than twenty years past, in violation of the said statute, lived a very irreligious life, and notoriously neglected the public worship of God.' It is therein alleged falsely and untruly, and the truth was and is, that the said Dr Bentley always was and is a devout, pious, and religious man, and was always accounted, reputed, and esteemed so to be, and this was and is true; and so much the said Robert Johnson hath heard and doth know and believe in his conscience to be true, and the party proponent doth allege and propound every thing jointly and severally.

2. And whereas it is also alleged in the said sixth article, of the said articles, that the said Dr Bentley, for more than twenty years last past, preceding the time of exhibiting the said articles, did notoriously neglect the public worship of God, and particularly by constantly and habitually absenting himself from divine service in the chapel of the said College, at the usual hours of morning and evening prayers: It is therein alleged falsely and untruly, and the truth was and is, that the said Dr Bentley, from the time of his being made Master of the College, and until he was about fifty years of age, which was about the year 1709, the said Dr Bentley constantly attended morning and evening prayers in the chapel, and that from that

s   273

time the infirmity of his constitution prevented his attending morning prayers, when at five or six o'clock in the morning, but he always attended when morning prayers were later at the times of celebrating the sacrament: That from 1709 he constantly attended evening prayers in summer, till he was about sixty years of age, which was about the year 1718 or 1719. That about that time the infirmity of his age and a tenderness contracted by his sedentary and studious life prevented his being so constant at evening prayers as he before had been. But the said Doctor, from about the said year 1718 to 1725 or 1726, was frequently at evening prayers, and at the celebration of the sacrament always when his health permitted. That from about the year 1718, when his age and the tenderness contracted as aforesaid, subjected him to almost constant colds and dangerous coughs by changing his habit and putting on a collegiate or academic one, yet he was so unwilling to be prevented attending chapel so constantly as he before had done, that in order to enable himself to stay in that spacious chapel, and to secure him from the cold and damp of the marble, the necessary time of prayers and administering the sacrament, he had a carpet carried by his servant to chapel for that purpose; but as his age and tenderness increased, and all means he could use proving ineffectual to prevent his indisposition, which he almost constantly contracted by being in so spacious a room in his collegiate or academic habit, about the year 1725 or 1726, two or three years before the said articles were exhibited, he was necessitated to decline going thither, or to any other place out of his own house, by advice of his physicians. And this was and is true, and the party proponent doth allege and propound as before.

3. That accordingly from that time the said Dr Bentley hath not, by reason of his tenderness and indisposition, gone out of his own house to visit any one Fellow of his own Society, or any one acquaintance in the University, nor once been in the College-hall, even at any public festival, though it adjoins to his own apartments. That from that time also, he being the King's Professor in Divinity, he has been forced to obtain a deputy at his own annual and considerable expense, to preside in his stead at disputations. That since that time, when his present Majesty did the University the honour of a visit, it

being the duty of the King's Professor in Divinity to receive him with a Latin oration in the University Schools, he, the said Doctor, performing the said exercise in person, did thereby get such an illness that he was for several days very dangerously ill, and accounted by his physicians as a dying man, and the party proponent doth allege and propound as before.

Articles X, XI. 4. That during all the time the said Dr Bentley hath been Master of the said College, there have been every year at least the number necessarily required by statute, and generally more, College preachers in his time, than there were in his predecessor's time for the like number of years, as appears by the College books and appointments of College preachers, to which the party proponent refers himself, and this was and is true, and the party proponent doth allege and propound as before.

5. That the Catechetical Lectures being by statute appointed only in order for the College preachers to be more commodiously chosen out of them, and there having never been a defective number of College preachers, there was not any necessity of appointing Catechetical Lecturers in order to choose College Preachers. But, however, there have been three times as many in the said Dr Bentley's time, as there were in the same number of years in his immediate predecessor's time, as appears by the usual appointments of lecturers, and this was and is true, and the party proponent doth allege and propound as before.

Articles XII, XIII. 6. That it does appear by the College books, to which the party proponent refers himself, that Mr Malled, who is alleged in the twelfth and thirteenth articles to have been refused to be put up to catechise in the year 1719, was actually put up for that purpose on the 4th of June, 1716, and so continued in 1719; and this was and is true, and the party proponent doth allege and propound as before.

Articles XXVII, XXVIII, XXIX. 7. That Dr Bentley was not present at, or any way privy to, the putting the seal to the instrument mentioned in the twenty-ninth article of the said articles objected to the said Dr Bentley. But the same was put in his absence by the Vice-master, after a meeting duly summoned, and agreed to be put by a majority of the sixteen seniors; and this was and is true, and the party proponent doth allege and propound as before.

8. That by the statutes as well as the usage of the College, the seal is not required to be put to any instruments in the presence of the sixteen seniors in College. For that by the said usage and statutes, the sixteen seniors in College are to be duly summoned, and if a majority of the said sixteen seniors agree to the putting of the seal, with the consent of the Master, or in his absence the Vice-master, the same is to be put accordingly. But in case any of the sixteen seniors in College shall not appear at the said meeting, the next senior Fellow in College in course, is to supply the vacancy; and this was and is true, and the party proponent doth allege and propound as before.

9. That it doth not appear by any of the College books that the seniors going out of College, have deputed any persons to act for them, or that ever any such deputations were made. But all College acts have been done at meetings composed of the proper seniors, and the next immediate seniors resident in College, without any deputation from the absent seniors; and this was and is true, and the party proponent doth allege and propound as before.

Article XXX. 10. That the meetings to transact the College affairs are appointed by the Master, or Vice-master, and the seniors are thereto always summoned, according as they appear in seniority resident in the College Books. And the said Dr Bentley hath not at any time given orders for summoning any persons in particular, but only in general to summon the seniors in the same manner as hath been always customary; and upon the 9th day of August, 1728, the sixteen seniors resident in College were duly summoned for the meeting upon the day following, being the 10th day of August, the day mentioned in the thirtieth article of the said articles. That sixteen Fellows duly assembled, of whom were the fifteen proper seniors then resident in College; that Mr Myers, who was the sixteenth proper senior then resident, and who had been duly summoned, but not attending, the next Fellow in seniority to him was summoned, and did assemble on the said

10th day of August, and the seal was put to the petition mentioned in the said article, by the direction of thirteen, or at least twelve, of the said sixteen so assembled; and that no juniors were purposely sent for, nor were any Fellows at that time resident in College absent from the said meeting who were of longer standing than any of those present, except Mr Myers, as aforesaid; and this was and is true, and the party proponent doth allege and propound as before.

11. That the Promoter himself being one of the sixteen so assembled, was so far conscious that the said assembly was regular, that though he, together with Dr Colbatch, the Casuistical Professor, and Mr Thomas Parne, two other Fellows of the said College, assembled on that occasion, did on that day draw up and deliver a protest in writing against the setting the seal to the said petition, yet he or they did not in the said protest even suggest that the said assembly had not been duly summoned, or that there were not sixteen assembled, or that the said sixteen were not the proper seniors resident in College; the said protest being founded wholly on the subject-matter of the instrument tendered to be sealed, and not on any irregularity of the said assembly, either as to the manner of summoning them, the impropriety of persons assembled, or the defect of the sufficient number; and this was and is true, and the party proponent doth allege and propound as before.

12. In supply of proof of the preceding article, the party proponent doth exhibit and hereunto annex the said original protest, and doth allege that the same is subscribed by and with the proper hand-writing of the said Dr Colbatch, Mr Parne, and the said Robert Johnson, the Promoter in this cause; and so much was and is true, and the party proponent doth allege and propound as before.

Articles XXXVIII, XXXIX, XL, XLI.   13. That the close, or piece of inclosed ground, in the parish of Kirby Kendal, in the thirty-eighth article mentioned, was copyhold of inheritance, and held by ——— Copland, of and from the said College, who were lords of the manor the same was held of, under a quit-rent of four shillings a year, and other duties and services. That the said Copland did, in 1708, mortgage the same to Mr Robert Shepheard, of Natland, in Westmoreland, and Mr William Wilson, of Kirkland, in the said county, for the sum of 34*l.*; that soon after the said Copland was convicted of felony, and was executed for the same, whereby the said piece of ground escheated to the said College, as lords of the said manor, subject to the said mortgage. That the charge of conviction of the said Copland amounted to ten pounds, and the said Copland leaving a wife and several small children, the neighbouring gentlemen and justices of the Peace petitioned the College not to take advantage of the said escheat, in compassion to the poverty of the said widow and family; that the said College, finding the annual value of the said piece of ground to be 3*l.* a year, agreed to re-grant out the same to Mr Josiah Lambert, he paying for the same 64*l.* out of which 44*l.* 15*s.* was to be deducted for the said mortgage and charge of conviction, and of the remaining, 19*l.* 5*s.* 9*l.* 5*s.* was given by the College as an act of charity to the said widow, and books were bought into the College Library with the remaining sum of 10*l.*; and this was and is true, and so much does appear by the College books, and an agreement of the Master and Seniors assembled together in 1712, in order to regrant the same; and this was and is true, and the party proponent doth allege and propound as before.

14. That the said piece of ground is not alienated for ever, nor by the deeds of conveyance purported to be so; but the same was only regranted out by the College to the said Josiah Lambert for life, only to be held of the said College at their will, under the same rents, dues, duties, and services, which the said —— Copland held the same by, as by the said original deed remaining in the said College will appear, and which, as lords of the said manor, they were enabled to do, in order to preserve and support their manor; and this was and is true, and the party proponent doth allege and propound as before.

Article LII.   15. That when the said Dr Bentley was made Master, the Master's lodge was in a very ruinous condition, little or nothing having been done towards repairing of it from the year 1640; and towards the repairs of the said lodge the said Dr Bentley gave out of his own proper money, in the year 1700, the sum of 100*l*. sterling; and in the same year, the said lodge being a considerable part of the fabric of the College, the Master and the eight Seniors finding the same to be much out of repair, unanimously agreed and ordered that the said lodge should be repaired, and finished, with new ceiling, wainscot, flooring, and other convenient improvements, which by the said statutes of the said College they have the power to do; and this was and is true, and the party proponent doth allege and propound as before.

16. That in pursuance of the said order, now remaining in the College books, the same was repaired and fitted up with convenient improvements, which did amount to the sum of 117*l*. and no more, which was necessary to be laid out thereon, and that the several sums of money which have been at any time laid out on the said lodge, and improvements of it, were ordered and approved of by the Master and Senior Fellows of the said College; and that the rest of the said fabric hath had as much laid out in repairing the same in Dr Bentley's time as the lodge hath had in proportion; and the said lodge is not in better condition, or better fitted up, than the lodges of several other Masters in the said University, though it is the residence of the Royal Family when they honour the University with their presence, as also of the Lords the Judges in their circuits; and this was and is true, and the party proponent doth allege and propound as before.

17. That about the year 1718, or 1719, the said Dr Bentley's infirmities and indispositions requiring a milk diet, and there being two pieces of ground belonging and near to the said College, in which the Senior Fellows had a right to turn their horses, and which were not of the yearly value of twenty shillings, he, the said Dr Bentley did apply to the said Seniors to hire the same of them, in order to keep a cow or two, at the yearly rent of two guineas, which the said Seniors let him have in the year 1720, at the said rent, by an order of the College for that purpose; and the same were not then, or at any other time, seized by him, as is falsely alleged in the fifty-second article exhibited against him; and this was and is true, and the party proponent doth allege and propound as before.

18. That the College being exempted from paying the duty of excise for beer brewed in their own brewhouse for their own use, and there being an old pigeon-house, with a lumber-room adjoining, belonging to the College, the same were fitted up by the approbation of the Seniors, for a place to lay the College stores, or grain in, when they should have occasion; but the said Dr Bentley did not convert the said two edifices, or any other edifices, into a large spacious granary, at the expense of 400*l.* or any other sum, for his own private use, to carry on the trade of a farmer, or maltster, as is falsely alleged in the said fifty-second article, which trade he never at any time used or followed, or ever used the said edifices or granary for his own use, or for any such like purpose; and this was and is true, and the party proponent doth allege and propound as before.

19. That whereas it is alleged in the said fifty-second article exhibited against the said Dr Bentley, that the said Dr Bentley hath, since the year 1715 or 1716, exorbitantly and unnecessarily laid out 2,000*l.* of the College stock on his lodge, garden, and other buildings, which in the said article are mentioned, it is therein alleged, falsely and untruly; and the truth was and is, that the sum of money laid out thereon did amount to 911*l.* and not more. And that in October, 1717, when his late Majesty, King George the First, designed to honour the University with his presence, some of his Majesty's surveyors being sent before to view the presence-room, called 'Henry the Eighth's Chamber,' and other rooms for his Majesty's entertainment, at the said Dr Bentley's lodge, the walls of the said chambers were found so decayed and weak, that they were then ordered to be underpropped and shored up for his Majesty's security during his stay there, and were thereupon pulled down and rebuilt, and a considerable part of the said 911*l.* were laid out in the same, and the rest thereof in the other buildings belonging to the College, and the whole sum was paid by order of the Seniors of the said College; and the party proponent doth allege that the other buildings mentioned in the said fifty-second article, and pretended to have been built for the use of the Master, in the back side of the said College, were not built for the use of the Master, as is falsely alleged in the said article, but for the use and conveniency of the Fellows of the said College; and this was

and is true, and the party proponent doth allege and pro-pound as before.

20. That whereas it is alleged in the said fifty-second article that Dr Bentley had made himself a bath in his garden, and caused it be supplied with water and other conveniences for bathing, the party proponent doth allege that there was a fountain near the place where the said bath now is, when the said Dr Bentley first came to be Master of the said College, and that the pipe which had for a century or two before supplied the same with water, was only lengthened by an addition of two feet of lead to supply the cistern of the said bath, and that there is no other summer-house in the said garden save the said bath; and this was and is true, and the party proponent doth allege and propound as before.

Article LIII. 21. And whereas it is alleged in the fifty-third article, that Dr Bentley built a fine new country house upon part of the College estate at Over, for the use of himself and family, fit for the reception of a person of rank and quality, which cost eight hundred pounds of the College money, though not then finished or furnished; it is therein alleged falsely and untruly, and the truth was and is, that the College being endowed with the great tithes of the parish of Over, and the glebe land belonging to said rectory and the parsonage-house being fallen to decay, by a former tenant running out his lease, it was agreed by the Master and Senior Fellows of the said College, to rebuild the said parsonage-house, which was done accordingly; that as the vicarage of the said parish is in the gift of the said College, and the vicar has no house to live in, and the profits of the said vicarage are exceed-ingly small, it was thought proper to rebuild the said house, so that it might not be inconvenient to the tenant or lessee of the rectory to let the vicar for the time being have two rooms or a floor for his use when necessary; that when the said house was rebuilt it was in lease to a tenant, and was so at the time the said articles were exhibited; that it was not built by Dr Bentley for the use of himself or family, that neither the said Doctor nor any of his family ever lived there, nor was any of his family ever there, or the Doctor himself, save only once when he went with the Seniors to view the said estate; that the said place is so far from being fit for the reception of a person of rank and quality, or for the residence of any person who can live elsewhere, that it is situate in the worst, the most dirty and unhealthful part of Cambridgeshire, on the brink of the great level of the Fen, and worse supplied with conveniences of life than any village in the said county; and this was and is true, and the party proponent doth allege and propound as before.

Article LVII. 22. That whereas it is alleged in the fifty-seventh article, that there is not any allowance by any of the statutes to the Master of the College for bread, beer, fuel, or other provisions for himself and family at home, yet, notwithstanding, that he hath consumed great quantities of the stores of the College to the amount of several hundred pounds a year; the party proponent doth allege that the said Dr Bentley hath never since he was Master of the said College received so much of the stock or stores of the College, or any other profits whatsoever from it, as by the statutes of the said College he is intitled to, due allowance being made for the decrease of the value of money, from the time when the statutes were given to the time of exhibiting the said articles; the Master of the said College having an allowance, by the 43d chapter of the said statutes, of 104l. a year for stipend and commons or provisions, and 4l. a year for livery, besides three servants and three horses to be kept and maintained at the College expense for his use; and by the 22d chapter of the said statutes, no deduction is to be made from his allowance for commons or provisions at such times as he shall be absent from the said College, as by the said 43d and 22d chapters of the said statutes, reference being thereunto had, may more fully appear; and this was and is true, and the party proponent doth allege and propound as before.

23. That whereas it is alleged in the said fifty-seventh article, that the said Dr Bentley hath consumed in bread, beer, and meal, one hundred and fifty pounds a year, it is therein alleged falsely and untruly, and the truth was and is, that he has not consumed in bread, beer, or meal a hundred pounds a year; and this was and is true, and the party proponent doth allege and propound as before.

Article LVIII. 24. That whereas it is likewise alleged in the fifty-eighth article, that Dr Bentley in the last year before the said articles were exhibited, spent of the College stock in linen and pewter ninety pounds, as will appear by the said College books; it is therein untruly alleged, and the truth was and is, that the said Dr Bentley had allowed him only in the said books thirty-five pounds three shillings and eight pence half-penny, as by the said books will appear; and this was and is true, and the party proponent doth allege and propound as before.

Articles LIX, 25. That some of the Fellows of the College LX, LXI. having in the year 1711 and afterwards, employed Mr Serjeant Miller in carrying on their contests in relation to some collegiate rights claimed by them before the Right Reverend Bishop Moore, the then Lord Bishop of Ely; and in carrying on a pretended prosecution against the said Dr Bentley, before the said Lord Bishop of Ely, and afterwards on the said Bishop Moore's death, a petition or two to his late Majesty in Council, and his said late Majesty or his Privy Council not proceeding therein, and the said Mr Miller being urgent on some of the Fellows for the expence he had been at on their account, it was in 1719, by some of the said Fellows mentioned to the said Dr Bentley, that it might probably be the opinion of his said late Majesty and his Honourable Privy Council, that the matters in difference should be ended and accommodated by themselves, and the said Dr Bentley was desired by the said Fellows to take the opinion of some of the King's learned counsel on a question to the following effect: whether, as the said contest carried on before Bishop Moore had been concerning some collegiate rights, concerning which the Fellows of the said Society had been near equally divided in their opinions, and no decision of the same had been made, the College might not equitably and justifiably pay the expenses of both sides out of the common stock of the said College, after the dividends to the Fellows and Scholars were paid, which question being thereupon stated to Mr Reeve and Mr Lutwyche, they were both of opinion the College might do so;

and this was and is true, and the party proponent doth allege and propound as before.

26. That some of the Fellows of the said College, in or about the month of July or August 1719, informed the said Dr Bentley, that many of the Fellows of the College being very desirous that an end might be put to the contests which had so long disturbed the College, had drawn up a certificate to the following effect, viz. 'I hereby declare that I sincerely wish that an end may be put to the contests depending, which have for so long time disturbed the College, and in order thereto, I desire that the charges of each side may be defrayed out of the public stock of the College'; and that the said certificate, or one to that effect, was at that time signed by two-thirds of the Fellows of the College, of whom the said Robert Johnson, the promoter, was one; and this was and is true, and the part proponent doth allege and propound as before.

27. That some time after (viz.), on the fifth day of December, 1719, during the stated annual statutable meeting of the Seniors, one of the senior Fellows of the College, came to Dr Bentley from the said meeting, and desired of him that, as so many of the Fellows had so fully declared their desire that an end might be put to the said contests, and the charges of both sides defrayed out of the common stock of the College, he would propose the said question to the Seniors, and call a meeting for that purpose, which accordingly the said Dr Bentley caused to be duly summoned, and the eight senior Fellows then residing in College, in pursuance of such summons assembled accordingly, when it was agreed by a majority of them, that the charges of both sides should be defrayed out of the common stock, and Mr Miller should give a discharge to every member of the said College for all claims occasioned by or depending on the said law-suit, but that no part of the charges of the said law-suit should be in any year paid, unless the College was in such a state of plenty that a whole dividend was first voted. And the said Dr Bentley did not make use of any indirect practices in order to obtain the consent of the Seniors so assembled; but the same was agreed to voluntarily and freely by five of the eight Seniors together with the said Master, so as afore-said summoned and assembled; and this was and is true,

and the party proponent doth allege and propound as before.

28. That whereas it is alleged in the fifty-ninth article, that Dr Bentley did fraudulently, unjustly, collusively, and unknown to the several members of the said College, make the contract and agreement in the said article referred to, with the said Serjeant Miller; the same is falsely and untruly alleged, and the truth was and is, that the said agreement was not only well-known to the several members of the College, but desired by them, and was agreed to by him at their desire, he, the said Dr Bentley, having had no intercourse by himself or any agent with the said Mr Miller for several years before the said agreement was entered into, nor had he any, either at that time or since, the persons who settled the same being agents for the College; and this was and is true, and well known to the promoter in this cause, and the party proponent doth allege and propound as before.

29. That whereas it is alleged in the said fifty-ninth article, that the contract or agreement with Mr Serjeant Miller, relating to the payment or allowance of four hundred and fifty-three pounds to him the said Serjeant Miller, was made by Dr Bentley with a view only to avoid the pursuit of justice, by engaging the said Serjeant to withdraw a certain petition that had been presented to his said late Majesty, in order to ascertain the visitatorial power; it is therein alleged falsely and untruly, and the truth was and is, that the only motive the said Dr Bentley had in coming into the said agreement, was the restoring the peace and quiet of the College, which the greatest part of the College so earnestly desired, and in that sense it was taken and understood by the then Fellows of the College, or the major part of them; and that he, the said Dr Bentley, was so far from avoiding to have the visitatorial power settled, that it was what he always wished and endeavoured to have done, and had even himself petitioned the Crown to direct the same to be settled before any of the said articles were exhibited; and this was and is true, and the party proponent doth allege and propound as before.

30. That whereas it is alleged in the said fifty-ninth article, that Dr Bentley procured the aforesaid sum of four hundred and fifty-three pounds to be paid to the said Serjeant out of the

College stock, over and above the sum of one hundred pounds to him before in hand paid; it is also falsely and untruly alleged, and the truth was and is, that the said sum of one hundred pounds was not paid to the said Serjeant by order or consent of the said Dr Bentley, but that the same and several other sums which had before been paid out of the said stock to the said Serjeant, were actually paid without and against his the said Dr Bentley's consent, and were paid the said Serjeant by the then Seniors in 1710 or 1711, and their adherents, to encourage him, the said Serjeant, to go on with the prosecution before Bishop Moore, against him, the said Dr Bentley; and this was and is true, and the party proponent doth allege and propound as before.

31. Whereas it is further alleged in the sixty-first of the said pretended articles, that the said Serjeant Miller in consideration of four hundred and fifty-three pounds, did by writing or instrument under his hand and seal, bearing date the nineteenth day of December, 1719, covenant and agree that he would not at any time after prosecute or proceed upon the before-mentioned petition to his said late Majesty, but would withdraw, or cause the same to be withdrawn; the party proponent doth allege, that at the meeting of the Master and Seniors, had on the fifth day of December, 1719, it was by a majority then present ordered and agreed, that the said Mr Miller should release the several Fellows of the said College from all demands he had upon them upon any account whatsoever; but that no order or agreement was then made that the said petition should be withdrawn; and if there be any such covenant in the said writing or instrument, the same was therein inserted at the desire of the promoter or others, the agents for the said Fellows, and not at the desire of the said Dr Bentley, he, the said Dr Bentley, having always been desirous, and having several times endeavoured to have the said visitatorial power ascertained by a judicial or other proper determination; and the party proponent doth allege, that the said Dr Bentley consented to the aforesaid agreement, at the desire of the major part of all the Fellows of the said College, who well liked and approved thereof, and in order to restore the peace of the said College, and that all or most of the said Fellows having been one way or other concerned in the said disputes, were desirous the same might be amicably adjusted,

and that the expense thereof might be paid out of the said College stock in the manner before set forth, as by the law and statutes of the said College they were empowered to do.

Appendix III

On Dr Bentley's Non-attendance
at Chapel

At his second trial at Ely House much was said about the master's favourite excuse about his health. Counsel made scathing remarks on the fact that there was 'something so odd, something so peculiar in his constitution, that the chapel should be the only place that did not agree with it'. Witnesses, especially from among his servants, were of the opinion that the doctor had a strong constitution and was of a healthy, robust constitution, that he was not kept abed a day in ten years although he often complained of the cold, that he was often walking in his garden while the bell was ringing for chapel or seen looking out of his window while others were going to chapel, that he might go to chapel when prayers were at nine, but not when they were at seven, that he always attended when the judges were entertained at the lodge or when the king was visiting. It was particularly noticed that he would come to chapel when there was an entertainment of music, and made more regular visits after he had been deprived of his degrees or when he was at his trial before Bishop Moore. What seems to have irked people especially was that he was never deterred by ill health from dining out in London or going on a fishing party, and that his frequent visits to London seemed to take no account of the season or the weather. The time came when his attendance at chapel was regarded as 'an extraordinary occurrence', noticed by the undergraduates, and an occasion for speculation as to what the cause might be. At the Master's Lodge, morning prayers were said while he was in his study, but he read evening prayers himself for his household.

Appendix IV

A Specimen of Dr Bentley's Efforts at English Verse

Apart from the surviving college exercise, 'The Papists' Conspiracy by Gunpowder' (p. 42 above), the only English verses which Bentley is known to have written were an Imitation of Horace Book III Ode II, which he was moved to write after reading (and admiring) an attempt at it by a Trinity student. Young Walter Titley's verses are to be found in Monk's *Life* (pp. 470–1), as are Bentley's. Dr Johnson is recorded by Boswell as having said of them: 'They are the forcible verses of a man of a strong mind, but not accustomed to write verse.'

> Who strives to mount Parnassus' hill,
>   And thence poetick laurels bring,
> Must first acquire due force and skill,
>   Must fly with swan's or eagle's wing.

> Who Nature's treasures would explore,
>   Her mysteries and arcana know;
> Must high as lofty Newton soar,
>   Must stoop as delving Woodward low.

> Who studies ancient laws and rites
>   Tongues, arts, and arms, and history;
> Must drudge, like Selden, days and nights,
>   And in the endless labour die.

> Who travels in religious jars,
>   (Truth mixt with errour, shades with rays;)
> Like Whiston, wanting pyx or stars,
>   In ocean wide or sinks or strays.

But grant our hero's hope, long toil
  And comprehensive genius crown,
All sciences, all arts his spoil,
  Yet what reward, or what renown?

Envy, innate in vulgar souls,
  Envy steps in and stops his rise,
Envy with poison'd tarnish fouls
  His lustre, and his worth decries.

He lives inglorious or in want,
  To college and old books confin'd;
Instead of learn'd he's call'd pedant,
  Dunces advanc'd, he's left behind:
Yet left content a genuine Stoick he,
  Great without patron, rich without South Sea.

Appendix V

About Bentley:
Instead of a Bibliography

Fons et origo of all that has been, and is likely to be, written on Bentley, is of course the *Life* by J. H. Monk. The quarto of 1830 resembles a family bible and needs a lectern or a reading-desk for handling The two-volume octavo second edition of 1833 is easily manageable by the ordinary reader. Monk's is one of the great 'suppressed' biographies of English literature, in the sense that Disraeli called Lord Shelburne 'one of the suppressed characters of English history'. It lacks the genius of Boswell's *Johnson* or the grace of Lockhart's *Scott*. But it does not weigh down on its subject with the tomb-like oppression of the standard Victorian *Life and Letters*. Not even a dean of Peterborough composing the life of an arch-deacon of Ely on the eve of the Victorian Age could inflict *rigor mortis* on Richard Bentley. After more than a quarter of a million words of generally marmoreal prose, the man remains alive and kicking. Skipping is not only to be permitted but to be encouraged, though the appendices which give the articles exhibited against the Master should on no account be missed. (Those relating to his trial before Bishop Greene are reprinted in the present volume as Appendix I. See also page 226 above.)

R. C. Jebb's *Bentley* in the English Men of Letters, 1882, is a wholly charming and accessible little book by one of the most learned Greek scholars of the nineteenth century, and, what is more rare, an elegant and readable writer of English prose. Jebb explains in his preface what is distinctive in his book. It was unlikely that he, or anybody else, could add anything important to Bentley's biography, but he has much of value to say about his works. Contributing to a series on 'English Men of Letters', he has half a dozen pages in his eleventh chapter on Bentley as a writer of English, an aspect of his genius that has never been sufficiently appraised.

Hartley Coleridge included an essay on Bentley in his *Biographia Borealis*, or *Lives of distinguished northerns*, 1833. It appears also in his *Worthies of Yorkshire and Lancashire*, 1836. It is a summary of Monk's *Life* along with a few impolite remarks on lack of synonymity of the terms 'scholar' and 'gentleman'.

Infinitely more worth reading is Thomas de Quincey's essay, included in Vol. VII of his *Works*, London, 1854–60. It was a review of Monk's *Life*, and, although it contains a summary of the life of Bentley, it is in the main an enthusiastic appraisal of the great scholar by a devoted champion of Greek and Latin literature. He is as indiscriminate in his praise for his hero as he is unjust to his enemies. 'In spite of vulgar prejudice,' he tells us roundly, 'Bentley was eminently right, and the College infamously wrong.' As for Dr Colbatch, he was 'a malicious old toad', a judgment that would have pleased Bentley himself. In a mealy-mouthed age and generation, de Quincey is refreshment to the spirit. Professor Jebb thought that de Quincey's 'whimsical judgments' need not be taken too seriously, but they deserve to be read by anyone who cares to experience some of the passionate partisanship he once aroused.

Macaulay's essay on *Sir William Temple* (1838) celebrates Bentley's victory in the Phalaris controversy with all the fervour of a Cambridge man rejoicing in his university's victory in the Boat Race. It is written with Macaulay's customary brilliance, but it leaves the impression that the Battle of the Books was a storm in a tea-cup, stirred up by Providence, or Clio, for the greater glory of Bentley and the University of Cambridge.

There are two twentieth-century examples of the literary essayist's treatment of the Bentley story in the acidulated-comic manner of the Bloomsbury school: Lytton Strachey's *Sad Story of Dr Colbatch* (1923, *Portraits in Miniature*), and Virginia Woolf's *Dr Bentley, an Outline*, included in the first volume of *The Common Reader* (1925).

* * *

Richard Bentley's *Works*, edited by Alexander Dyce, supplies an accessible text for English readers:
Volumes I and II contain both his essays on *The Letters of Phalaris* (1697 and 1699), and *Epistola ad Joannem Millium.*

Volume III contains the *Boyle Lectures*, together with letters Newton wrote to him on his employment of *Principia Mathematica*; together with the *Sermon on Popery, Remarks upon Free-thinking* a propos of Anthony Collins, the *Proposals* for an edition of the New Testament, and his *Answer* to the *Remarks* of Conyers Middleton.

Bentley's *Correspondence* was edited by (1) Christopher Wordsworth, 2 vols., London 1842–3, and (2) Charles Burney junior, London 1807: this volume, *Richardi Bentleii Epistolæ*, contains letters exchanged between Bentley and Graevius.

*   *   *

Two first-hand authorities on Bentley's character and career are:
Richard Cumberland (1732–1811), author of many sentimental comedies long forgotten, but once described as 'the last and the best of the Sentimental School', was the son of Bentley's favourite daughter, Joanna, and was born in the Master's Lodge at Trinity. His *Memoirs of Richard Cumberland, written by himself,* was published in 1806, and contains our best record of the Master's domestic life. Mudford's *Life of Richard Cumberland* (1812), and S. T. Williams' study of his life and dramatic works (Yale University Press 1917), are also worth consulting.

Edward Rud, who was a Fellow of Trinity in the early period of Bentley's quarrel with the Fellows, left a diary which is preserved in the Wren Library. It was edited by H. R. Luard on behalf of the Cambridge Antiquarian Society in 1860. This little volume also contains some letters of interest in connection with Bentley's courtship of Joanna Bernard, and one from Mrs Bentley containing a recipe for making a kind of biscuit to which her lord seems to have been partial. When Rud went off to a living in the north of England, he seems to have spent a great deal of time in brewing beer, and his diary contains much record of the mode of domestic brewing in those times.

*　　*　　*

The climax of Bentley's career as a literary critic came in 1732 with his publication of his notorious edition of Milton's *Paradise Lost*. This has never been reprinted. J. W. Mackail delivered the Warton Lecture for 1924 on Bentley's edition. It is to be found in Volume XI of the *Proceedings of the British Academy*. Other reflections on Bentley's treatment of Milton's epic are to be found in William Empson's *Milton's God*, F. L. Lucas' *Decline and Fall of the Romantic Ideal*, and Christopher Ricks' *Milton's Grand Style*. The compendium for reference of Miltonic criticism is: *Milton's Editors and Commentators*, from *Patrick Hume to Henry John Todd*, 1695–1801. This may be found in Vol. 19–20 of *Acta Universitatis Dorpatensis Humaniora* (Tartu, 1930).

It is in his editing, or 'restoring', of Milton's *Paradise Lost* that Bentley gives us his prescription for retrieving a poet's own words, when in doubt, or in the absence of a manuscript. Briefly, the prescription is 'Sagacity and happy Conjecture'. It is this to which Jacob Mähly referred when he spoke of 'his real genius and perhaps unequalled power of divination in the field of conjectural criticism'. At p. 1 of his *Richard Bentley, Eine Biographie*, he calls it *seine vielleicht einzig da stehende, wahrhaft geniale Divinationsgabe auf den Gebiete der Conjectural kritik*. But then, these things often sound better in German.

Appendix VI: A Chronology of Dr Bentley's Life

	ÆT	LIFE	MAIN WORKS	HISTORICAL EVENTS
1662		Jan 27, birth at Oulton, Yorks		
1672	10	Wakefield School		
1676	14	St John's College, Cambridge		
1680	18	BA		
1682	20	Master at Spalding School. Tutor to J. Stillingfleet		
1683	21	MA		
1685	23			James II
1688	26			The Glorious Revolution
1689	27	To Oxford with J. Stillingfleet		William and Mary
1690	28	Ordained chaplain to Bishop Stillingfleet		
1691	29		Letter to Mill	
1692	30	Delivers the Boyle Lectures		Sir William Temple's *Essay on Ancient and Modern Learning*
1693	31	Prebendary of Worcester	Fragments of Callimachus	
1694	32	Nominated King's Librarian Takes up residence at St James's		Wotton's *Reflections on the Ancient and Modern Learning*
1695	33	Chaplain in Ordinary to the king. Fellow of the Royal Society		Boyle's *Phalaris*
1696	34	Reparation of Cambridge University Press DD.		
1697	35		First Essay on Phalaris in 2nd Ed. of Wotton's *Reflections*	

Appendix VI: A Chronology of Dr Bentley's Life—continued

	ÆT	LIFE	MAIN WORKS	HISTORICAL EVENTS
1698	36	Master of Trinity College		Boyle against Bentley (Jan.)
1699	37		*Dissertation on the Letters of Phalaris* or 'Bentley against Boyle' (Mar.)	
1700 (Feb. 1)	38	Installed as Master of Trinity Vice-Chancellor		
1701 (Jan. 7)	39	Marriage to Joanna Bernard		
1702	40	Archdeacon of Ely		Queen Anne Declaration of War against France
1702–4	40–2	Reforms at Trinity		Blenheim
1710	48	Fellows Petition Bishop Moore		
1711	49		*Horace*	Dismissal of Sarah, Duchess of Marlborough Harley. Founding of South Sea Company
1713	51	Cited to Ely House by Bishop of Ely	Remarks on the *Discourse of Free-Thinking* of Anthony Collins	
1714	52	1st Trial at Ely House (July) Death of Bishop Moore		Death of Queen Anne Accession of George I
1715	53	*Sermon on Popery* Fellows Petition the Crown		Jacobite revolt
1716	54	Regius Professor of Divinity.		
1717	55	Visit of George I		

Year	Age	Bentley	Works	National events
1718	56	Bentley arrested and deprived of Degrees by Senate		
1720	58	Bentley proposes edition of New Testament		The South Sea Bubble
1721	59			Walpole 1st Lord of Treasury
1724	62	Bentley's degrees restored		
1726	64		*Terence*	
1728	66	George II visits Cambridge Bentley's illness		
1729	67	Cited to Ely House by Bishop Greene. Veto by King's Bench		
1732			Bentley's edition of *Paradise Lost*	
1733		2nd Trial at Ely House Sentenced to deprivation of the Mastership (1734)		
1734–7	73–5	Efforts to secure execution of sentence of deprivation Bentley remains in possession Death of Bishop Greene		
1738	76			
1739	77		*Manilius*	
1740	78	Death of Bentley's wife		Opening of War of Austrian Succession
1742	80	July 14, death of Richard Bentley at the Master's Lodge		Resignation of Walpole
1749		Death of Dr Colbatch		

Index

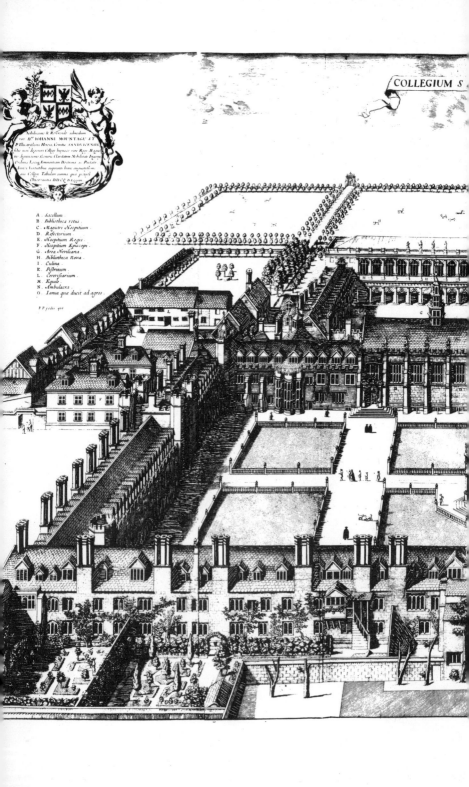

COLLEGIUM S

A Sacellum.
B Bibliotheca vetus.
C Magistri Hospitium.
D Refectorium.
E Hospitium Regis.
F Hospitium Episcopi.
G Area Nobiliaria.
H Bibliotheca Nova.
I   Culina.
K Pistrinum.
L Cerevisiarium.
M Equile.
N Ambulacra.
O Ianua quæ ducit ad agros.